Syed Abul Hasan 'Ali Nadwi

Islamic Heritage in Cross-Cultural Perspectives

1. Gandhi's Responses to Islam; by Sheila McDonough. (ISBN 978-81-246-0035-1)
2. Fawā'id al-Fu'ād — Spiritual and Literary Discourses of Shaikh Niẓāmuddīn Awliyā; Originally Compiled by Amīr Ḥasan 'Alā' Sijzī Dehlawī; English Translation with Introduction and Historical Annotation by Ziya-ul-Hasan-Faruqi. (ISBN 978-81-246-0042-9)
3. Change and Continuity in Indian Sūfism — A Naqshbandi-Mujaddidī Branch in the Hindu Environment; Thomas Dahnhardt. (ISBN 978-81-246-0170-9)
4. Islamic Thought and Movement in the Subcontinent — A Study of Sayyid Abu A'lā Mawdudi and Sayyid Abul Hasan Ali Nadwi; Sheikh Jameil Ali. (ISBN 978-81-246-0491-5)
5. Ṣūfī Thought of Shaikh Sayyid 'Abdul Qādir Jīlānī and Its Impact on the Indian Subcontinent; Manzoor Ahmad Bhat. (ISBN 978-81-246-0545-5)
6. Islamic Resurgence: Sayyid Abul Ḥasan 'Ali Nadwī and his Contemporaries; Abdul Kader Choughley. (ISBN 978-81-246-0573-8)
7. Sayyid Abul Ḥasan 'Ali Nadwī: Life and Works; Abdul Kader Choughley. (ISBN 978-81-246-0611-7)
8. Evolution and Development of Islamic Jurisprudence in Central Asia; Dr Showkat Hussain Dar. (ISBN 978-81-246-0723-7)

Islamic Heritage in Cross-Cultural Perspectives, no. 9

Syed Abul Hasan 'Ali Nadwi

An Eminent Scholar, Thinker, and Reformer

Syed Muhammad Rabey Hasani Nadwi

Translated by

Mohammed Moidul Haque

DK PRINTWORLD

Publishers of Indian Traditions

Cataloging in Publication Data — DK

[Courtesy: D.K. Agencies (P) Ltd. <docinfo@dkagencies.com>]

Nadvī, Muḥammad Rābi' Ḥasanī, 1929-

[Maulānā Sayyid Abūlḥasan 'Alī Nadvī. English]
Syed Abul Hasan 'Ali Nadwi : an eminent scholar, thinker, and reformer /
Syed Muhammad Rabey Hasani Nadwi ; translated by Mohammed Moidul Haque.
p. cm. – (Islamic heritage in cross-cultural perspectives; no. 9)
Translated from Urdu.
Includes bibliographical references and index.
ISBN: 9788124607466

1. Nadvī, Abulḥasan 'Alī, 1913-1999. 2. Muslim scholars – India – Biography. I. Haque, Mohammed Moidul, 1947-. II. Title. III. Series: Islamic heritage in cross-cultural perspectives ; no. 9.

DDC 297.092 23

ISBN 13: 978-81-246-0746-6

First published in India in 2014

Printed and published by:
D.K. Printworld (P) Ltd.
Regd. Office : *Vedaśrī*, F-395, Sudarshan Park
(Metro Station: Ramesh Nagar)
New Delhi – 110 015-11
Phones : (011) 2545 3975, 2546 6019; *Fax* : 2546 5926
e-mail : indology@dkprintworld.com
Web : www.dkprintworld.com

Contents

Publisher's Note vii

Translator's Note ix

Preface xi

Introduction – by Dr. 'Abdullah 'Abbas Nadwi 1

1. **Biography: A Brief Overview** 11

2. **Education, Upbringing, and Formation of Personality** 29

   Key Factors in the Formation of Personality 29

   Outstanding Qualities and Moral Character 46

   Internal Rectification and Devotion to Allah 59

3. **Public Life and Services** 71

   D'awah 71

   Social Reform 82

   Advice to the Leaders of India and Muslim Countries 94

   Reform of the System of Education and Mentoring 106

4. **Movements and Institutions** 117

   Academy of Islamic Research and Publications 117

   World Forum of Islamic Literature 130

   Payam-e-Insaniyat 141

Deeni T'alimi Council 149
All India Muslim Majlis-e-Mushawarat and AIMPLB 157
Nadwatul 'Ulama 167

5. **Travels to Foreign Countries** 179
To Arab Countries 179
To Europe and North America 197
To Neighboring Countries 205
Burma 205
Malaysia 207
Pakistan 210
Bangladesh 214
Sri Lanka 216

6. **Publications** 219
Sheikh Nadwi's Publications 219
Publications by Others on Sheikh Nadwi 237

Glossary of Arabic Terms 241
Index 245

Publisher's Note

Syed Abul Hasan 'Ali Nadwi (1913-99) was one of the most respected and influential scholars of the twentieth-century Islamic world. He was a gifted speaker and a prolific writer. He authored more than 50 books and hundreds of papers on history, literature and theology in both Arabic and Urdu. His writings have been translated into several languages including Bengali, Chinese, English, French, Gujarati, Hindi, Indonesian, Malaysian, Persian, Spanish, Tamil and Turkish.

Very few scholars have been so revered and recognized in both the Arab and non-Arab parts of the Islamic world. His command of language, style of presentation and grasp of subject matter made his writings immensely attractive to the modern educated people. He was able to articulate his point of view in a way that impressed intelligent and analytical minds and inspired them to think in a rational way.

He dedicated his entire life to foster mutual respect and understanding among followers of different faiths and religions, especially between Hindus and Muslims of India and the Islamic world and the West. He was a visionary who looked at the entire mankind as a single family which could prosper only if its members care about each other and strive to establish peace and justice in the world.

He played a key role in founding and establishing several national and international organizations and institutions including the Oxford Centre for Islamic Studies, World Forum of Islamic Literature, Muslim World League, Islamic University

(Saudi Arabia), Academy of Islamic Research & Publications and Payam-e-Insaniyat (Message of Humanity).

Several biographies of Syed Abul Hasan 'Ali Nadwi have been published in recent years, but the one that stands out most among them is the one which was authored by Syed Rabey Hasani Nadwi, the current rector of Nadwatul 'Ulama, Lucknow. Since Syed Rabey Hasani Nadwi was not only Syed Abul Hasan 'Ali Nadwi's nephew and student, but also his most trusted associate and confidant for several decades, he was able to recount the story of Syed Abul Hasan 'Ali Nadwi in the most accurate and authentic way.

D.K. Printworld is honored to present the English translation of the above-mentioned biography which Syed Rabey Hasani Nadwi authored in Urdu in 2005. We hope that it serves as an inspiration and guidance to those who desire to serve the humanity and establish peace in the world.

Editor
D.K. Printworld

Translator's Note

In the name of Allah, the Compassionate, the Merciful
Praise be to Allah and His blessings be on Prophet Muhammad, his progeny and Companions

This is the translation of Sheikh Syed Abul Hasan 'Ali Nadwi's biography which was written in Urdu by his nephew and close associate Sheikh Syed Muhammad Rabey Hasani Nadwi in 2005. Sheikh Syed Abul Hasan 'Ali Nadwi was one of the greatest scholars, thinkers and reformers of the twentieth century. He clearly stands out among his contemporaries and it is hard to find anyone else who is revered and recognized to the same degree in both the Arab and non-Arab parts of the Islamic world. He was a gifted writer and speaker. He was a true descendant of *salaf saliheen* (pious people of the earliest period of Islam) in simplicity, humility and piety. He served his country and Muslims all over the world in many different capacities with great distinction for over sixty years before he passed away in 1999.

Sheikh Nadwi started his literary career at the age of 23 or 24 when he wrote the biography of his ancestor Syed Ahmad Shaheed (d. 1831) who had led one of the greatest reform movements in India in the nineteenth century. Sheikh Nadwi wrote in both Arabic and Urdu. Many of his writings were originally in Arabic and they were later translated into Urdu and other languages. His command of Arabic was such that even native learned Arabs envied him. He published over 200 articles and books in Arabic and over 300 in Urdu. Many of his writings have been translated from Arabic and Urdu into several languages including Bengali, English, French, Hindi, Malaysian, Persian and Turkish.

He has left behind a huge array of speeches and writings. Many have already been translated into English and the rest will hopefully be translated in future. Thus the main purpose of presenting this biography in English is to introduce him and his work to the English-speaking people so that they can benefit from his work. Since many of his speeches and writings are addressed specifically to Muslims living in non-Muslim countries, they can find in his work invaluable guidance for preserving their faith and traditions in foreign lands.

I have attempted to keep the translation as simple as possible. With that in mind, I have avoided embedding Arabic terms in the text in Arabic script. However, I have embedded those Arabic terms (in italics) which are now appearing more frequently in English literature and it is hard to find exact English words for them. Some of these terms are *d'awah, deen, hadith, iman, millat, sunnah, taqwa, 'ulama* and *ummah*. Also, some of these terms have multiple meanings which depend upon the context in which they have been used. For example, *ummah* and *millat* may mean Muslims, nation, followers or mankind and *deen* may mean religion, Islam or way of life, etc. So to assist the reader in getting the closest meaning, I have included in parentheses the meaning which appears the most appropriate.

There are many who have helped me in completing this translation. I wish to thank all of them, especially Dr. Shah 'Ebadur Rahman (former professor of English at Ummul Qura University, Makkah, Saudi Arabia) and Dr. Rehmat Ali (former professor of Economics at Jamia Millia Islamia, Delhi).

May Allah accept this meager effort and make it a means of forgiveness for everyone who took part in this endeavor!

9 November 2013 **Mohammed Moidul Haque**

Preface

In the name of Allah, the Compassionate, the Merciful
Praise be to Allah and His blessings be on Prophet Muhammad, his progeny and Companions

A PROMINENT scholar and former judge of the Supreme Court of Syria was asked in a radio interview, "Which is your most beloved city?" He replied, "My home city of Damascus and then Lucknow, the city of my friend Sheikh Syed Abul Hasan 'Ali Nadwi". Similarly, a prominent scholar of Iraq once remarked to an Indian official, "We know India due to Lucknow and we know Lucknow due to Sheikh Syed Abul Hasan 'Ali Nadwi". These and similar compliments, which were heard in the Arab world, speak about the international stature of Sheikh Nadwi.

How did Sheikh Nadwi develop into such a personality? We need to look at the factors that contributed to the formation, mentoring and nurturing of his personality. The factor that stands out most is the environment of his home and family. On one hand, it was very distinguished in religiousness, nobility, morality, literature and education. On the other hand, it was deeply involved in India's struggle for freedom from the British rule.

Sheikh Nadwi's grandfather Hakeem Syed Fakhruddin Khayali (d. 1908) was a poet and a scholar. His father Hakeem Syed 'Abdul Hai Hasani (d. 1923) was a historian and a biographer. His brother, Dr. Syed 'Abdul 'Ali Hasani (d. 1961), was an eminent physician and a fusion of the old and new.

His mother (d. 1968) was a pious, softhearted and learned woman credited with a published anthology of poems. His sister was an author. Above all, his forefather Syed Ahmad Shaheed (d. 1831) was a true example of *ruh-baan bil lail wa fur-saan bin na-haar* (monastic during night and warrior during day).

Sheikh Nadwi was a fusion of numerous personalities of extraordinary caliber and an amalgamation of their distinguished qualities. He was a man of literature and composition. His patriotism for his country, India, was unwavering. He was always eager for the country's progress and prosperity. He always strove to create an atmosphere of mutual love and brotherhood among various communities. He was always eager to see Muslims excel in education and morality.

He had seen the period during which India was a British colony and had closely witnessed the brutalities and injustices of that regime. He had seen how savagely Indians in general and Muslims in particular were treated by the British rulers. This had created in him an intense yearning for independence and freedom. So when India gained Independence, he strongly felt that every community must have full freedom to preserve its identity and to live according to its own religious beliefs and values. He also felt that an environment must be created that fostered love and respect among different communities and encouraged them to live in peace and harmony with each other. Thus when he entered public life, he started working on two fronts: (1) education and character building, and (2) social reforms.

Allah had blessed him with very powerful pen and speech. He used both of these skills effectively to promote educational and social reforms. Using public platform, he reminded masses of their obligations towards their community and country. He approached influential people and leaders individually to remind them to serve the country and contribute to its progress and prosperity. He always appreciated and supported those who were engaged in any kind of service to the community, country or humanity. His approach was simple and clear and was purely based on well-wishing for all. That is why he was respected by leaders of different communities and affiliations and they all saw him as a sincere and kindhearted person.

He was a distinguished scholar of Islam. He enjoyed tremendous amount of respect and affection among Muslim scholars all over the world. He was originally from Rae Bareli, Uttar Pradesh, India, but was brought up and educated in Lucknow which is the capital of the State of Uttar Pradesh, India.

His role as a leader and thinker in dealing with the educational, social, and religious affairs of Muslims and his contributions in these areas are widely recognized. In addition to taking special interest in the affairs of Muslims, he was also committed to the welfare of the entire country and all communities.

In the area of education, he concentrated mainly on Nadwatul 'Ulama (an Islamic institution of higher learning in Lucknow, India) which was established about a century ago in order to bring together the best of both the traditional and modern education. During the last four decades under his leadership, Nadwatul 'Ulama gained the stature of an internationally recognized and respected institution. He also established an organization known as the Deeni T'alimi Council for the purpose of ingraining a solid foundation of Islam in Muslim children in the very early stage of their education so that they could protect their faith while living in the Hindu-majority environment of secular India. He remained head of the Council until his death.

On the social and religious front, Sheikh Nadwi remained actively involved in the efforts of the All India Muslim Personal

Law Board (AIMPLB) which was established in 1973 for the purpose of protecting and preserving the Islamic *shari'ah* (code of conduct) in India. After the death of its founding president Qari Muhammad Taiyab Qasmi in 1983, Sheikh Nadwi was appointed the president and served in that capacity until his death in 1999. He played a pivotal role in tackling key issues faced by the Board during his tenure. While actively leading efforts in India, he also rendered his services to Muslim countries and communities outside India.

In addition to being concerned about Muslims, he also took deep interest in the welfare and betterment of the entire humanity. For this very purpose, he started the movement known as Payam-e-Insaniyat (Message of Humanity) in which he involved good-hearted people of all religions and denominations and reminded them about their obligations to the country and humanity. Thus he served at all levels – community (Muslims), national and international – and received acclamation from all corners. Wherever he saw a need, he tried to do his part. Wherever he saw some weakness or slackness, he boldly voiced his opinion. He did not hesitate in presenting correct Islamic perspective of an issue and safeguarding the interests of the *millat* (Muslims).

His approach was such that he would give due respect and recognition to the person with whom he was speaking and would use the language that was most appropriate to the position and status of that person. Even when he criticized someone, he did so in a loving and respectful manner. That is why even his harsh words were well received by others. Whenever he got an opportunity to talk to leaders and influential people of a country, he presented his viewpoint with no motive other than that of well-wishing and without any material gain in mind. Details of such encounters can be found in his autobiography and other writings.

His scholarly and thoughtful writings gained immense popularity both inside and outside the Indian subcontinent, especially in the Arab world. Some of his books were recognized in the Arab world among the best three or four of the century.

He presented literature as a tool that could be used to serve Islam and humanity. This role of literature was recognized by the Muslim world and consequently an international organization known as Rabita al-Adab al-Islami al-'Alami (World Forum of Islamic Literature) was founded and he remained its head until his death with the headquarters in Lucknow. Not only was he a vocal champion of this cause, but he himself produced some extraordinary work of literature which truly represented his vision.

The elements of *islah batin* (internal rectification) and *tazkiyah nafs* (spiritual purification) were deeply engrained in Sheikh Nadwi's character and thinking. This was the result of his close association with the pious and spiritual personalities who meticulously followed *sunnah* (traditions of Prophet Muhammad) and were endowed with spiritual qualities. This, in turn, had developed in him qualities of *zuhd* (asceticism from worldly pleasures), *istighna* (expecting nothing from anyone except Allah), contentment and cognizance of the life hereafter. As a result, he became very endearing to people and his call became quite appealing to them.

The expanse of Sheikh Nadwi's work was very wide and diverse. His efforts included so many facets of the community, national and global interests that it is very rare to find a person who could involve himself in so many different endeavors at the same time. That is why his death was felt as a huge loss by every group and every segment of the society. Many groups acknowledged that it would be very difficult to fill the vacuum created by his death. Thus it becomes the responsibility of all of us to continue the efforts that he was carrying in his lifetime. People like him are born only rarely. The Urdu poet Shaad 'Azeemabadi has rightly said:

> Even if you search for us from country to country, you will not find us as we are not available
>
> O, the people of today, value us as we are only rarely available if not completely non-existent.

Numerous writings by various authors have appeared about Sheikh Nadwi's life and work. *Meer-e-Karwan* by Dr. 'Abdullah 'Abbas Nadwi (d. 2006) is one of them. Sheikh Nadwi himself wrote his autobiography entitled *Karwan-e-Zindagi* that consists of seven volumes and includes detailed description of important events that took place in his lifetime. Given his superior style of writing, who else could have written better than him and who else could have given a more accurate account of what was happening around him? Thus his autobiography could have been sufficient by itself. But, while he has written elaborately (in his autobiography) about the events pertaining to Muslims and his country (India), he has written very little about his own personal life. However, one must have a good knowledge of his personal life and character to fully understand his vision, accomplishments and achievements.

Some people felt that this gap could be filled by someone who belonged to Sheikh Nadwi's family and was very close to him. With that in mind, they approached me. I was hesitant in the beginning, but finally agreed to it. However, my engagements were such that I was unable to dedicate myself to this task. A plausible compromise was that I would dictate my thoughts and recollections to someone who would then compile them in the form of a manuscript. Syed Mahmood Hasan Hasani Nadwi was chosen for that task.

Syed Mahmood Hasan Hasani Nadwi is the older son of

my niece[1] (daughter of my brother). He stayed close to Sheikh Nadwi during later part of Sheikh Nadwi's life. He is endowed with a fine literary taste. Because of his closeness to Sheikh Nadwi, he had a very good understanding of Sheikh Nadwi's vision and thinking. Thus his selection for this task was quite appropriate and he completed it quite satisfactorily. Whenever I had time, I dictated to him my thoughts and recollections and he finally put them together in the form of this book. The fact is that this book could not have become a reality without his diligence and hard work.

What I have stated in this book is what I have closely witnessed and observed. Thus I hope that it fulfills the need for which people wanted me to write this biography and I hope that it will not be without benefit.

Why was I chosen for writing this biography? Maybe, because I had the opportunity of being closest to Sheikh Nadwi right from the days I was a student until he departed from this world. Though Sheikh Nadwi was my maternal uncle, he was given full responsibility of our (me and my brothers) guardianship by my father Syed Rasheed Ahmad Hasani who was speech and hearing impaired. My grandfather Syed Khaliluddin Ahmad Hasani (nephew of Syed Shah Ziaun Nabi Hasani) who was a prominent landlord had made special arrangement for my father to acquire necessary skills to take care of his personal and household needs. Thus my father's responsibilities were limited to taking care of matters pertaining to land and agriculture and he made our maternal uncles (Sheikh Nadwi and his older brother Dr. Syed 'Abdul 'Ali Hasani) fully responsible for our education and upbringing.

It was also the time when India was getting close to gaining

[1] She passed away on 14 Shaban 1426 AH (19 September 2005) after a brief illness in Lucknow and was buried in her ancestral graveyard in Rae Bareli.

its Independence. But the resources were very limited and the British influence on the society was so strong that it was generally believed that one could succeed and flourish in life only by acquiring the education that was patronized by the British. Nevertheless, the maternal side of our family was fully committed to religious education and upbringing.

My maternal grandfather Sheikh Hakeem Syed 'Abdul Hai Hasani (father of Sheikh Nadwi) was a distinguished religious scholar and physician. He was also the rector of Nadwatul 'Ulama. He had chosen the path of religious education for his sons Dr. Syed 'Abdul 'Ali Hasani and Sheikh Nadwi.

Similar was the case with our maternal grandmother (mother of Sheikh Nadwi). She was the most religious person in the family and had great influence on her son Sheikh Nadwi and two daughters – my mother (Saiyadah Ammatul 'Aziz) and my aunt (Saiyadah Amatullah Tasnim). Since my maternal grandfather (Sheikh Nadwi's father) had died at an early age, my maternal grandmother had to play a much bigger role in the upbringing and education of her children.

Anyway, my mother (Sheikh Nadwi's sister) made our maternal uncles (Dr. Syed 'Abdul 'Ali Hasani and Sheikh Nadwi) responsible for overseeing our education and upbringing and our father fully supported her even though he himself was more inclined towards modern and secular education under the influence of some of his relatives on the paternal side. That is how my brothers and I were brought up under the supervision and guardianship of our two uncles – Dr. Syed 'Abdul 'Ali Hasani and Sheikh Nadwi.

Furthermore, it just happened that I, out of all of my brothers, was most fortunate in benefitting from Sheikh Nadwi. Most of my education took place under his direct supervision. Maybe, due to this very reason, I got more opportunities to serve and assist him in his academic works, especially those which were in Arabic. I frequently accompanied him in travels to foreign countries (mostly to Arab countries). I was heavily involved in proofreading his manuscripts and publishing them. Thus I was very fortunate to have the opportunity to work closely with him. It enabled me to understand his mission and vision and allowed me to earn his confidence and trust.

As his nephew, I received his affection. As his student, I developed deep reverence for him. By working closely with him, I became fully acquainted and acclimatized to his thinking. Probably, these were the reasons why people thought of me as the one who should write his biography.

I was related to Sheikh Nadwi from both the maternal and paternal sides. Both of my grandfathers (father of my mother and father of my father) were cousins and came from the same forefather a few generations back. This relationship is a matter of honor for me and I feel elated in accepting the task of working on this biography. May Allah accept it!

Syed Mahmood Hasan Hasani Nadwi was very instrumental in preparing the manuscript and bringing it into a publishable form. My nephew Syed Bilal 'Abdul Hai Hasani Nadwi (son of late Sheikh Syed Muhammad Al-Hasani) who was very close to Sheikh Nadwi in his last years and Iqbal Ahmad Nadwi (a teacher in Nadwatul 'Ulama) were also of great assistance to me in this effort. I greatly value their contributions.

I am also indebted to Dr. 'Abdullah 'Abbas Nadwi for being kind enough to write the introduction of this book. He passed away on first Zul Hijjah 1426 AH (1 January 2006) in Makkah, Saudi Arabia, and was buried in Jannatul-Mo'allaa (a graveyard in Makkah) after hundreds of thousands of people attended his funeral prayer in the Grand Mosque, Makkah.

I am also grateful to my younger brother Syed Muhammad

Wazeh Rasheed Hasani Nadwi for reviewing this book and giving useful suggestions. I must also express my gratitude to Qari Habeeb Ahmad Lucknowi for his efforts and monetary assistance which he provided in publishing this book. May Allah immensely reward him and all of those[2] who helped in bringing this task to fruition! May Allah make it beneficial for the entire mankind and a means of reward for all of us! Amen!

9 June 2005 **Syed Muhammad Rabey Hasani Nadwi**

---

[2] Maulvi Anis Ahmad Nadwi deserves special mention for his assistance.

Introduction

IT has been five years since Sheikh Syed Abul Hasan 'Ali Hasani Nadwi passed away and the sixth year is in progress. During this period, several articles and books have been published in both Arabic and Urdu highlighting different aspects of his life. One of them is the biography that Syed Bilal 'Abdul Hai Hasani Nadwi has written. It gives a complete portrait of Sheikh Nadwi's life. Bilal Nadwi is the son of Sheikh Syed Muhammad Al-Hasani (d. 1979) who was a highly gifted and renowned writer of the Islamic world and was very dear to Sheikh Nadwi.

Writing biographies of religious scholars and pious people has been a speciality of this family as is exemplified by *Nuzhatul Khawatir*[1] (Arabic) which was authored by Sheikh Nadwi's father Hakim Syed 'Abdul Hai Hasani (d. 1923). Sheikh Nadwi's own autobiography *Karwan-e-Zindagi* is another extraordinary work in that tradition. In *Karwan-e-Zindagi,* Sheikh Nadwi has shed light on important events of his life which include the formation and accomplishments of the All India Muslim Majlis-e-Mushawarat, Deeni T'alimi Council, Payam-e-Insaniyat, All India Muslim Personal Law Board, and World Forum of Islamic Literature. He has also covered the tragic events of the invasion of Egypt by Israel and the separation of Bangladesh (from Pakistan).

---

1 It is an extensive biographical dictionary of over 4,500 Islamic scholars of the Indian subcontinent. It consists of 8 volumes and about 3,500 pages.

Sheikh Nadwi was very candid in addressing Arabs and his talks were unflattering and unbending. In doing so, he was actually fulfilling an obligation which could very well be legal, moral, or political, but the main driving force was his inner zeal, fervor, and passion that ran through every fiber of his body.

There are many who have written about Sheikh Nadwi and have expressed their feelings, love, and respect for him. I also happen to be one of them and have paid my tribute by writing *Meer-e-Karwan*. But the fact is that the person who could have written most forcefully and eloquently about Sheikh Nadwi could be none other than Sheikh Syed Muhammad Rabey Hasani Nadwi. May Allah bless him to serve for many years to come! Sometimes, it occurs to me that he is actually a true replica of Sheikh Nadwi. Now his look also has become like that of Sheikh Nadwi.

One of Allah's special favors to Sheikh Nadwi was that He gave him a successor like Sheikh Rabey who is indisputably his true heir. Thus my inner desire was that Sheikh Rabey should have written about Sheikh Nadwi. What others have come to know secondhand, Sheikh Rabey had witnessed them with his own eyes. People have heard that the qualities of selflessness, serving *deen* (Islam), and sacrificing everything for it had come in Sheikh Nadwi because of his mother's upbringing and supplications. For Sheikh Rabey, it was not a matter of hearing these things from someone. Rather, all this was happening right in front of his own eyes in the home of his grandmother (Sheikh Nadwi's mother) who used to remain engaged in *dhikr* (remembrance of Allah), long *d'ua* (supplications), and *tahajjud* (pre-dawn prayers).

Sheikh Rabey was with Sheikh Nadwi at all times, whether at home or in journey. He represented Sheikh Nadwi on many occasions and spoke on his behalf many times. If Sheikh Nadwi accepted any responsibility, it was Sheikh Rabey who was to implement it.

Sheikh Rabey did not write this biography in a conventional way. Instead, he dictated little by little his account of important events which he had personally observed and experienced. Thus the book that you have in your hands is a collection of those recounts.

I do not mean to belittle what others have written on Sheikh Nadwi. In fact, everyone has done so with full affection and regard for him. No one was forced to write and everyone has expressed his feelings and observations in his own unique way. Nothing is redundant, as a poet has said: "Every flower has its own color and fragrance". In the last five years, many articles, books, biographies, both in Arabic and Urdu, have appeared and more are still coming.

In the second chapter of this book, Sheikh Rabey has presented an excellent picture of Sheikh Nadwi's early life. Mentioning all the prominent persons who were born in the family since 1857, he has written that Sheikh Nadwi's maternal side, despite being *zamindar* (absentee landowners) and well off from the worldly point of view, was firmly committed to religious values and practices. Thus both *zamindari* (landlordship) and religiousness were going on hand in hand and the family was able to inculcate in its members qualities of piety, modesty, *d'awah* (calling people towards Allah and His divine religion), sacrifice, supplication, spiritual purification, and humility. It was as if both these streams were merging into each other. If I could, I would rephrase Sheikh Rabey's analysis in the words of Shah Waliyullah Dehlavi (d. 1762) that both the material and spiritual forces were working together in the family with proper balance and without any conflict. The clay with which Sheikh Nadwi's skeleton was kneaded had neither the element of monasticism of hermits and monks nor the element of endless greed of worldly people.

All the biographers of Sheikh Nadwi agree that the factors that played a role in the formation of Sheikh Nadwi's personality are the upbringing of his mother, teaching of Sheikh Ahmad 'Ali Lahori, *d'ua* of Sheikh Syed Hussain Ahmad Madni, recognition of his potential by Sheikh Ashraf 'Ali Thanwi, spiritual mentoring of Sheikh Muhammad Ilyas Kandhlawi, Shaikhul Hadith Muhammad Zakariya Kandhlawi, and Sheikh 'Abdul Qadir Raipuri and affection and *d'ua* of many others including Shah Muhammad Wasiyullah Fatehpuri, Shah Muhammad Yakoob Mujaddidi, and Sheikh Muhammad Ahmad Phulpuri of Partapgarh. All these factors, with the blessings of Allah, culminated into the versatile personality of Sheikh Nadwi.

Sheikh Rabey has written nearly the same thing; his assessment is of course most authentic as it is a matter of his own home and he has witnessed all of these with his own eyes. However, my own humble opinion is slightly different. In my view, the outward and inward training of Sheikh Nadwi's mother and older brother Dr. Syed 'Abdul 'Ali Hasani turned him [from raw material] into a piece of gold and precious gem. He then became the focus of attention of all the eminent jewelers and diamond makers who were blessed with the skill of polishing human character and personality. As we have read, Shaikhul Hadith Muhammad Zakariya Kandhlawi, Sheikh Muhammad Ilyas Kandhlawi, Shah Muhammad Yakoob Mujaddidi, and Shah Muhammad Wasiyullah Fatehpuri spotted Sheikh Nadwi's talent and potential in their very first encounter with him and he became very close to them in a very short period of time. What was the reason?

> Was it the miracle of his (Ibrahim's) glance or that of her (Ismail's mother) lap

Who taught Ismail the etiquette of being a worthy son?[2]

Sheikh Nadwi's mother planted the seed of worthiness in him and his older brother nurtured it. Then wherever he went, he bloomed into a rose.

Sheikh Rabey has written all this in his own elegant way. I have expressed it in my own rustic way. Nevertheless, these were the factors which played key role in shaping the personality of Sheikh Nadwi.

When Sheikh Nadwi opened his eyes, he found himself as a member of the family of Syed Ahmad Shaheed (d. 1831) whose feats and accomplishments were still inspiring Muslims to sacrifice their lives for the sake of Allah. It was in fact Syed Ahmad Shaheed from whom Sheikh Nadwi inherited the zeal for *d'awah* and *tabligh* (propagation) and the understanding that they (*d'awah* and *tabligh*) must be plain, simple and free from any pomp and show and must reach kings as well as paupers.

Sheikh Nadwi addressed Shah Saud and Shah Faisal of Saudi Arabia, President Ziaul Haq of Pakistan, Shah 'Abdullah of Jordan, Shah Hasan of Morocco as well as poor peasants of the villages of Lucknow and gave them *d'awah.* When addressing someone, he used the method that was most appropriate to the level of understanding of that person and attempted to infuse the divine message of Allah in that person's heart. His strategy of working in India was same as that of Mujaddid Alf Thani (d. 1624) whom Allah had enabled to foresee the danger at the right moment and steer Muslims of India to preserve Islam in their lives.

It is true that Allah alone is the ultimate protector of His divine religion, but He uses humans for this service and I am

---

2 It refers to the ultimate obedience of Prophet Ismail to his father Prophet Ibrahim (Abraham) . Who inculcated this quality in Prophet Ismail – father or mother?

sure that Sheikh Nadwi will be counted among such people, if not in this world, certainly in the hereafter. He started his adult life with *d'awah,* always remained firmly connected to Allah and breathed his last while reciting the Quranic verse:

> Give him good tidings of forgiveness and noble reward.
> — *Yaseen,* 36:11

Sheikh Nadwi's vision of education was not confined to the walls of a *madrasah* (religious seminary). He had closely studied educational systems of the East and West. Through the lens of history, he had understood what were the needs of different times and which qualities and skills were required in different eras to discharge the duty of *d'awah* effectively. The curriculum that he had designed was the outcome of this study and vision. And since Sheikh Syed Muhammad Rabey Hasani Nadwi was deeply involved in its implementation, it was most fitting for him (Sheikh Rabey) to shed light on this topic as well and he has done it elegantly in the pages that follow.

Regarding literature, Sheikh Nadwi held the view that it does not merely entail decorating and displaying words in a beautiful manner. In the words of Sheikh Sayyid 'Ali Al-Tantawi:

> The clutter of words that we find in our literature books today is not real literature. The real literature is what the Indian scholar Sheikh Abul Hasan 'Ali Nadwi has understood and demonstrated in his books *Qasas-al-Nabiyyin* (Arabic), *Al-Qira'at-ur-Raashidah* (Arabic) and *Mukhtaaraat Min Adab-al-Arab* (Arabic).

About these books, Syed Qutb Shaheed (d. 1966) said:

> I myself have been involved in writing and reviewing books for children, but the truth is that the books of Syed Abul Hasan 'Ali Nadwi are the best of all.

Sheikh 'Abdul 'Aziz Rafa'i, an expert in education from Riyadh said:

> I wrote a book on Sayyidna K'ab bin Malik (a Companion of Prophet Muhammad) and analyzed his poetry. But it was Sheikh Abul Hasan 'Ali Nadwi who opened the literary beauty of his poetry to me.

These were some of the comments that I have seen in different journals and books, but Sheikh Rabey understood much better than me as to what was Sheikh Nadwi's vision of education.

Sheikh Rabey writes:

> Sheikh Nadwi through his own study and that of his associates, who were educated in the modern system of education, knew very well the reasons of the ascendancy of Europe. He understood that the Western nations did not attain worldly supremacy over others because they were genetically superior to others. Rather, they achieved it through their education, discoveries and innovations. He was fully convinced of the veracity and truthfulness of Islam and the ways of the Prophet Muhammad and believed that if Muslims could combine Islamic practices with the know-how of the West, they could achieve better than the Western nations.

Sheikh Rabey further writes:

> Sheikh Nadwi was aware of the importance of both branches of education – secular (modern) and religious. With respect to the secular education, we need to examine which parts of it are necessary for survival in the society and then make students acquire expertise in those fields. With respect to the religious education, the goal should be to develop in students (1) the conviction that Islam offers the most natural and comprehensive system for the mankind, and (2) the ability to discharge the duty of *d'awah* as this is the most basic qualification for being deemed as the best nation. He held the view that a curriculum must be designed to develop these skills in the new generation. Regarding the institutions of secular education, he felt that since their curriculum of social and human sciences was

> designed mostly by the materialistic and irreligious-minded people, they were not compatible with the needs and temperament of the Muslim *ummah*.

Not only did Sheikh Rabey understand Sheikh Nadwi's vision of education, but he fully internalized it. Same was true for Sheikh Syed Muhammad Al-Hasani[3] as well. These two (Sheikh Rabey and Sheikh Syed Muhammad Al-Hasani) were unique in this respect as they had fully absorbed Sheikh Nadwi's vision of education and had become the eyes through which Sheikh Nadwi used to see. I thus feel that no one could have written about Sheikh Nadwi's vision of education as Sheikh Rabey has done in this book.

Sheikh Nadwi's concept of Islamic literature was different from what was prevalent in Egypt. In his view, Islamic ideas and teachings should be mixed with literature in the same way as sugar or salt is mixed with flour. This was the reason why Arab educators preferred his books to their own and not because they were printed on glossy paper with colorful titles.

Sheikh Nadwi in fact revolutionized Islamic literature by redefining its role, meaning, and structure. People started realizing that Islamic literature had degenerated significantly in the last few centuries and it needed to be revived. Thus when the scholars of Egypt and Syria started a movement to revive Islamic literature, they entrusted Sheikh Nadwi to lead the way which resulted in the publication of journals such as *Al-Mishkaat* (Arabic) from Morocco, *Al-Adab Al-Islami* (Arabic) from Saudi Arabia, and *Karwan-e-Adab* (Urdu) from India.

Until recent past, a piece of literature was deemed Islamic if it included even a trace of Islamic material. However, the trend has changed now and the Arab countries, especially Saudi Arabia, are producing literature which contains

[3] Sheikh Muhammad Al-Hasani passed away on 14 June 1979.

substantial amount of Quran and *hadith* (traditions of Prophet Muhammad). The Saudi books have been adopted by Jordan in its secondary school curriculum. Similar books have been developed in Egypt as well and they are being used in the Gulf countries, Morocco, Algeria, and Mauritania. Thus the literature books which have been developed recently in the Arab countries for elementary and secondary schools are truly rich in Islamic material.

Sheikh Nadwi never hesitated in voicing his opinion against any attempt that was aimed at damaging or defaming Islam. When the Indian government started promoting Hindu mythology (in schools) and downgrading Islam as a religion of rituals and dogmas, he vigorously objected to it and fully supported Qazi 'Adeel 'Abbasi who had spearheaded a campaign against it.

It was not important to him whether a noble effort had started from his own home or from somewhere else. He did not care whether credit would be given to him, to his family, to his forefathers, or to his institution. What was important to him was that the words of Allah should be the ultimate goal of our intellect and understanding and the name and respect of Prophet Muhammad should be held high. He always kept in high esteem Deoband,[4] Saharanpur[5] and every place where the name of Allah was being remembered and he despised every place that was devoid of it.

When the wave of Arab nationalism of Gamal Abdel Nasser was sweeping the entire Middle East, he denounced it with full force. And he did it despite the fact that he belonged to a minority community of India and had no say in the government

---

[4] Deoband (India) – home of the renowned Islamic institution Darul 'Uloom.

[5] Saharanpur (India) – home of the renowned Islamic institution Mazahirul 'Uloom.

while Gamal Abdel Nasser was considered a Pharaoh-like king of 50 million people between the rivers of Nile and Euphrates and had the support of the superpowers. It was nothing but the Hashmi[6] zeal and spirit which had inspired him to do so as was done by his ancestor Syed Ahmad Shaheed in the nineteenth century.

Many articles and books have been published on Sheikh Nadwi in both Arabic and Urdu and they are still continuing. His name has become so revered that anything that is associated with him is published by the Arab press with great pride. Commentaries, critiques and reviews are being published regularly. This is the blessing of Allah and the result of His acceptance which is the ultimate objective of every human being. His writings are being read and studied today with the same vigor and interest as they were read in his lifetime.

In my view, had not Sheikh Rabey written this book, there would have remained a significant vacuum in the Islamic literature. By writing this book, not only has he fulfilled the rights of his uncle (Sheikh Nadwi), but has also rendered a great service to the Islamic community. May Allah accept this effort!

29 May 2005

'Abdullah 'Abbas Nadwi
Makkah Mokarramah
Saudi Arabia

---

[6] The Prophet was known as Hashmi as Hashim was his forefather.

1

Biography
A Brief Overview

SHEIKH Syed Abul Hasan 'Ali Hasani Nadwi was born on Friday, Muharram 6, 1332 Hijri (5 December 1913) in the village of Takiya Kalan (also known as Dairah Shah 'Alamullah). This village is located in Rae Bareli, which is a district in the State of Uttar Pradesh of India. His early education and upbringing took place in this village. This village was inhabited only by his family members who were generally educated and belonged to the middle class.

Sheikh Nadwi's father Sheikh Hakim Syed 'Abdul Hai Hasani (d. 1923) passed away when Sheikh Nadwi was only nine years old. He was a distinguished Islamic scholar, well-known writer and physician. He earned his living by practicing medicine. He was also the rector of Nadwatul 'Ulama which is an Islamic institution of higher learning.

Sheikh Nadwi's mother (d. 1968) was a very pious woman of exemplary character. She was very learned and well versed in literature. She put Sheikh Nadwi on the path of religion and religious education instead of worldly pursuit and modern education.

Sheikh Nadwi was the youngest among his brothers and sisters. He had two older sisters who were very caring and affectionate to him. Influenced by their father and other family members, both sisters were very inclined towards religion and learning. As a result, Sheikh Nadwi also developed a strong liking for books at a very early age, even before he was able to comprehend them.

Following the footsteps of his father, Sheikh Nadwi's elder brother Dr. Syed 'Abdul 'Ali Hasani (1893–1961), who was 20 years older than Sheikh Nadwi, completed religious education and then studied Yunani (Greek) medicine. Thereafter, he studied modern medicine (M.B.B.S.). But, before he could complete his education, his father passed away creating a huge void and the family was faced with great hardship. Nevertheless, he managed to complete the study of medicine. He then went into medical practice and became a very successful physician. He also filled the void that was created in the family by his father's death in an extraordinary manner and paid special attention to Sheikh Nadwi's education and upbringing.

Sheikh Nadwi completed his education under his brother's close supervision and then got appointed as a teacher at Nadwatul 'Ulama in 1934. As a student, Sheikh Nadwi had taken special interest in *hadith* (traditions of Prophet Muhammad), *tafseer* (exegesis of Quran), and literature. Subsequently *tafseer* and literature became his main subjects of teaching. Since his interest in Arabic literature was very strong and he had very good command of it, his ability to understand and interpret Quranic verses was exceptional.

In Arabic literature, Sheikh Nadwi had two main teachers. Sheikh Khalil bin Muhammad Arab taught him during his student days and developed in him keen interest and competency in Arabic literature. Later, when Sheikh Nadwi himself became a teacher, he benefitted from Sheikh Taqiuddin Hilali (of Morocco) who helped him master the fine points of Arabic literature. With respect to Urdu literature, he benefitted mainly from learned persons of his own family, especially Sheikh Abul Khair Barq.

In *tafseer*, he benefitted mainly from Sheikh Ahmad 'Ali Lahori (d. 1962) who was a renowned authority of *tafseer* and an expert in the discipline of *tazkiyah nafs* (spiritual purification) and *lil-laa-hiyat* (doing everything for Allah). He made several trips to Lahore and attended Sheikh Lahori's *tafseer* classes on a regular basis. He also studied *Hujjat-Allah-al-Balighah* (a book in Arabic by Shah Waliyullah Dehlavi) under Sheikh Lahori's supervision and established spiritual allegiance with Sheikh Lahori for spiritual purification.

Sheikh Nadwi studied *hadith* at Nadwatul 'Ulama under Shaikhul Hadith Haider Hasan Khan Tonki (d. 1940) and at Darul 'Uloom, Deoband, India, under Shaikhul Hadith Syed Hussain Ahmad Madni (d. 1956).

At the age of twenty-three, Sheikh Nadwi wrote his first book *Seerat Syed Ahmad Shaheed* (Urdu) which is a biography of his ancestor Syed Ahmad Shaheed (d. 1831). Syed Ahmad Shaheed was a great reformer and had led a massive reform movement in India in the first half of the nineteenth century. The book was well received by the educated class and served as an introduction of Sheikh Nadwi to religious-minded educated people of the Indian subcontinent. He had started this book in 1936 and completed it in three years.

The book created a zeal in Sheikh Nadwi himself to do something concrete and inspired him to travel across the entire subcontinent to know about those who were engaged in various types of Islamic work. Based upon what he observed and experienced in those visits, he decided to dedicate his life to the effort of *d'awah* — reminding Muslims of their obligations towards Islam, Muslims and humanity.

In that trip (after the publication of *Seerat Syed Ahmad Shaheed*), Sheikh Nadwi met several scholars and leaders including the renowned poet and philosopher Dr. Muhammad Iqbal (d. 1938). Though he had met Dr. Iqbal several times in his previous visits to Lahore, this was the first meeting with him after the publication of *Seerat Syed Ahmad Shaheed*; it was also his last meeting with the poet.

Sheikh Nadwi was deeply impressed by Iqbal's poetic expressions of the grandeur of Islam and held in high esteem the poems in which Iqbal had presented Islamic ideology of pride and self-esteem (*khud-daari*). As a result, Sheikh Nadwi, in his writings, appreciated Iqbal's viewpoint that Islamic pride, leadership of the world, self-confidence, and lofty goals (in personal lives) should be considered Allah's special bounties and be actively pursued. These themes and Iqbal's concept of *khudi* (self-recognition) resonate prominently throughout Sheikh Nadwi's writings.

Sheikh Nadwi also met Sheikh Syed Abul A'ala Maududi (d. 1979). He liked Sheikh Maududi's style of addressing modern educated people and enthusiastically acknowledged its importance and effectiveness.

He established spiritual connection with Sheikh Ahmad 'Ali Lahori (d. 1962) and Sheikh 'Abdul Qadir Raipuri (d. 1962), earned their affection and received their *khilafah* (permission to guide others on their behalf). He greatly benefitted from their guidance and advice.

He also closely observed the movement of *d'awah* and *tabligh* (known as Jama'at Tabligh) of Sheikh Muhammad Ilyas Kandhlawi (d. 1944). He fully understood the importance of Sheikh Ilyas's work and wholeheartedly participated in it. It enabled him to earn special attention and close company of Sheikh Ilyas. He used to recount the days of his company with Sheikh Ilyas as the best moments of his life.

Sheikh Nadwi had come in contact with Shaikhul Hadith Muhammad Zakariya Kandhlawi (d. 1982) while he was still in his early youth and continued getting closer to him as the time passed by. Shaikhul Hadith, in his last days, felt closest to Sheikh Nadwi among his associates. Sheikh Nadwi considered Sheikh Zakariya Kandhlawi as his elder and mentor.

In order to remind educated Muslims about their responsibility of *d'awah*, Sheikh Nadwi wrote an extraordinary book (in Arabic) entitled *Ma Dha Khasarul 'Alam ba Inhetatul Muslimeen* (published in English as *Islam and the World: The Rise and Decline of Muslims and Its Effect on Mankind*). He wrote this book when he was only 32 or 33 years old. It was published in 1950 by a reputed publisher of Egypt. This book became extremely popular in the Arab world and far exceeded the popularity that his first book *Seerat Syed Ahmad Shaheed* had enjoyed in the subcontinent. Arabs recognized it as one of the best books of the twentieth century. It became so popular that there was hardly any Islamic-oriented Arab student or teacher who had not read and appreciated it.

The book *Ma Dha Khasarul* . . . was actually the outcome of Sheikh Nadwi's thorough study of the history of Muslims, their ascension to the position of world leadership, their downfall, and the emergence of Europe as the dominant world power. It provided an objective and critical analysis of the current situation of Muslims in the light of historical facts.

Sheikh Nadwi performed his first *hajj* (pilgrimage to Makkah, Saudi Arabia) in 1947, the second in 1950 and the third in 1951. Between the second and third *hajj*, he visited several Arab countries including Egypt, Syria, Sudan, Jordan, and Palestine. He delivered lectures at various places and met many important personalities. People were impressed that he was able to present his ideas and thoughts directly in Arabic like a native speaker (without any translator). His fluency in Arabic was the result of the extraordinary effort that he had made in learning and mastering the language. He was equally effective and articulate in Urdu.

As the time passed by, he became so occupied and involved in the work of *d'awah* that it became difficult for him to continue teaching with full devotion. As a result, he finally resigned from the teaching position at Nadwatul 'Ulama in 1944 after ten years of service and offered to teach only on a voluntary basis whenever he would have time.

Now he had become very well known in both the subcontinent and the Arab world. He was invited by Damascus University to deliver a series of lectures. He went to Damascus for a month in 1956 and delivered several lectures there. Those lectures became the first part of his book *Tarikhe Dawat wa Azimat* (published in English as *Saviours of Islamic Spirit*) which he later expanded into five volumes and covered the period from the early days of Islam to the twelfth century Hijri (eighteenth century). It has been published in Arabic as well.

His contributions in academics, research, and *d'awah* earned him high recognition among Muslims and he was chosen to head several educational, literary, and religious institutions. In December 1959, a conference on religious education was convened in Basti, Uttar Pradesh, India. An organization known as Deeni T'alimi Council (Religious Education Council) was formed there and he was chosen as its president. In the same year, on his initiative, the Academy of Islamic Research and Publications was established in Natwatul 'Ulama for the purpose of disseminating sound Islamic thought and ideology to modern educated Muslims and he was appointed as its head.

In 1961, while he was on an academic and *d'awah* tour of Kuwait, he received an invitation to visit Hejaz.[1] In response to that invitation, he went to Hejaz in 1962 when Jami'ah Islamiyah (Islamic University) was founded in Madinah, Saudi

---

1 Hejaz consists of Jeddah, Makkah, Madinah, etc. in Saudi Arabia.

Arabia, and he was appointed to its advisory council. In the same year, Rabita al-'Alam al-Islami (Muslim World League) was also founded and he was appointed as one of its founding members. Around the same time, an Islamic center was established in Geneva, Switzerland, by Dr. Sa'id Ramadan (d. 1995) who was a prominent Islamic scholar from Egypt and Sheikh Nadwi was appointed as one of its founding members.

A year later, when the Hindu–Muslim communal riots erupted in the eastern part of India in 1963, Muslims became very depressed and disheartened, and it was feared that if something was not done urgently to remedy the situation, Muslims would become a defeated and dejected lot in India. To ponder over and discuss this matter, Sheikh Nadwi convened a meeting of prominent Muslims from the entire country at Nadwatul 'Ulama. On that occasion, an organization known as the All India Muslim Majlis-e-Mushawarat was founded and he was appointed as one of its founding members.

In 1961, when the then rector of Nadwatul 'Ulama Dr. Syed 'Abdul 'Ali Hasani (Sheikh Nadwi's elder brother) passed away, Sheikh Nadwi was appointed as the rector. Prior to that appointment, he had served as the dean of education at Nadwatul 'Ulama for several years.

During the period from 1960 to 1977, the problem with his eyes was so severe that he could not read or write on his own. Despite that limitation, all of his scholarly work continued and many of his important writings came during that very period. It is hard to imagine how he accomplished so much without proper eyesight. His students used to read to him and he used to give dictation to them.

In 1974, he started the movement known as Payam-e-Insaniyat (The Message of Humanity) with the objective of widening the scope of *islah* (reform) and *d'awah* to the entire population (including non-Muslims) of the country. It had a very positive effect on the educated people of all religions and denominations.

From the very beginning of his career, Sheikh Nadwi had the vision that education should be tailored to fit the needs of the *millat* (Muslims) and *'aqidah* (faith), and the *millat* should be prepared to fill the needs of the entire humanity – the theme that he heavily emphasized in his writings and speeches. He worked diligently on developing a suitable curriculum for that purpose. He himself prepared several books on Arabic language and literature which became highly popular all over the Muslim world, including the Arab countries. In addition, he also guided and supervised his students in preparing books which gained recognition and became popular.

To emphasize and deliberate on the above-mentioned role of education, he convened an international conference at Nadwatul 'Ulama in 1975. It coincided with the completion of 85 years of Nadwatul 'Ulama and thus was named as the Eighty-fifth Educational Conference of Nadwatul 'Ulama. The conference was very successful and was attended by prominent figures from all over the Muslim world.

In 1975-76, the government of India started enforcing the policy of birth control with excessive force and brutality and declared the state of emergency in the country. Sheikh Nadwi boldly condemned it and said that it was grossly wrong and undemocratic. To convey his concern, he wrote a letter to the then Prime Minister Mrs. Indira Gandhi and met her personally. He also drew attention of the general public towards the deteriorating condition of the country. Due to such efforts and general discontent of the public, the Congress party failed to secure enough seats in the next election and was removed from power after ruling the country for almost 30 years.

In 1977, he traveled to USA to attend a conference that

was organized by an organization known as the Muslim Students Association. In that trip, he also got surgery performed on his eyes and his eyesight was restored to a satisfactory level. He stayed in USA for two months and visited several cities. He reminded Muslims living there about the importance of preserving their identity in a distant country.

In 1978, he visited Pakistan to attend an Islamic conference. During that trip, he delivered lectures at several major universities and religious institutions. Those lectures have been published in the form of a book entitled *Dawate Fikr wa Amal* (Urdu).

In the beginning of 1979, he visited United Arab Emirates (UAE) and met several prominent and influential persons there. He cautioned them against the increasing influence of wealth and modern culture, and reminded them about their moral and religious obligations.

In 1980, in recognition of his academic and religious services, Sheikh Nadwi was awarded the King Faisal Award which was instituted in Saudi Arabia in the memory of King Faisal (d. 1975). Sheikh Nadwi donated the monetary sum that came with the award to various educational and charitable institutions. In the same year, an international conference was held on *Seeratun Nabi* (life of Prophet Muhammad) in Qatar in which he delivered a very powerful speech which was widely acclaimed. The centennial anniversary of Darul 'Uloom, Deoband, India, was held in the same year and the speech that he delivered there was considered to be the most important speech of the event.

In 1981, Sheikh Sultan Bin Muhammad Al Qasmi of Sharjah came to Nadwatul 'Ulama, Lucknow, to meet Sheikh Nadwi. Sheikh Nadwi welcomed the Sultan and reminded him of his obligations towards Islam, Muslims and his own people. In the same year, an international seminar was held at Nadwatul 'Ulama under his supervision, the theme of which was "Islamic

Content in Arabic Literature and Other Languages". Participants in the seminar came from all over the world and included prominent persons such as Syed 'Abdul 'Aziz Rafai (former secretary of the Council of Ministers of Saudi Arabia), Dr. 'Abdur Rahman Rafat al-Basha, Dr. Zakaria Barri (Minister of *Awqaaf* of Egypt), and Sheikh 'Abdullah Ibrahim Al-Ansari (*Nazim* of Religious Affairs of Qatar).

In the first week of September 1981, Sheikh Nadwi went to Hejaz to attend important meetings of the Islamic University of Madinah and the Muslim World League. On that occasion, he presented an important paper entitled "Daurul Hadith fi Takweenil Manakhil Islami wa Siyanah" (published in English as Hadith and the Promotion of Islamic Climate and Attitudes).

In October 1981, he was conferred the honorary degree of Doctor of Literature by the University of Kashmir.

In 1982, he visited Sri Lanka. In the same year, he presided over an international seminar on "Islam and Orientalists" that was held at Darul Musannefin, Azamgarh, India.

In 1983, the Oxford Centre for Islamic Studies was established at University of Oxford, England, and Sheikh Nadwi was appointed as the founding chairman of the trustees. The establishment of such a center in a secular institution like University of Oxford was an extraordinary achievement.

In 1983, when the then president of All India Muslim Personal Law Board (AIMPLB) Sheikh Qari Muhammad Taiyab Qasmi passed away, Sheikh Nadwi was elected as the president of AIMPLB.

In the beginning of 1984, an international organization known as the World Forum of Islamic Literature was established for the purpose of promoting Islamic literature for which Sheikh Nadwi had been working for more than four decades. He was appointed as its founding president. In

1981, an international seminar was held at Nadwatul 'Ulama to further discuss the need of such an organization and was attended by prominent scholars and writers from all over the Islamic world.

In 1986, spearheading AIMPLB's efforts to protect the Islamic *shari'ah* (code of conduct), Sheikh Nadwi (as the president of AIMPLB) and Sheikh Syed Minnatullah Rahmani (as the general secretary of AIMPLB) met the then prime minister of India several times and successfully persuaded him to get a bill passed in the parliament to preserve the Muslim Personal Law. It was considered a major achievement in the history of AIMPLB.

In 1986 as well, he went to Istanbul, Turkey, to attend a conference of the World Forum of Islamic Literature. On the return trip to India, he stopped in Pakistan and met President General Ziaul Haq who had come from Islamabad to Karachi to meet him. In his meeting with the president, Sheikh Nadwi reminded him that he should strive to improve relationship with India. The president promised to work for it. In the same year, he attended an Islamic seminar that was held in Algeria and presented a paper there. He also met several prominent persons of the Islamic world there and exchanged views with them.

In 1987, he visited Malaysia on the invitation of a prestigious educational institution and delivered lectures at various educational institutions and organizations. He also delivered a speech at the International Islamic University of Malaysia emphasizing the need and importance of *d'awah*. After returning from there, he developed ulcer in his stomach due to which he had to discontinue activities for several months.

In 1988, when Sheikh Nadwi traveled to Saudi Arabia to attend a meeting of the Muslim World League, he also visited Abu Dhabi. It was his first trip to UAE for the sole purpose of *d'awah*. Engineer Muhammad 'Uthman of Hyderabad and I had accompanied him in that trip. Dr. Taqiuddin Nadwi who was already there was of great assistance to us during that trip. Sheikh Nadwi addressed a semi-governmental gathering and reminded the audience that the society ought to be based on Islamic teachings and should adopt a balanced path in order to become truly Islamic. That speech was well received by the audience and was later published as a booklet entitled *Tarsheedus Sahwatil Islamiyah*[2] (Arabic).

In that trip, Sheikh Nadwi also addressed the female wing of a university. The brother of Dr. Muhammad Al Mubarak (with whom Sheikh Nadwi had very close relationship) was the dean at the university at that time and was very helpful in arranging programs. He reminded students and teachers of the university about their responsibilities, the need of shaping their lives according to Islamic values, and the importance of preserving their character and personality to face modern challenges. He also met several dignitaries including the vice-chancellor of the university and the special envoy to the president of the Emirates, Sheikh Zayed.

In 1990, during Sheikh Nadwi's visit to Saudi Arabia, a program was arranged to introduce the Oxford Centre for Islamic Studies to Saudi officials. He, along with a few other members of the center, met Ameer Sultan who was the defense minister as well as the head of the committee for Islamic *d'awah*. In that meeting, there was a detailed talk on the topic of Islamic *d'awah*.

Thereafter, Sheikh Nadwi and other members of the Oxford Centre delegation went to Riyadh where they met Ameer Suleman (the governor of Riyadh province), Ameer 'Abdullah (the crown prince who later became the king), and Ameer Ahmad (deputy interior minister). In this way, the effort of the Oxford Centre in creating awareness among the

---

2 Approximate translation of the title: Guiding the Islamic Awakening.

people of Europe about Islam was introduced. He also used that opportunity to remind the Saudi officials that only a balanced and middle-of-the-road path of Islam could prove effective in combating the general tendency of masses of blindly following the Western culture.

In the meantime, the issue of Babri Masjid had become very inflamed and complicated in India. After returning from the trip, Sheikh Nadwi met the then Prime Minister Rajiv Gandhi regarding this matter and asked him to find an immediate solution and not to allow the situation to deteriorate further. He also advised Gandhi that the correct solution to the problem was to restore the places of worship to their status at the time of Independence (i.e. 1947).

In addition to meeting the prime minister, Sheikh Nadwi also proposed to talk to the Shankaracharya (Hindu priest) of Chennai, India. This proposal had actually come jointly from Sheikh Nadwi and three others namely, Sheikh 'Abdul Karim Parikh, Mr. Yunus Saleem and Mr. Krishan Kant. Mr. Saleem was the governor of the State of Bihar; Mr. Kant was the governor of the State of Andhra Pradesh and later became the vice-president of India. They all traveled to Chennai to meet the Shankaracharya.

The Shankaracharya agreed with the idea that the *masjid* should remain intact and promised to work for it. To achieve that, he suggested that (1) a committee should be formed and assigned as the caretaker of the *masjid,* (2) the Shankaracharya should head the committee, and (3) there should be included a few Hindus in the committee as it would help the Shankaracharya in handing over the *masjid* to Muslims. Sheikh Nadwi came to Delhi and presented this proposal to the Muslim committees which were handling this matter, but they did not accept it. Sheikh Nadwi then decided not to pursue this matter any further and the issue remained squarely in the hands of those committees which were less inclined to negotiate.

Unfortunately, the situation continued getting worse and the *masjid* was ultimately demolished in 1992 making the situation extremely explosive. The Muslim committees which were very vocal in this matter up to this point felt very demoralized by this incident and consequently handed over their responsibilities to AIMPLB. AIMPLB accepted the responsibility and formed a special committee which is currently pursuing the matter through legal and judicial means.

In 1993, the centennial celebration of the Parliament of the World's Religions was held in Chicago, USA. One of the organizers of the event was Dr. Hamid 'Abdul Hai who is the younger brother of Dr. Ahmad 'Abdul Hai (a prominent surgeon of Patna, India) who was very close to Sheikh Nadwi. Dr. Hamid 'Abdul Hai had sent an invitation to Sheikh Nadwi for the event saying that it would be a good opportunity to represent Islam. Since Sheikh Nadwi was already going to Oxford, England, he accepted the invitation. The other incentive for accepting the invitation was that he would be able to meet those whom he had met in his last visit to Chicago in 1977.

Since Sheikh Nadwi had decided to stay in Oxford until the end of the program there, he reached Chicago only a day before the end of the conference. The schedule was such that he would address on the last day of the conference and as such he went to the venue. When he reached the place, there was still some time left before the start of the program. The place was packed, people of all different religions were arriving and some of them had started reciting *bhajan* (Hindu devotional song or hymn) and *mantra* (chant). Sheikh Nadwi was provided a place where he could wait. But he felt that the atmosphere was so full of darkness (spiritually) that he did not want to stay there for a moment and insisted on leaving the place.

I was present with Sheikh Nadwi on that occasion. The dilemma was that the entire trip was arranged and undertaken for the very purpose of participating in the conference and the expenses were borne by the conveners. Since Dr. Hai was like a middleman, he was put in a very awkward position. But seeing Sheikh Nadwi's uneasiness, Dr. Hai wholeheartedly agreed to his wish and said that he would not subject him (Sheikh Nadwi) to any discomfort even though it might look awkward. Later, Sheikh Nadwi apologized to Dr. Hai and thanked him for his patience and understanding. He stayed in Chicago for a couple of days to meet his acquaintances there. He then went to New York and stayed there for a day before returning to India.

In the same year (i.e. 1993), he got an opportunity to visit Tashkent, Samarqand, and Bukhara. The reason of that visit was that the Oxford Centre for Islamic Studies (of which he was the chairman) had persuaded the president of Uzbekistan to convene a seminar on Imam Bukhari (a pioneer in the science of *hadith*) and establish a university in Imam Bukhari's name to conduct study and research on Imam Bukhari's life and work.

The city of Samarqand was proposed as the site of the university. There were *madaris* (religious schools) in that city in the past and their buildings are still present. The grave of Timur Lang (also known as Tamerlane) is in this city. Also, graves of those who had come there with Qutham bin 'Abbas (a companion of Prophet Muhammad) are there. The proposal for the university was accepted by the government and dates were set for the inauguration. Many scholars of *Bukhari Sharif* (the book of hadith compiled by Imam Bukhari) from all over the world were invited to this event. Since Sheikh Nadwi was the chairman of the Oxford Centre for Islamic Studies and I am one of its trustees, we were also invited to this event.

Sheikh Nasir 'Ali, a teacher of *Bukhari Sharif* at Nadwatul 'Ulama was also invited.

We reached Samarqand via Tashkent. *Muhadditheen* (scholars and experts of *hadith*) from various parts of the world were already present there and a very good atmosphere had come into existence. Several good papers were presented in the seminar. The architectural model of the proposed university was presented and it was liked by all. Sheikh Abul Fattah Abu Ghodda was among the participants. His presence made the environment more pleasant. With his assistance, a trip to Bukhara was arranged.

On the way to Bukhara, we stopped at the village where Khawaja Bahauddin Naqshbandi used to live and was buried. After briefly stopping there, we went to the city of Bukhara. We went to the Jama Masjid of Bukhara where Imam Bukhari used to teach. We also visited the adjacent *madrasah* (religious school) which is still there, but is in poor condition. We met students there and found that some of Sheikh Nadwi's books were in the curriculum. After staying in *madrasah* overnight, we came back to Samarqand. The people who went on this journey benefited immensely from the conversations between Sheikh Nadwi and Sheikh Abu Ghodda. After returning to Samarqand, we went to visit archeological sites. Sheikh Salman Nadwi, who was close to Sheikh Abu Ghodda, was also with us in that trip.

In his 1996 visit to the holy city of Makkah, Sheikh Nadwi was presented the key of K'aba (cube-shaped structure in Makkah which is known as the House of Allah) and was privileged to open its door. Although he was blessed to have entered K'aba in earlier visits also, this was the first time he had the opportunity to open its door.

In 1997, Sheikh Nadwi went to Lahore, Pakistan, to participate in an international seminar of World Forum of Islamic Literature. He met Pakistani President Farooq Ahmed

Khan Leghari there. President Leghari expressed his love and respect for Sheikh Nadwi. A few months later, he met in Jordan Ameer Hasan who was officiating for the King of Jordan at that time. He treated Sheikh Nadwi with utmost love and respect.

In 1998, Sheikh Nadwi was awarded the Islamic Personality of the Year Award in Dubai. A few months later, he received the Sultan Hassanal Bolkiah International Award from the Sultan of Brunei; this award is given jointly by Brunei and the Oxford Centre for Islamic Studies. He donated the monetary sum that came with these awards to educational and religious institutions and to some individuals who were engaged in the service of religion and education.

He departed from this temporary abode on Ramadan 22, 1420 Hijri (31 December 1999), a little before the Friday prayer, while he was at his ancestral home in Dairah Shah 'Alamullah, Takiya Kalan, Rae Bareli. The burial took place in the night of Ramadan 23 in the ancestral graveyard where his ancestor Shah 'Alamullah (d. 1685) and his father, mother, brother, sisters, and nephews are buried. The village of Takiya Kalan was founded by Shah 'Alamullah Hasani who was a very prominent Islamic personality of his time and the Mughal Emperor Aurangzeb 'Alamgir (d. 1707) was one of his close patrons.

Sheikh Nadwi had been suffering from ill health and weakness for several years. About ten months before he passed away, he had a stroke, the effect of which had gradually subsided, but the weakness remained. The death was apparently caused by heart failure. At the time of his death, his tongue was busy with the recitation of the beginning verses of the Quranic chapter of *Yaseen*.

His death generated a lot of grief and sorrow all over the Islamic world. Funeral prayers, in absentia, were held in many parts of the world. In the Grand Mosque of Makkah and the

Prophet's Mosque of Madinah, funeral prayers were performed by huge gatherings on the twenty-seventh night of Ramadan. Later on, seminars and meetings were held at numerous places in his memory and they are still continuing. Several institutions and academies have been established in his memory. Several magazines published special issues to commemorate his life and work. Several national and international awards such as the Shah Waliyullah Award[3] and the ISESCO Award[4] were conferred on him posthumously which his students and relatives collected on his behalf.

May Allah have mercy on him, grant forgiveness to him, and enter him into paradise in the company of the prophets, the trustful, the martyrs, and the upright!

---

3 Awarded by the Institute of Objective Studies, Delhi, India.

4 Awarded by the Islamic Educational, Scientific and Cultural Organization (ISESCO).

2

Education, Upbringing, and Formation of Personality

Key Factors in the Formation of Personality

THE formative years of Sheikh Abul Hasan 'Ali Nadwi (1913-99) were spent in the noble and literate surroundings of northern India. India was under the British rule and his maternal family was belonged to the *zamindar* (absentee landlord) class. After the uprising of 1857, Muslims were facing revenge at the hands of British rulers and had become quite depressed and demoralized. Many, especially those who lacked sound Islamic education and upbringing, had been greatly influenced by the British culture and system of education. Modern education had become more attractive to them while the importance and respect for religious education and religious people had diminished in their eyes. Yet, the *'ulama* (Islamic scholars), despite being small in number, continued their efforts to keep the lamp of guidance lighted and burning.

Both maternal and paternal sides of Sheikh Nadwi's family came from the same forefathers and lived in the same village. Though the maternal side belonged to the *zamindar* class, it was firmly committed to religion and was fully aware of its importance. His maternal grandfather Syed Shah Ziaun Nabi Hasani was a well-recognized spiritual figure of his time and a lot of people in his locality had spiritually benefitted from him. However, because of the prevailing environment, a number of family members (on Sheikh Nadwi's maternal side) were influenced by modern education. Thus a hidden tussle between the modern and religious education was going on within the family which was affecting younger generation in several ways.

Sheikh Nadwi's mother was greatly influenced by her father and she possessed very strong *iman* (belief) and *yaqeen* (conviction) in Islam. Sheikh Nadwi's father was himself a distinguished Islamic scholar. Thus he received religious support and supervision from both of his parents. Yet, the environment in which he was living was full of conflicting forces and attitudes.

When Sheikh Nadwi was only nine years old, his father passed away. Thereafter, Sheikh Nadwi's elder brother Dr. Syed 'Abdul 'Ali Hasani who was very similar to his father in temperament and nature, became his guardian. Dr. 'Ali was well versed in both the religious and modern education; religious education had given him firm faith and conviction in Islam and modern education had given him self-confidence and freedom from inferiority complex.

Sheikh Nadwi had full faith in his mother's religious values and she was equally eager to implant them in her son. Furthermore, he had the supervision of his brother who was a well-balanced individual. Thus, after the age of nine, he had two guardians — mother and brother — and was able to develop a good understanding of worldly matters as well as a temperament of piety and religiosity. The economic hardship that the death of his father had brought upon the family had also helped him develop qualities of contentment and *zuhd* (asceticism).

Sheikh Nadwi, in addition to acquiring religious knowledge, had also enriched himself with modern and contemporary knowledge. This gave him self-confidence and shielded him from becoming a victim of inferiority complex in front of those who possessed modern education. He got the qualities of contentment and religiousness from his mother and those of self-confidence and broadness in outlook from his brother.

By the time Sheikh Nadwi finished his formal education, he immensely realized the importance of the efforts which were needed to bring Indian Muslims out of the state of depression and low self-esteem. With that in mind, he studied the life of his ancestor Syed Ahmad Shaheed and his reformist movement and presented his study in the form of a book entitled *Seerat Syed Ahmad Shaheed* (Urdu) which served as an inspiration to revive enthusiasm, self-confidence, and pride among conscientious Muslims. The book became very popular and proved very instrumental in shaping his vision as well. It also marked the beginning of his efforts of *d'awah* (calling people towards Allah) which kept on expanding in scope and diversity throughout his life.

The kind of nurturing and upbringing that Sheikh Nadwi received in his childhood and the kind of teachers and mentors that he met in his later years were special favors of Allah to him. As he has mentioned in his autobiography, his home environment and his elders played a key role in shaping his character, personality, and vision. One of the family elders he often used to mention was his maternal uncle Hafiz Syed 'Ubaidullah who had a very pleasant and loving personality. It was the effect of such upbringing and mentoring that made him unique among his contemporaries.

The environment and people around him engrained many qualities in him. He was always eager to benefit others; he was extremely cautious in receiving any benefit for himself; he treated everyone with due respect; he was very humble; he gave due recognition to everyone for that person's ability; he always kept the aspect of *d'awah* dominant in all of his work; he endured loss for himself, but never allowed others to suffer; he did not take revenge on anyone whether the other person was his enemy or an opponent; he fulfilled the rights of others; he suppressed his own needs for others; he gave full respect to elders and did not hesitate in benefitting from them; he was affectionate to those who were younger than him; and was always eager for their guidance and progress.

In his efforts of social reform, *d'awah*, mentoring, and dissemination of the message of truth, Sheikh Nadwi came across people of all types and backgrounds including rich, poor, ordinary, and powerful. The rich and powerful respected him, but he never sought any material benefit from them. If something was offered to him, he avoided accepting it. With the poor and ordinary people, he maintained brotherly and sympathetic relationship.

While Sheikh Nadwi was a child, his mother paid full attention to the development of right attitude and good manners in him with special emphasis on two things – religiousness and *ikhlas* (sincerity) – as was practiced by the family elders such as Syed Shah Ziaun Nabi Hasani, Syed Ahmad Shaheed, and Shah 'Alamullah. She used to relate their qualities and stories to him in fascinating ways.

Though she loved Sheikh Nadwi dearly, she was never lenient to him. She admonished him not to indulge in wasteful and frivolous activities. She encouraged him to be kind and helpful to the poor and needy. She always encouraged him to pursue high and ambitious goals. He in his adolescent years participated in sports such as hockey, volleyball, swimming, and hunting.

Sheikh Nadwi's mother was the most religious and sagacious person in the family. She was also very knowledgeable and well versed in literature. She always restrained Sheikh Nadwi from engaging in useless activities, harboring feeling of superiority complex, being inconsiderate to others, and not fulfilling rights of others. She always guarded him against discriminating between people on the basis of wealth, social status, caste, or occupation. Here is an example to illustrate this point.

Sheikh Nadwi once hit the son of a maidservant. When the maidservant reported it to Sheikh Nadwi's mother, she (Sheikh Nadwi's mother) called both of them and asked the maidservant's son to hit back Sheikh Nadwi. The maidservant was very reluctant to let her son hit Sheikh Nadwi, but Sheikh Nadwi's mother insisted that he must do so. When the maidservant refused to let her son hit Sheikh Nadwi, Sheikh Nadwi's mother herself took the hand of the maidservant's son and made him hit Sheikh Nadwi.

This was the kind of upbringing that grounded in Sheikh Nadwi the character due to which he never considered anyone low or insignificant and never became abusive to anyone. This remained his character even after becoming famous and prominent. Sometimes, he had to face wrath and rage of others and was subjected to very harsh treatment. So far I know, despite being in a position of taking revenge, he never did so. Once when a group of people started a campaign against him in newspapers, not only did he refrain from replying back, but he also forbade everyone from doing so on his behalf and left the matter to Allah. The result was that those who were campaigning against him had to retract their allegation and he came out unscathed. At times, the situation became extremely tough, but he did not react to it and ultimately his name was cleared.

The way Sheikh Nadwi's mother raised him was truly exceptional. But, more than that, the way she made *d'ua* (supplications) for him was very special. She used to make *d'ua* in the form of couplets that she had composed; those couplets were later published as a booklet entitled *Bab-e-*

Rahmat[1] (Urdu). An examination of those couplets gives an idea as to what kind of pathos and passion she had in her *d'ua*. She was a pious woman and was very particular about *awraad* and *wazaaif* (regimen consisting of recitation of Quran and remembrance of Allah) and *tahajjud* (pre-dawn prayer).

When she became widow, Sheikh Nadwi was very young. Thus her responsibility towards him increased significantly. Her heart was broken and she was under great hardship. It is hard to imagine what kind of *d'ua* she was making in that condition. If someone would have listened to her *d'ua* and looked at the conditions around her, it would have been very hard to imagine that even a small portion of her *d'ua* would come to fruition. But she had firm faith in the acceptance of her *d'ua*. The result was that all of her *d'ua* ultimately came to full fruition although most of them had remained unfulfilled in her lifetime. Had Allah shown to her in her grave the fruits of her *d'ua*, it must have made her extremely happy. She had prepared a manuscript *Ad D'ua wal Qadr*[2] (Urdu) in which she had expressed her hopes for the acceptance of her *d'ua*; it was handwritten and was very touching.

When Sheikh Nadwi reached the age of adolescence, he got the guardianship of his elder brother Dr. Syed 'Abdul 'Ali Hasani. Dr. 'Ali was well versed in both the traditional and modern subjects. He had received special supervision of his father. He was well aware of the deplorable condition of Muslims and knew what they needed to do to get out of that situation and regain the place of respect and honor. He wanted to prepare his younger brother (Sheikh Nadwi) for that challenge. With that in mind, he provided Sheikh Nadwi with opportunities to visit elders who could potentially serve as his mentors. He also exposed Sheikh Nadwi to the body of

---

1 Approximate translation of the title: Door of Mercy.

2 Approximate translation of the title: Supplication and Destiny.

literature that could develop in him the capacity to lead and reform.

Sheikh Nadwi went to Lahore and stayed in the company of Sheikh Ahmad Lahori (d. 1962) who was a renowned spiritual mentor and scholar. Through Sheikh Lahori, he met Sheikh Ghulam Muhammad Deenpuri who was a very prominent spiritual figure of his time, took *bay'ah* (oath of spiritual allegiance) with him and earned his affection and blessing. During his stay in Lahore, he also met Dr. Muhammad Iqbal (d. 1938), the Poet of the East, whom he often-quoted in his writings.

He went to Darul 'Uloom, Deoband, India (an Islamic institution of higher learning) to study *hadith* (traditions of Prophet Muhammad) under the supervision of Sheikh Syed Hussain Ahmad Madni (d. 1956). The company of Sheikh Madni gave him immense spiritual benefit. It elevated his piety, *lil-laa-hiyat* (doing everything for the pleasure of Allah) and the spirit of living and dying for the sake of Allah.

He went to Delhi to meet Sheikh Muhammad Ilyas Kandhlawi (d. 1944) who was carrying the effort of *d'awah*. He took part in Sheikh Ilyas's work and noticed significant change in himself. He was greatly affected by Sheikh Ilyas's deep concern and compassion for Islam, Muslims, and mankind. He was also impressed by the effectiveness of Sheikh Ilyas's method of *d'awah*, his sincerity and conviction in the promises of Allah.

He then met Sheikh 'Abdul Qadir Raipuri (d. 1962), an eminent spiritual figure, and Shaikhul Hadith Muhammad Zakariya Kandhlawi (d. 1982). He benefitted immensely from both of them and remained indebted to them during his entire life.

In addition to the above-mentioned personalities, Sheikh Nadwi benefitted from others as well who were involved in any effort of *d'awah* and *islah*.

It was a great favor of Allah to Sheikh Nadwi that he got excellent teachers. He was taught in a system that closely resembled the classical method of teaching – a system that is more natural, beneficial, and requires a student to master one subject at a time before advancing to the next. He received instructions in each subject by renowned and distinguished teachers who taught their subject with its unique taste and flavor. Thus he was able to build a sound foundation in each subject and master its fine points as well.

His early childhood education began at home under the supervision of his uncle Sheikh Syed 'Azizur Rahman Hasani who taught him Urdu, Persian and other basic subjects. Sheikh Hasani, who was in-charge of the library at Nadwatul 'Ulama, was very good at teaching young children. He taught Sheikh Nadwi with great affection, but was also very strict in discipline.

The next phase of Sheikh Nadwi's education was focused on the Arabic language. Since his father was a prolific writer of Arabic, there was already an atmosphere of interest in Arabic at home. His elder brother Dr. Syed 'Abdul 'Ali Hasani had studied both Arabic and English, and was familiar with the modern techniques of teaching a language as well. Dr. 'Ali held the view that the tradition of making a student first master all the rules of grammar before teaching him text and literature is an impediment to learning a language; teaching text and literature before teaching grammar is more natural and is similar to teaching a child his mother tongue; it enables the student to understand and use the language at the same time.

Dr. 'Ali obtained for Sheikh Nadwi reading materials which were prepared in Egypt and engaged Sheikh Khalil bin Muhammad Arab to teach them to Sheikh Nadwi. Sheikh Khalil was a learned scholar of Arab descent and was living in the same locality as Sheikh Nadwi. Though Sheikh Khalil was educated at Nadwatul 'Ulama, he had retained his native skills of Arabic language. He taught Arabic to Sheikh Nadwi as if he was teaching it to a native Arab student.

Sheikh Khalil was very affectionate to Sheikh Nadwi and treated him like his own nephew. He obtained and taught latest reading books that were published in Cairo and Beirut. He tried to instill in Sheikh Nadwi the feeling that Arabic was Sheikh Nadwi's mother tongue. This had profound effect on how Sheikh Nadwi learned and mastered Arabic. The benefit was so great that Sheikh Nadwi remained grateful to Sheikh Khalil throughout his life.

Sheikh Khalil, in addition to teaching Arabic, was also very particular about developing proper manners and learning skills. If needed, Sheikh Khalil did not hesitate in disciplining Sheikh Nadwi for which he had permission from both his mother and elder brother. To illustrate this, Sheikh Nadwi has written an anecdotal piece namely *Taufiq-e-Ilahi* (favor of Allah) in his autobiography *Karwan-e-Zindagi* which is presented here:

> During the period I was taught by Sheikh Khalil, a situation came which looked ordinary, but had very decisive consequences for my study of the Arabic language and literature. One day, I told my English teacher Khaliluddin Hanswi that I would not be able to take lesson from him because of some reason and shut the door on him which made him feel very insulted. Later, Khaliluddin Hanswi related that incident to Sheikh Khalil who used to respect him a lot. Upon hearing this, Sheikh Khalil, who was very short tempered by nature, became very upset and wanted to admonish me. He took permission from my elder brother and admonished (beaten) me severely which was much more than what was warranted by the incident. Later on, Sheikh Khalil realized it and apologized to me.
>
> Somehow, the news reached my mother in Rae Bareli. She asked me about severe beating by Sheikh Khalil. At that time, Allah guided me and I pleaded on behalf of Sheikh Khalil and defended his action. My mother was satisfied

> and my education continued. I believe that that action of mine was nothing but the favor of Allah as it paved the way for me to develop interest in the Arabic language and literature and serve *deen* (Islam) and knowledge through it in future. Had I proven myself innocent and my dear and affectionate teacher to have crossed the limit in reprimanding me, things would have been quite different and I would have been deprived forever of the blessings of Sheikh Khalil's teaching and the success that I attained in the Arabic language and literature later.
>
> "This is from the favor of my Lord to test me whether I will be grateful or ungrateful." – Holy Quran, *An Naml*, 27: 40

Sheikh Nadwi continued to develop competency in Arabic like that of a native Arab under the supervision of Sheikh Khalil and became so fluent and proficient that even Arab scholars and writers envied him. Sheikh Nadwi always felt indebted to Shiekh Khalil and used to often remember him with respect and gratitude.

With respect to the Arabic language and literature, Sheikh Nadwi was blessed with one more favor. At the time Sheikh Nadwi was about to complete his studies at Nadwatul 'Ulama, Sheikh Taqiuddin Hilali, a highly experienced and respected scholar of Arabic from Morocco, came to India. Sheikh Nadwi's elder brother Dr. 'Ali used to greatly value and appreciate Arab scholars. Thus when he came to know about Sheikh Hilali, he got him appointed as a teacher of Arabic language and literature at Nadwatul 'Ulama. This gave Sheikh Nadwi an opportunity to benefit from Sheikh Hilali for three years. Sheikh Nadwi often used to mention with gratitude the benefits that he received from Sheikh Hilali.

Sheikh Hilali emphasized on pure classical usage of Arabic words and their derivatives and did not tolerate any adulteration even though it might have gained currency among Arabs. To illustrate the caliber and authority of Sheikh Hilali, Sheikh Nadwi used to describe a real story. Once, with respect to some Arabic words, an argument ensued between Egypt's prominent scholar Sheikh Rasheed Raza and the renowned writer and philosopher Ameer Shakeeb Arsalan. To settle the argument, they made Sheikh Hilali as the arbitrator and agreed to accept his decision. This shows the level of respect and authority that Sheikh Hilali enjoyed among scholars of Arabic language. Sheikh Hilali was very rigid in his approach and thinking. If he considered something wrong, he was not willing to compromise with it at any cost. That is how he was in the day-to-day life also.

During Sheikh Hilali's stay at Nadwatul 'Ulama, a number of other newly-appointed teachers (in addition to Sheikh Nadwi) also benefitted from him as his students. They included Sheikh Mas'ud 'Alam Nadwi, Sheikh Muhammad Nazim Nadwi, and Sheikh Abul Lais Islahi Nadwi.

Sheikh Mas'ud 'Alam Nadwi started the Arabic monthly magazine *Al-Dhiya* (Arabic) from Nadwatul 'Ulama. Sheikh Syed Sulaiman Nadwi and Sheikh Taqiuddin Hilali were its sponsors. Sheikh Abul Hasan 'Ali Nadwi and Sheikh Muhammad Nazim Nadwi were its co-editors.

Sheikh Mas'ud 'Alam Nadwi was more in agreement with Sheikh Hilali's opinion that the modern denotation and usage which had crept into the Arabic language in recent times should not be used if they were different from their classical counterpart even though they might have become commonly used phrases among the Arabs. However, Sheikh Abul Hasan 'Ali Nadwi was more flexible in his approach and held the view that if someone from among the genuine native Arabs was using modern denotation, there was no need to be so strict about it.

Sheikh Abul Hasan 'Ali Nadwi's approach added beauty to the language and made it more acceptable and preferable. Sheikh Hilali's approach was geared more towards preserving the classical nature of the language. Sheikh Nadwi agreed with that in principle and considered adherence to it essential whenever possible.

The next phase of Sheikh Nadwi's education was focused towards the study of *hadith*. He had the privilege of benefitting from several renowned scholars in this area. He first studied it under the tutelage of Sheikh Haider Hasan Khan Tonki (Shaikhul Hadith of Nadwatul 'Ulama) who was a distinguished scholar of *hadith*. Since Sheikh Tonki had good relationship with Sheikh Nadwi's relatives living in Tonk (a place in the State of Rajasthan, India), he gave Sheikh Nadwi special attention. Sheikh Nadwi finished the highest book of *hadith* under Sheikh Tonki and received the certificate of completion of *hadith* from him. Sheikh Nadwi used to give the same certificate to his students.

To gain further enrichment in *hadith*, Sheikh Nadwi stayed for about six months in Darul 'Uloom to attend classes given by Shaikhul Hadith Syed Hussain Ahmad Madni. He then went to Lahore to attend classes of *tafseer* (exegesis) of Quran given by Sheikh Ahmad 'Ali Lahori. He also attended the course on *Hujjat-Allah-al-Balighah* (a book in Arabic written by Shah Waliyullah Dehlavi) which was taught by Sheikh Lahori in a very special way and completed it with distinction. Thus Sheikh Nadwi specialized in three branches – Arabic language and literature, *hadith*, and *tafseer* of Quran.

Sheikh Nadwi benefitted from three more prominent scholars. One of them was his own brother Dr. Syed 'Abdul 'Ali Hasani who guided him to study a wide range of subjects and encouraged him to become well versed in all branches of knowledge – both religious and contemporary. He made Sheikh Nadwi study books of great scholars such as Shaikhul Islam Ibn Taimiyah (d. 1328), 'Allamah Ibn Qaiyam (d. 1350), 'Allamah Ibn Jauzi (d. 1200), and Imam Ghazali (d. 1111). In addition, he also wanted Sheikh Nadwi to be well aware of the past and present conditions of the Muslim *ummah*.

The second person was Sheikh Nadwi's uncle (husband of his father's sister) Sheikh Syed Talha Hasani who was a professor at Oriental College of Lahore, Pakistan. His study of literature, history, and religion was very broad and he was also very good at grooming students academically. He worked diligently to help Sheikh Nadwi develop proper vision and excellent academic ability and social skills.

The third person was Sheikh Syed Sulaiman Nadwi who was the dean of education at Nadwatul 'Ulama and enjoyed a very distinguished position among his contemporaries due to his scholarship. Sheikh Nadwi often sought his guidance in Quran, Arabic language, literature, and history.

The above-mentioned persons were the main architects of Sheikh Nadwi's academic career. But it had been his practice that whenever he had an opportunity to meet any expert of a subject, he would try to benefit from him through some discussion or exchange of views. He never felt shy of benefitting from anyone, even from his students.

When Sheikh Nadwi started getting opportunities to join international organizations and institutions, he also got opportunities to meet scholars and experts of international repute. In those meetings, he did not limit himself to administrative and organizational activities only. Rather, he found opportunities for scholarly and intellectual discussions also. This allowed him to constantly enrich his knowledge and expertise. This made him so versatile that he was regarded as a scholar of international caliber and was frequently sought by reputable groups and organizations for patronage.

Allah had shown special favors to Sheikh Nadwi in shaping his personality both as a scholar and a person. The kind of grief and sense of helplessness that was brought upon him by the death of his father at such a tender age must have attracted Allah's special mercy that comes to an orphan of noble character and good moral. He was also blessed with the special care and *d'ua* of his mother. These two factors had played an important role in shaping his personality.

Sheikh Nadwi also went through a number of health problems – things that often elevate a person to new heights if he is determined and ambitious. At very young age, he developed chronic dysentery and suffered from it for a very long time. That illness had made him very weak and he had to endure a lot of hardship in his academic pursuits and *d'awah* travels.

From his physical appearance, it was easy, especially for physicians, to sense that he had suffered from a lot of sicknesses during his childhood and youth years. In one of his trips to Lahore, a doctor suggested that he was suffering from either bone or intestinal tuberculosis and thus had only a short time to live. Later, when he went to Lahore again after several years and met that doctor, Sheikh Nadwi felt somewhat amused by the thought that the doctor would be amazed to see him still alive.

Despite suffering from chronic dysentery, Sheikh Nadwi continued his travels to remote villages for *d'awah* which aggravated his sickness and caused excessive bleeding. It used to make his brother Dr. 'Ali very worried that something untoward might happen during those journeys. Dr. 'Ali, who had specialized in both the Greek and modern medicines, after trying several lines of treatment, was finally able to cure that disease.

Soon after getting over the disease of chronic dysentery, Sheikh Nadwi developed the problem of excessive coughing. He used to cough so profusely and frequently that he did not pass even five minutes without coughing. The coughing had become his signature to indicate whether or not he was present. Excessive coughing had affected his nervous system also. All kinds of treatment were done, but there was no relief. But when he went to Damascus as a visiting professor in 1956 and stayed there for a month, the problem disappeared on its own without any treatment and never reoccurred.

Shortly thereafter, he suddenly developed problems with his eyes. He went to the Aligarh Muslim University Medical College for treatment. One of his eyes was operated, but it did not help much. He then had to go to Bombay for a major surgery which was performed by a prominent surgeon. Since it was a major surgery, there were many precautions needed after the surgery.

While he was still recovering from the eye surgery, major Hindu–Muslim communal riots broke out in Jamshedpur (Bihar, India) and Rourkela (Orissa, India). To address that problem, a meeting of community leaders was convened at Nadwatul 'Ulama in August 1964. The All India Muslim Majlis-e-Mushawarat was formed at that very time. Since he was the host, he had to participate in meetings and deliver a speech – something that was against the precautions required by the surgery. Furthermore, it was later found that there had occurred in the previous surgery some mistake due to which his eyes were adversely affected and led to the development of glaucoma.

For the treatment of glaucoma, he went to the famous eye hospital of Sitapur (Uttar Pradesh, India) and stayed there for one-and-half months. The treatment was only partially successful. The pain used to subside after surgery only to come back with the same severity in three to four days requiring another surgery. The result was that the surgery had to be repeated six or seven times. Due to repeated surgeries, the eye had become severely bruised. The month of Ramadan arrived in the meantime and we had to pray Eid prayer inside the hospital.

After coming back from Sitapur, he started homeopathic treatment for his eyes. The pain subsided, but the vision still remained problematic. This situation lasted for ten to twelve years. During that period, he was unable to do any reading or writing on his own and always needed someone to assist him. Despite these difficulties, he continued his work unabated and many of his important writings came during that very period. He also needed someone to assist him in moving from one place to another, but did not stop traveling.

Finally in 1977, the eye which had almost completely lost vision was operated by a prominent eye doctor in Philadelphia at the end of his trip to USA. The sight in that eye was successfully restored and he continued using it for the rest of his life.

He then developed the disease of gout which sometimes used to cause excessive pain. But he continued his academic, religious and *d'awah* activities at the same pace.

In the early part of Sheikh Nadwi's youth, while he himself was suffering from chronic dysentery, an important incident took place involving his nephew Syed Mahmood Hasan (d. 1942). Syed Mahmood Hasan was about seven years younger than Sheikh Nadwi and was suffering from multiple diseases since his very childhood. Once he became so sick that he had to be admitted to the European ward (a special ward) of the Lucknow Medical College Hospital and Sheikh Nadwi had to stay with him in the hospital for a few days, day and night.

It was the beginning of Sheikh Nadwi's youth and thus it was quite natural for him to be easy going and lighthearted. But the few nights that he spent in the hospital with his nephew shook him very much. From time to time, he heard cries of pain and suffering coming from different corners of the hospital. A cry would also come from his own nephew who would call him for help. But Sheikh Nadwi, being unable to do anything to alleviate his nephew's pain, would run to the nurse who also would not be able to do much. Sheikh Nadwi used to say that the few nights that he spent in the hospital affected his outlook of life so much that his lightheartedness changed into seriousness forever and he developed an acute sense of responsibility towards life.

Sheikh Nadwi's nephew came home from the hospital after treatment, but his bout with other diseases continued. He was diagnosed to have TB for which there was no cure at that time and he passed away eight or nine years later when he was still very young. Those events had profound effect on Sheikh Nadwi's character and personality. They made him more determined, resilient, patient, and compassionate.

At the time Sheikh Nadwi finished his education, conditions and prospects were very unfavorable for the education that he had obtained and the course of life that he had chosen to pursue. Even some of his close relatives and acquaintances held the view that the path of religious education was a hindrance in achieving progress and they believed that it was only the English education and modern lifestyle that could guarantee success. In this regard, some of them would express their views in a sympathetic and lamenting way and some, especially those who were of his age, would pass sarcastic remarks. He had to endure those unpleasant comments, but his mother and brother were fully supportive of him in this ordeal.

A similar situation came when he was once visiting his uncle in Lahore. Some of his uncle's friends got impressed with Sheikh Nadwi's intelligence and suggested that a person of his caliber should be given English education and be prepared for ICS (Indian Civil Service) instead of putting him through religious education. Such was the mindset of the so-called educated people of that time and he had to tolerate their sarcastic and derogatory remarks.

Despite all these difficulties, he continued pursuing the path which had the promise of making him a better person and capable of serving and benefitting Islam, Muslims, and the mankind. Ultimately, Allah blessed him to become as outstanding and enviable as he became.

Outstanding Qualities and Moral Character

Sheikh Syed Abul Hasan 'Ali Nadwi was a person of multiple dimensions and diverse talents. He was an eminent thinker and reformer. He was an accomplished teacher and mentor. He was a prolific writer and a distinguished scholar.

He had anchored his life around two key elements: (1) wishing well for the entire mankind, and (2) remaining committed to a cause, whatever it may be, with dedication, sacrifice, asceticism (*zuhd*), and contentment. He also possessed qualities of humility, politeness, prudence, farsightedness, and high aspirations. These qualities enabled him to resolve numerous problems, and gain respect and recognition among leaders of the society.

There were two qualities which were very evident in his life: (1) he was very accommodating, and (2) he always refrained from hurting anyone. He had a place in his heart for all those who were involved in any constructive effort for the betterment of Islam, Muslims, and humanity. He recognized and respected their contributions and good qualities provided they were not working to hurt the core principles and values of *deen* (Islam) and *millat* (humanity).

In his opinion, differences in jurisprudential matters, ways of thinking, and methodology should not cause conflict and disunity among different factions of Muslims so long as they are not harmful to *deen* and *millat.* With that principle in mind, Sheikh Nadwi looked at the educational institutions such as Darul 'Uloom (Deoband), Mazahirul 'Uloom (Saharanpur), Madarasatul Islah (Sarai Mir), and Jami'ah Salfiyah (Banaras) with utmost respect and regard. In the same way, he duly acknowledged contributions and services of organizations such as Jami'at 'Ulama Hind, Jam'at Islami, and the Muslim League. He maintained cordial relationship with responsible persons and officials of these institutions and organizations and lent his support to them whenever it was needed.

He was also very careful not to cause any harm to anyone. He was so particular in this respect that if someone insulted or offended him, he did not reply back to that person and instructed his associates also to do the same. If he met such a person, he did not complain to him and treated him as if nothing had happened. It was not that he did not feel the pain of insult and disrespect, but he had deliberately chosen the path of tolerance and forgiveness.

There was no room for revenge or ill-boding in Sheikh Nadwi's character. He kept away from finding faults of others. If he considered someone disreputable and knew his shortcomings, he did not expose them to anyone. There were people who were hostile to him and wanted to hurt him, but he did not despise or expose them. His associates, assuming that he was unaware of the intent of such persons, informed him about their hostility so that he could protect himself from them. But they would often find out that he already knew about them and deliberately kept quiet. Due to this approach, many who were first unfriendly or hostile to him ultimately became close to him.

Sheikh Nadwi's commitment to serve, protect, and preserve *deen* and *millat* was unshakable. When he found someone doing any damage to *deen* or *millat,* he took it very seriously and voiced his opinion fearlessly which was very evident in his speeches and writings. Despite having utmost love and respect for Arabs, he vehemently opposed the idea of Arab nationalism. Despite having great respect and love for the Turks for their past accomplishments, he strongly condemned the anti-Islamic actions of the Turkish government.

He used his pen and speech to the fullest whenever there was a need to defend and protect *deen*. When a campaign was launched in India to taint Islamic practices with non-Islamic customs, he forcefully opposed it and wrote articles and delivered speeches to condemn it. He also launched a nation-wide campaign demanding that every community must be allowed to freely practice its religion and the majority community must not impose its religious and cultural traditions on minority communities.

Sheikh Nadwi kept himself aware of the social, educational, and political needs and challenges of Muslims and extended support to different efforts without getting sidetracked by the minor differences that existed between them with respect to their viewpoints or mode of operation. Since he was among the founders of the AIMPLB, All India Muslim Majlis-e-Mushawarat, and Deeni T'alimi Council, he was heavily involved in them. But he also fully appreciated and recognized the constructive efforts of organizations such as Jami'at 'Ulama Hind and the Muslim League.

In the area of education, while he had a very strong connection with religious institutions, he fully supported the institutions of secular education such as Aligarh Muslim University and Jamia Millia Islamia, acknowledged their importance and lent his support to them when needed. He believed that it was the obligation of everyone to make necessary effort to protect, preserve, and promote interests of the *millat* and every group was obligated to rise above its own individualistic approach and ideology for this purpose. He adhered to this principle wholeheartedly and lent his support to different efforts to the best of his ability. It was the result of this approach that all groups of Muslims, despite having differences among themselves, united behind him and considered him their supporter and well-wisher.

Though he extended support to various groups having very diverse viewpoints and ideologies, it did not mean that he did not have an opinion of his own. In fact, he had his own firm opinion in every matter and did not compromise with something that was fundamentally wrong and ill-founded. His basic premise was that minor differences should be ignored for a larger benefit.

Sheikh Nadwi's services to *deen* and *millat* were not limited to India and the subcontinent only. They extended to the entire Islamic world – to Malaysia and Indonesia in the east and to Afghanistan, Iran, Turkey, and Arab countries in the west. He also reached Muslims living in Europe and America. Wherever he saw a need, he offered his assistance. Wherever he saw a weakness or failing, he voiced his concern and offered suggestions for remedy. In order to convey right perspective of Islam and protect interests of Muslims, he reached masses through public speaking, and persons of power and influence through personal meetings, discussions, and negotiations.

When he addressed someone, he gave full recognition to that person's contributions and used the method that was most appropriate to the position and status of that individual. He presented his viewpoint with full force. But, even in his criticism, he was so compassionate and loving that the addressee did not feel offended and took even his tough words in a positive way. He took advantage of the opportunities that he got to meet important leaders of India and abroad and conveyed his message to them only with the welfare of people in mind and without any desire to gain material benefit for himself. Details of such encounters may be found in his autobiography. He was blessed with the extraordinary skill of combining good gesture with harsh criticism. I have myself witnessed him doing this on many occasions with great skill, courage, and wisdom.

In his social and community works, Sheikh Nadwi followed the prophetic example: while addressing someone, the speaker must be mindful of the language and level of understanding of the addressee, must be genuinely sincere and sympathetic to the addressee, and must have an earnest desire to solve the problem.

Sheikh Nadwi took guidance from the stories of prophets which the holy Quran has described about how they conveyed the message of truth and from the life of Prophet Muhammad. He also took cues from past reformers and saviors who strove in different periods of history, faced unique challenges, and employed methods that were most appropriate to their unique situations.

He kept in front of him the example of Imam Ahmad bin Hanbal (d. 855) who remained steadfast and committed to the words of *haq* (truth) despite being subjected to severe tests and hardships; Imam Ghazali (d. 1111) who, despite reaching the highest levels of scholarship, remained concerned about his own inner purification and spiritual progress; Imam Ibn Taimiyah (d. 1328) who, through his writings, fought against social evils and immoral practices, and defended fundamental religious values; Jalaluddin Rumi (d. 1273) who brought changes through his poetic marvel; Mujaddid Alf Thani (d. 1624) whose emphasis on *tawheed* (oneness of Allah) was unwavering and who attempted to reform rulers of his time without becoming confrontational; Khawaja Moinuddin Chishti (d. 1230), Khawaja Nizamuddin Aulia (d. 1325), and Sheikh Sharfuddin Yahya Maneri (d. 1291) who used very pragmatic and effective methods to bring spiritual reforms and changes; Hakimul Islam Shah Waliyullah Dehlavi (d. 1762) who worked in an era of political turmoil and social upheaval and tried to bring social reform and establish a system of education and guidance; and Syed Ahmad Shaheed (d. 1831) and his companions who strove to purify faith and practice and revived the traditions of *hijrah* (emigration for the sake of Allah) and *jihad* (struggle for propagation and establishment of truth).

Sheikh Nadwi also kept in front of him the life of his ancestor Syed Shah 'Alamullah Hasani (d. 1685) who was very firm in practicing *tawheed* and *sunnah* (traditions of Prophet Muhammad) and was very relentless in refuting and combating *bid'ah* (innovation in Islamic practices). Shah 'Alamullah Hasani was a *khalifah*[3] (deputy) of Syed Adam Binnauri (d. 1644) who was a *khalifah* of Mujaddid Alf Thani (d. 1624). Syed Shah 'Alamullah Hasani intended to migrate to Madinah, Saudi Arabia, but changed his mind upon persuasion of some saintly person and decided to settle in a barren place known as Takiya Kalan in the district of Rae Bareli, Uttar Pradesh, India.

Shah 'Alamullah Hasani built a *masjid* in Takiya Kalan. His family lived on very meager resources, carried on the work of reform, propagation, and education in the surrounding areas and made all kinds of sacrifices. Syed Ahmad Shaheed (d. 1831) was born in this family. In recent times, Sheikh Nadwi carried on the mission and work of the family. Sheikh Nadwi's paternal lineage reached Syed Shah 'Alamullah Hasani through his uncle Syed Muhammad Ishaq and maternal lineage reached him directly.

Sheikh Nadwi benefitted from the examples of the above-mentioned personalities. He also looked at the history of the past nations to derive guidance for tackling the problems of today. Sheikh Nadwi's example was like that of a honey bee which gathers nectar from various flowers and makes honey for the benefit of people. The honey bee has a sting also which she uses when attacked or assaulted. But Sheikh Nadwi was different in that respect. He never took revenge on anyone. There were many instances in which he could have retaliated, but he chose to keep quiet and remain patient.

Sheikh Nadwi was very good at quickly recognizing a

---

[3] *Khalifah* – One who has permission to render spiritual guidance on behalf of his teacher.

truth and getting good grasp of an issue. He could also quickly sense dangers of a fallacy or misguided effort. In such situations, he used his pen and speech to combat the danger and remedy the situation.

The unity of *ummah* (Muslims) and its collective and core interests were most important to him. Whether it was to promote goodness, fight an evil, combat a threat from the enemies of Islam, unite the *ummah* or help it regain its lost glory, he was always eager to offer his services, be it physical or intellectual.

He treated his relatives, both close and distant, according to *sunnah*. While visiting a distant town or country, if he found someone who was related to him even remotely, he went to that person's home and conversed with him in a loving and polite way. If he found someone who was a friend of his (Sheikh Nadwi's) father, he went out of way to meet him and his children. He was eager to earn rewards (in the hereafter) of being nice to relatives. If some relatives gave him cold shoulder or hard time, he exhibited tolerance and did some favor to them. He acted according to the *hadith* which encourages maintaining and mending relationship even with those who want to sever it.

He treated his non-relatives also with due respect. The practice of treating a *momin* (believer) with utmost respect was very evident in his life. He treated even his servants as his equal and made them sit next to him while eating. This was the result of his mother's upbringing and training through which she had instilled in him these qualities in his very childhood.

Sheikh Nadwi was also deeply committed to the welfare and dignity of the entire mankind. Once, Sikhs, a minority community in India, became the object of atrocity and brutality at the hands of the majority community. When he came to know about it, he became very restless, warned people about its consequences and issued a very passionate appeal to stop the carnage. It had a very positive effect. The situation calmed down and the people returned looted items to their owners.

Sheikh Nadwi's life was full of simplicity and humility. His dress was simple, according to *shari'ah* (code of conduct) and without any pomp and show. Those who were close to him amply witnessed it and some have mentioned it in their writings as well. There was nothing out of ordinary in his household. He treated members of his household with full recognition of their position. He had an uncle who was financially distressed and had become very weak due to old age. Once he got his clothes soiled. Sheikh Nadwi, despite being a scholar of international repute, himself took the soiled clothes to the river and washed them saying that he was his uncle and it was his responsibility to wash his uncle's clothes.

Sheikh Nadwi's treatment to his mother and brother was exceptional. He considered serving his mother a great honor. After his father passed away, he considered his brother as his guardian and greatly benefitted from his guidance.

Sheikh Nadwi treated his sisters with utmost love and respect. After the death of his mother, he used to treat his eldest sister (my mother) like his mother and used to sit with her with great love and affection. It was his daily routine to sit with her for some time during his stay in Rae Bareli. The other sister was Amatullah Tasnim Sahiba. She was older than him and was very knowledgeable in Arabic. After the death of her husband, Sheikh Nadwi included her as a member of his own household. He loved and respected her a lot and continued doing so until her death. He also had two cousins (daughters of his mother's sister). After they became widow, he included them also in his household and treated them with due respect.

Sheikh Nadwi's wife was the daughter of his maternal uncle (brother of his mother). Due to this relationship, he kept her nieces (daughters of his wife's sister) in his own house during their childhood and made arrangement for their education and upbringing. They were even married from his home though their parents were still alive.

Sheikh Nadwi did not have any children of his own. He treated his nephews and nieces as his own children and took full responsibility of their education and upbringing. The result was that we [Shiekh Rabey and his brothers] followed the path which was dear to him.

In his personal life, Sheikh Nadwi was very particular and punctual in *'ibadah* (worship) and *dhikr* (remembrance of Allah). Though his punctuality of daily congregational prayers was visible to everyone, that of his *dhikr* and recitation of Quran was hidden from the public eye. He recited the Quranic chapter *Yaseen* more than ten times everyday and rendered its rewards to his deceased relatives and elders. In this rendering, he included people from the early days of Islam up to his own time and everyone who had done any favor to him. He used to do it everyday without fail with full concentration and devotion. He was also very particular about reciting a portion of Quran everyday in the morning after fulfilling his needs.

Despite being so particular and punctual in these practices, he tried not to expose them to others. Also, instead of repeatedly reminding others about them, he kept such a posture that others automatically felt reminded. He was also very particular about *tahajjud* (pre-dawn prayer), maybe, since his very childhood. When I came under his guardianship, I started living with him in the same room and saw him praying *tahajjud* (pre-dawn prayer) on a regular basis.

The desire to serve *deen* (Islam) and *ummah* (mankind)

was deeply rooted in him. He was mentally preoccupied with it at all times. All of his writings, speeches, and participation in various programs were driven by this motive. In this connection, he sometimes had to meet leaders and heads of countries. In such meetings, he kept himself vigilant that he was doing so solely for the pleasure of Allah. He never sought any material gain for either himself or his relatives. If he was offered a gift, he excused himself from that.

He received four international awards: (1) Shah Faisal Award from Saudi Arabia, (2) Quran Majeed Award from Dubai, UAE, (3) Sultan Hassanal Bolkiah International Award from the Oxford Centre for Islamic Studies, United Kingdom, and (4) Seeratun Nabi Award from Islamabad, Pakistan. Each award carried a sizeable amount of money which he gave away to educational institutions, religious persons, and needy individuals. He did not use even a single penny from those awards although he himself was not financially well off. He lived of the small income that he received from the publication of his books.

In order to fulfill all the responsibilities that he had assumed to serve *deen* and *ummah*, Sheikh Nadwi used to utilize his time very carefully. He had divided his time into several segments for different activities and was very particular about utilizing them accordingly. He encouraged others also to do the same.

He had chosen several individuals to assist him in different activities and utilized a person only in the area that was of interest to that individual. Thus he had individuals assisting him in matters pertaining to Nadwatul 'Ulama, Deeni T'alimi Council, Academy of Islamic Research and Publications, All India Muslim Majlis-e-Mushawarat, AIMPLB, Payam-e-Insaniyat, Tahrike Islahe Mo'asherah, and other outfits. The most prominent among them was Sheikh Manzoor N'umani who, while in good health, used to be Sheikh Nadwi's closest associate and adviser. Besides him, Dr. Ishteyaq Hussain Quraishi, Sheikh Qazi Muhammad Moinullah Indori Nadwi, Dr. 'Abdullah 'Abbas Nadwi, Sheikh 'Abdul Karim Parikh, Prof. Anees Chishti, Qazi 'Abdul Hameed Indori, Sheikh Syed Muhammad Murtaza Mazahari, and Sheikh Burhanuddin Sanbhli assisted him in various capacities. The list included this humble author also.

One of Sheikh Nadwi's special skills was that he never utilized a person in an area or activity that was assigned to someone else. In this way, he kept a person focused on the task that was designated to that person. The main criterion in the selection of a person for a task was that person's ability and performance. Thus everyone was assigned to the activity which was most suited to that person. He was very good at identifying and recognizing people's skills and talents. He always cared about proper training, nurturing, and progress of those who were working with him. In this way, he played an important role in preparing a generation of young people for the service of *deen* and *millat*.

He had a very big and kind heart. To fulfill the need of a person, he used to do everything possible within his reach. In case he could not fulfill the need of a person, he comforted that person with his kind and courteous words. He was so mindful of the feeling of others that he allowed a person (whom he had assigned some task) to continue working on a task until that person himself wanted to be excused from it. In the same way, he was very watchful in making sure that no one was hurt by his actions or words. If he felt that someone might have been hurt by him, he tried to compensate that person in some way and did not hesitate in seeking forgiveness from him.

Kindness and tolerance were the main characteristics of Sheikh Nadwi's personality. He was very affectionate and lenient with weak and young people. He was very considerate towards them and used to put minimum burden on them. He used to put himself in hardship to save them from difficulties and was always eager for their welfare and progress. The result was that young people, especially students, had developed a love for him that lasted for life. His treatment to the young people who were not related to him was such that they would sometimes start thinking that they were his equal, but he did not care about it.

He exhibited special tolerance and patience in dealing with his elders and peers. If they differed from him or opposed him in some matter, he did not reply back to them. Instead, he remained courteous and helpful to them and advised his associates also to do the same. There were occasions when it seemed necessary and convenient to rebut the opposition, but he refrained from doing so which sometimes surprised his associates. He used to say that if our relationship with Allah was good, He would help us and we would not be harmed. Thus we witnessed many instances in which the opposition's attempt to harm him did not succeed and he finally prevailed.

Helping the poor and needy was one of Sheikh Nadwi's special traits. He used to help them so secretly that it would be known only to him or to his very close associates. He paid special attention to widows, orphans, and disabled persons and used to give them a fixed amount on a regular basis.

He used to show special regard to elders whether they belonged to his own circle or not. In this respect, he sometimes would go to such an extent that people would think that such a treatment was unwarranted. But that was his temperament. In fact, he was just practicing what has been reported in *hadith* about the conduct of Prophet Muhammad.

In his private life, he was friendly, well mannered, humble, tolerant, generous, and helpful. That is why those who came in contact with him loved him and remained very close to him.

Sheikh Nadwi was very hospitable toward guests and was very particular not to cause any inconvenience or discomfort to them or hurt their feelings. He was very mindful while talking to them and did whatever was necessary to make them feel honored and respected.

In spending money, he was very mindful about how and where to spend. He was neither spendthrift nor stingy. Allah had protected him from both the extremes.

He was very cautious in accepting gifts. He always checked whether or not the element of greed was present in his heart at the time of accepting a gift. If he suspected any trace of it, the least he did was that he did not use it for himself.

Treating others with dignity, showing respect for the humanity, fulfilling needs of the poor and needy, helping people in difficulties, making sacrifices for the progress of Muslims, country, and the mankind, striving to uplift Islam, and wishing well for everyone – these were the qualities that made Sheikh Nadwi very likeable and he was looked at by different segments of society with utmost love and respect. Outside the subcontinent, he was immensely loved and respected in the Arab world. This was evident from the huge number of condolences that were received upon his death from all over the world.

In his death, the world has lost a great benefactor, an eminent thinker, and an excellent leader. It has created a vacuum which only Allah knows how to fill. May Allah bless him with great bounties of the hereafter and recompense the country and *ummah* (mankind) for this great loss!

Internal Rectification and Devotion to Allah

The elements of *tasawwuf* (mysticism), *ihsan* (sublime God-consciousness), and *tazkiyah batin* (internal purification) were deeply imbued in the life of Sheikh Abul Hasan 'Ali Nadwi. But they were often overshadowed by his overwhelming engagement in the effort of improving condition of Muslims and presenting Islam to non-Muslims. As a result, most people were unable to see this aspect of Islam in his life. Not only was he associated with the discipline of *tazkiyah batin*, but he had thoroughly studied influential literature on it and had undergone strenuous exercises to excel in it.

Sheikh Nadwi's study of the discipline of *tazkiyah batin* began with Imam Ghazali's monumental book *Ahya ul 'Uloom* which he read at an early age. He was also greatly influenced by the thinking and supervision of his mother and elder brother. His mother was the daughter of Sheikh Syed Shah Ziaun Nabi Hasani who was a renowned spiritual personality of his time and she was known to have been most affected by him in the family.

Sheikh Nadwi's mother kept a very vigilant eye on Sheikh Nadwi from his very childhood and always labored hard to steer him in the right direction. Whenever she found him showing even the slightest inclination towards the worldly interests of his peers, she immediately put a stop on it. She always described to him examples of pious and spiritual people and encouraged him to be like them. She often talked about her father Syed Shah Ziaun Nabi Hasani, his *khalifah* (deputy) Sheikh Syed Muhammad Amin Nasirabadi and Sheikh Nadwi's paternal grandfather who was also a distinguished spiritual elder of his time.

Only about a hundred years ago, the famed personality of Sheikh Syed Ahmad Shaheed (d. 1831) had emerged in the family and the stories of his spirituality, piety, and sacrifices were still fresh in the minds of family members and they used to often talk about him. All of these had created in Sheikh Nadwi an inclination towards *tazkiyah batin* from the very childhood.

Dr. Syed 'Abdul 'Ali Hasani had closely observed his father and was earnestly following his footprints. As a result, he was also closely associated with the pious and learned people of his time. He was a disciple of Sheikh Syed Hussain Ahmad Madni and used to be his host in Lucknow.

Sheikh Nadwi, after finishing his formal education, wanted to establish a spiritual connection with some spiritual elder. For that purpose, he approached Sheikh Ghulam Muhammad Deenpuri who was a renowned spiritual elder of Punjab. Sheikh Deenpuri in turn directed him to his *khalifah* Sheikh Ahmad 'Ali Lahori. Sheikh Lahori accepted Sheikh Nadwi as his disciple and instructed him to remain isolated from public as well as his relatives for a specified period of time and stay in a room in Badshahi Masjid (in Lahore) by himself. Since the *masjid* was away from the populated area, it used to become very lonely in the night – something that Sheikh Lahori deemed necessary for *tazkiyah batin*. In addition, Sheikh Lahori also prescribed a regimen of *awraad* and *adhkaar* (words recited to remember Allah) to attain excellence in internal purification. Through these means, Sheikh Nadwi was able to attain the desired level of spirituality and was later conferred *khilafah* (permission to render spiritual guidance to others) by Sheikh Lahori.

That was the time when Sheikh Nadwi was in his prime youth – the age at which very few individuals are able to keep away from worldly interests and activities. But he was very determined and spiritually enlightened. He was very particular about his *awraad*, *adhkaar*, and *tahajjud* (pre-dawn prayer) and he maintained these in future also when he was teaching and taking care of his home and family.

In addition to remaining in close contact with his spiritual mentor Sheikh Ahmad 'Ali Lahori, Sheikh Nadwi also maintained relationship with other elders. He also visited Hakimul Ummat Ashraf 'Ali Thanwi (in Thana Bhawan, a small town located in Muzaffarnagar, Uttar Pradesh) and used to attend Sheikh Thanwi's gatherings during his visits to Lucknow.

Gradually Sheikh Nadwi became very close to Sheikh Muhammad Ilyas Kandhlawi and Sheikh 'Abdul Qadir Raipuri, and gained their special trust and attention. His relationship with Sheikh Raipuri developed further and he became one of Sheikh Raipuri's prominent *khulfah* (spiritual deputies). Although Sheikh Nadwi had *khilafah* (permission to guide others) from several other elders, he usually guided people in the tradition of Sheikh Raipuri and most of his associates took *bay'ah* (oath of spiritual allegiance) in this tradition.

Sheikh Nadwi had permission to render spiritual guidance in all four major traditions of *tasawwuf*. In adition, he also had permission in the tradition of his ancestor Sheikh Syed Ahmad Shaheed which is known as Muhammadiyah tradition; he gave permission to some of his *khulfah* to render spiritual guidance in this tradition.

In addition to having close connection with Sheikh Raipuri, Sheikh Nadwi maintained close contact with other elders of *tasawwuf* as well and visited them on a regular basis to seek their blessings. Thus he used to go to Bhopal's Shah Muhammad Yakoob Mujaddidi who was a high-ranking Sheikh of the Mujaddidiyah tradition, Allahabad's Shah Muhammad Wasiyullah Fatehpuri who was a prominent *khalifah* of Hakimul Ummat Ashraf 'Ali Thanwi, Shah Muhammad Ahmad Partapgarhi who was a *khalifah* in the tradition of Shah Fazlur Rahman Ganj Moradabadi, Sheikh 'Abdus Shakoor Farooqi Lucknawi, Haji 'Abdul Ghafoor Jodhpuri, and Sheikh Muhammad Ahmad.

By maintaining good relationship with these spiritual elders, Sheikh Nadwi had won a special place in their hearts. Their diversity helped him develop the ability to combine many different traits in his personality which in turn proved very effective in mentoring and guiding his own associates.

During the lifetime of Sheikh Raipuri, if someone approached Sheikh Nadwi for *bay'ah*, he directed that person to Sheikh Raipuri for it. However, if that person had some hesitation in taking *bay'ah* with Sheikh Raipuri or was insistent upon taking *bay'ah* with Sheikh Nadwi, he accepted that request out of necessity. Sometimes, Sheikh Raipuri also directed people to take *bay'ah* with Sheikh Nadwi.

In addition to maintaining very close connection with Sheikh Raipuri in spiritual matters, Sheikh Nadwi also consulted him in all of his other activities and engagements. In fact, he used to approach Sheikh Raipuri as if he was seeking his permission in those matters. Before undertaking any foreign trip, he used to first go to Raipur (town where Sheikh Raipuri was residing) and seek Sheikh Raipuri's approval.

Once he got an opportunity to go for *hajj* (pilgrimage to Makkah). He went to Sheikh Raipuri and informed him about it. Sheikh Raipuri, due to some reason, did not give his consent as a result of which Sheikh Nadwi dropped his plan. During that conversation, Sheikh Raipuri looked at Sheikh Nadwi's face and found total compliance and obedience in him.

Next year, Sheikh Raipuri himself made arrangement for Sheikh Nadwi to go for *hajj* and accompanied him in that trip saying that it was the reward for listening to his advice the previous year without any hesitation. Besides enjoying the privilege of performing *hajj* with Sheikh Raipuri, Sheikh Nadwi was also able to derive many other benefits from that trip. He visited Egypt, Sudan, and Syria and got an opportunity to observe various Islamic movements in those countries. He also met prominent scholars and religious elders and exchanged his ideas with them regarding religious, academic, and *d'awah* (calling people towards Allah and His divine religion) efforts. Thus it was not merely a *hajj* trip. It in fact gave Sheikh Nadwi a rare opportunity and experience that helped him greatly in his future endeavors.

In that very trip, Sheikh Nadwi also got the opportunity to go inside the Baitullah (cube-shaped structure in Makkah which is known as the House of Allah). Sheikh Raipuri and those who were traveling with him were also able to avail that opportunity. The person-in-charge of the key to the Baitullah, Sheikh Shaibi had become so close to Sheikh Nadwi that he opened the Baitullah the next day also for those who had missed the opportunity on the first day.

In Syria, Sheikh Nadwi met Sheikh Ahmad Haroon Al-'Asal Al-Hajjar who was a highly-respected spiritual elder of Al Ghazaliyah tradition of *tasawwuf*. Sheikh Al-Hajjar had significant influence in Damascus and its surroundings and people of all walks of life were benefitting from him. Sheikh Nadwi became very close to him during that visit.

Allah had blessed Sheikh Raipuri with a very special talent. He had a very good understanding of the conditions of Muslims of the entire Islamic world and he understood it very well as to what was needed to improve their condition and alleviate their suffering. He, through his associates, kept himself fully informed of what was happening around the world. Thus on the eve of Sheikh Nadwi's trips to foreign countries, he used to advise Sheikh Nadwi as to what kind of suggestions and advice Sheikh Nadwi should give to the rulers and influential people of those countries.

After Sheikh Raipuri passed away in 1962, Shaikhul Hadith Muhammad Zakariya Kandhlawi became Sheikh Nadwi's closest elder who was very kind and affectionate to Sheikh Nadwi. It was due to this closeness and trust that Shaikhul Hadith Muhammad Zakariya Kandhlawi wanted Sheikh

Nadwi to write the foreword of all of his (Shaikhul Hadith's) books that were published in Arabic. One can gauge the affection and attachment that Shaikhul Hadith had for Sheikh Nadwi by looking at the following letter that he wrote to Sheikh Nadwi from Madinah, Saudi Arabia, on 22nd Jumada Awwal 1393 Hijri (24 June 1973):

> I did not forget you in *d'ua* (prayer) either in Makkah or Madinah. And I don't remember missing on any day sending *salaat* (blessing) and *salaam* (salutation) to the Prophet on your behalf. You will not disagree with me that I do not feel with anyone as comfortable as with you.

By remaining in close contact with prominent spiritual elders of his time, Sheikh Nadwi was able to understand different methods and traditions of spiritual mentoring and purification. This enabled him to utilize a variety of techniques in mentoring and grooming his own associates. If there was an associate who belonged to a certain environment and had the potential of carrying out the effort of *islah* (reform) effectively there, Sheikh Nadwi utilized methods that prepared that associate to do the work effectively in that very environment.

Sheikh Nadwi designated several of his associates as his *majaz* (deputy) to carry out the work of guiding and mentoring people on his behalf, both in India and foreign countries. He gave such permission to those about whom he felt that they could effectively serve Islam and develop good moral character in people. It included several who attained prominence in this respect; Sheikh 'Abdur Rasheed N'umani is one of them.

Sheikh Nadwi's method of spiritual mentoring was based on *hadith* and *sunnah* (traditions of Prophet Muhammad). He did not emphasize on any specific regimen of *tasawwuf* as much as on sincerity of intention, service to *deen* (Islam), and adherence to *sunnah*. He prescribed a lighter regimen of *adhkaar* to those who were engaged in teaching or learning of *deen* or in any other service of *deen*. Generally, he prescribed only those *adhkaar* which were less burdensome on human body and mind. The recitation of Quran and *adhkaar* which are derived from *sunnah* formed the core of what he prescribed to his disciples. In *adhkaar, kalimah tawheed* (words proclaiming the oneness of Allah) served as the main anchor and he recommended its recitation in a way that affected the heart.

At the time of taking *bay'ah* (oath of spiritual allegiance) from his disciples, Sheikh Nadwi uttered the same words that the Prophet Muhammad used to utter and had been mentioned in Quran in reference to *baitun-nisa*[4] (oath of allegiance of women). He emphasized on the belief in the oneness of Allah, His power, His decree, and in seeking His help in every matter.

In his own daily routine, in addition to reciting *adhkaar,* Sheikh Nadwi was very particular about recitation of Quran. He recited *Surah Yaseen* (thirty-sixth chapter of Quran) several times a day and made *d'ua* (supplication) thereafter. In his *d'ua,* he included all of his relatives, elders, friends, those who had asked him for *d'ua* and all individuals and groups who were serving Islam and promoting Islamic teachings. He was so punctual in this practice that he never missed it and he used to do it in such a way that only those who were very close to him knew it.

It was also his daily routine to recite certain verses of Quran to seek protection from evils, diseases, harms, and calamities. He recited *Surah Al-Kahf* (eighteenth chapter of Quran) every Friday which was his habit from the very childhood.

The main qualities which Sheikh Nadwi had extracted from the lives of his elders and mentors were (1) humility, (2) respect for others, (3) service to *deen* (religion), (4) concern for the betterment and progress of humanity, and (5) concern for a system of education that would make students aware of the

---

4 Al-Mumtahina, Ayah no. 12.

vices and challenges of their time, prepare them to meet those challenges and equip them with the ability to serve *deen* and *millat* (Muslims and humanity). He used to focus on nurturing these qualities in his associates and students and guide them accordingly.

He appreciated everyone who had anything positive to offer towards *deen*. He gave due respect and recognition to those who possessed qualities pertaining to *deen*. Sometimes he gave so much respect to a person that people around him thought that he was overestimating that person by not knowing his real worth. But, the fact was that he was doing so simply as an act of respect that was due to a *momin* (believer).

Sheikh Nadwi greatly valued those who were striving and making sacrifices for the betterment and progress of Islam and Muslims. On the other hand, he was deeply hurt by those who were hurting the cause of Islam and Muslims. He had seen and understood the Islamic world. He had visited Europe and America. The hostile attitude of the anti-Islamic forces had made him very concerned and he used to remain restless at all times for the same. He used his pen and speech with full dedication for the benefit of Islam and Muslims even though it sometimes required risking his own prestige and standing. He used to say that it was not a big sacrifice to put on line one's prestige and position for the sake of truth. There were plenty of such examples in his life.

Not only did he publicly voice his opinion against the efforts that were aimed at harming Islam and Muslims in India and elsewhere, but he also spoke to the leaders and authorities with courage and advised them accordingly. And he did so even in situations where he himself was in danger of being harmed, but Allah protected him in every situation due to his sincerity. If he noticed any deficiency in the approach or thinking of an Islamic organization, he pointed it out with courage and wisdom. Sometimes, people were surprised by his courage and felt that it was not the right time to speak out, but he went ahead without fearing for consequences. His approach of giving utmost respect to an individual and appreciating even the smallest good of a person was so effective that even his harsh words were taken in stride by people.

In the eyes of Sheikh Nadwi, all the above-mentioned qualities fell well within the realm of *tasawwuf* which is nothing other than fulfilling the requirements of *iman* (faith) and developing its temperament. He had in front of him the following verses of Quran in which the characteristics of a believing person are described:

> Successful indeed are the believers who are humble in their prayers, who shun vain conversation, who are payers of the poor-due and who guard their modesty
>
> – *Al-M'uminun*, 23:1-4

He was very particular about developing these qualities of *iman* in the society in order to bring reform. Before the conditions in Burma (now Myanmar) became very hostile to Muslims, he had sternly warned them to correct their *iman* and social life lest they might be afflicted with great difficulties. He had given similar warnings in his speeches to the people of Lebanon and Syria before revolution and upheaval gripped them. In his visits to Kuwait and Dubai also, he implored people to adopt the life of true believers and live a life according to the will of Allah.

He considered all of these activities to be part of *tasawwuf* and often reminded his disciples to the same. He also prescribed to his disciples the traditional regimens of *tasawwuf* which were derived from Quran and *hadith* or were recommended by authentic spiritual elders in accordance with *sunnah*. His approach, which was developed under the supervision and guidance of his esteemed elders, proved very beneficial to even those who were not so akin to the traditional regimens of *tasawwuf*.

He was very particular about not hurting anyone even though he might himself suffer. Sometimes, those who wanted to meet him or seek some kind of assistance from him would put him in a difficult situation. But he tolerated them and never let them know about his inconveniences. In some instances, because he could not fulfill their request or there was some misunderstanding, they started a campaign to defame him. But his response was not to reply back to such allegations. He even refrained from mentioning them in his gatherings as he considered it to be an act of backbiting.

He stayed away from backbiting at all costs even though it involved someone who had hurt him. He was never heard saying anything bad about anyone in his gatherings unless it pertained to protecting *deen* and *millat* from a possible damage. Even in those situations, he avoided personal attacks or criticism. Even with those who opposed him openly, he was nice and respectful instead of being revengeful. If one of his associates told him that the person whom he was giving such a good treatment had in fact done such and such harm to him, he simply replied, "I am aware, but this is my way".

Some people, in opposing him, gave him such a hard time that he became very distressed. But he only said, "Allah will decide in this matter. We are not going to retaliate." Generally, such people realized their mistakes after some time and subsequently changed their attitude towards him.

On one hand, he refrained from retaliating to those who harmed or mistreated him and, on the other, he wished well for everyone. Time and again, he was faced with very trying and difficult situations, but he always showed tolerance, kindness, and leniency and refrained from reacting to those allegations. He always followed the example of a true *momin*.

He kept his eyes on his own shortcomings and avoided looking for faults of others. In solitude, he used to cry, repent, confess, and seek forgiveness. He used to express his needs to Allah with deep anguish by reciting the Quranic verse.

> My Lord! I am needy of whatever good You send down for me. – *Al-Qasas*, 28: 24

He also used to recite other prayers and supplications including the Quranic verse:

> I only complain of my suffering and my grief to Allah.
> – *Yusuf*, 12: 86

Overwhelmed by the concern and worry for dying in the state of *iman* (firm faith), he often used to recite the Persian saying:

> *Khodaya 'aaqibat mahmood gardaan*
>
> O God! Make my end pleasant.

In dealing with his relatives, Sheikh Nadwi practiced the *sunnah* of *sila-rahmi* (establishing and mending relationship with relatives) and gave them love and co-operation. In case of those relatives who had caused him severe harm, he not only ignored their behavior, but also treated them nicely and gave special help and co-operation to them.

In Sheikh Nadwi's opinion, all these practices fell within the realm of *tasawwuf*, *ihsan*, and *tazkiyah batin* as is evident from the books that he has written about the elders of *tasawwuf* and *tazkiyah nafs*. To those who took *bay'ah* with him, he advised them to read sermons and biographies of elders. His recommendations included books, lectures, and sayings of Sheikh Ashraf 'Ali Thanwi, *Fazail-e-'Aamaal* (published in English as *Teachings of Islam*) by Shaikhul Hadith Muhammad Zakariya Kandhlawi, his own books *Dastoor-e-Hiyat* (published in English as *A Guidebook for Muslims*), *Seerat Syed Ahmad Shaheed* (Urdu) and *Sawaneh Maulana Abdul Qadir Raipuri* (Urdu), *Zade-e-Safar* (Urdu) by Amatullah Tasnim Sahiba, and *Mo'ariful*

Hadith (published in English as *Meaning and Message of the Traditions*) by Sheikh Manzoor N'umani. He also recommended recitation of Quran with translation.

His greatest emphasis was on correcting and strengthening *'aqidah* (faith). One must have full conviction that there is no one except Allah who gives life and death, health and sickness, children and sustenance. No one except Him controls destiny of good or bad and no one except Him is worthy of worship. One must always remain mindful that it is He who creates and it is He who sustains.

After *'aqidah*, he emphasized most on *salah* (daily obligatory prayers). These must be performed at their prescribed times with full observance of devotion and *sunnah.* Negligence and slackness in *salah* cannot be recompensed in any way.

He also emphasized heavily on correcting *niyah* (intention). One must perform every deed, whether it pertains to this life or the hereafter, with the intention of getting reward and pleasure of Allah. The same must also be observed in matters pertaining to social dealings and activities in order to receive rewards for them.

He also used to remind people to observe the *sunnah* of Prophet Muhammad in every aspect of life, adhere to Prophet's instructions and study the life of Prophet. Instead of prescribing too many regimens, he used to prescribe only what one could easily do.

3

Public Life and Services

D'awah

THE work of *d'awah* (calling people towards Allah and His divine religion), *islah* (reform), and *tarbiyah* (mentoring) was basically the responsibility of prophets and it remained connected with *wahi* (divine revelation) until the departure of the final prophet, Prophet Muhammad, from this world. Thus all the prophets discharged their duties under the guidance of divine revelation.

When *wahi* discontinued, Allah preserved both what was revealed to Prophet Muhammad in the form of Quran and what was revealed to him outside Quran and made them secure and permanent until the day of *qiyamah* (the Doomsday) so that the followers of Prophet Muhammad could continue the work of *d'awah, islah,* and *tarbiyah* in the same way as prophets used to do. Thus *'ulama* (scholars of Islam) and those who have knowledge of Quran and *sunnah* (traditions of Prophet Muhammad) have continued this duty to this day by deriving guidance for their effort from the holy Quran and the life of Prophet Muhammad.

Sheikh Syed Abul Hasan 'Ali Nadwi came from a family which had been consistently engaged in the effort of *d'awah.* He had heard the accounts of his family elders. He had also studied the history of reformers and *sufia* (mystics) of India. While writing the biography of Syed Ahmad Shaheed (d. 1831), he had thoroughly studied his movement of *d'awah, islah,* and *tarbiyah*. When the book came out, many *'ulama* got inspired and they used the life and methodology of Syed Ahmad Shaheed as a guide for themselves. At that time, the renowned scholar and thinker Sheikh Manzoor N'umani (d. 1997) asked Sheikh Nadwi, "Now that you have written this book, do you have any plan for future?" At this, Sheikh Nadwi and Sheikh Manzoor N'umani decided to visit centers which were carrying the efforts of *d'awah, islah,* and *tarbiyah* in different parts of India at that time.

Thus they went to Sheikh Muhammad Ilyas Kandhlawi in Delhi, Shaikhul Hadith Muhammad Zakariya Kandhlawi in Saharanpur, Sheikh 'Abdul Qadir Raipuri in Raipur, and Sheikh Ahmad 'Ali Lahori in Lahore. While in Lahore, they also met Sheikh Syed Abul A'ala Maududi who was carrying the effort of *d'awah* in a certain way and his writings were proving very effective in introducing Islam to modern educated people.

The work of Sheikh Ilyas impressed them most and they started participating in it with full dedication. Sheikh Maududi also looked at the effort of Sheikh Ilyas and acknowledged its benefits, but continued working on his own pattern. Though they (Sheikh Nadwi and Sheikh Manzoor N'umani) had fully dedicated themselves to the effort of Sheikh Ilyas, they also kept in touch with all other efforts of *deen* (Islam) which were going on at other places in accordance with the *sunnah* of the Prophet. They also studied works and methodologies of important personalities who had led such efforts in the past in India.

One of the special qualities of Sheikh Nadwi was that wherever he found any good – in an individual or a group, in books or practice – he tried to benefit from that in his effort. Thus he deemed it appropriate to carry the effort of *d'awah* in three segments of population: (1) common Muslims, (2) modern educated Muslims, and (3) people of power and influence.

He felt that it had become very common among those who were engaged in the effort of *d'awah* to divide themselves into isolated groups, each group confining its efforts to a specific segment of population. *'Ulama* and *sufia* generally worked among common Muslims. Modern educated people tended to concentrate only on the educated class. Those who worked among the powerful and influential people generally followed the methods which had evolved in Europe and they expanded most of their talent and energy in either championing or refuting those ideas instead of bringing real reform in the society.

Sheikh Nadwi considered the approach of the past *'ulama* and *sufia* appropriate for working among common Muslims. That is why he liked the method of Sheikh Muhammad Ilyas Kandhlawi and other elders like him and adopted it for working among that segment of population. However, to reach the modern educated people, he utilized his pen and speech in a way that was appropriate to their temperament and understanding. In case of the powerful and influential people, he used the method of Mujaddid Alf Thani (d. 1624) who had approached the ruling class of his time through letters and personal contacts without becoming confrontational to them. Sheikh Nadwi stayed away from the prevailing practice of merely offering hollow support or unwarranted criticism.

Sheikh Nadwi used a balanced and comprehensive approach based upon the examples of the past elders and reformers. To reach common people, he used the examples of Hasan Basri, Ibn Jauzi, and 'Abdul Qadir Jilani. To reach *'ulama* and elite groups, he used the examples of Imam Ghazali, Ibn Taimiyah, Ibn Qaiyam, and Shah Waliyullah Dehlavi. To reach the powerful and influential people, he used the examples of Mujaddid Alf Thani and Khawaja Ubaidullah Ahrar, a prominent elder of the Naqshbandiyah tradition of Sufism.

In his work of *d'awah*, Sheikh Nadwi greatly benefitted from his study and teaching of *tafseer* (exegesis) of Quran. He took cues from the examples of prophets which Quran has described about how they invited people towards *deen* (divine religion) on different occasions and in different circumstances. He tried to understand and absorb the wisdom behind their approach and methodology. In his speeches, he made frequent references to Quranic verses some of which are as follows:

> Call unto the way of your Lord with wisdom and fair exhortation, and reason with them in a better way.
>
> – *An Nahal,* 16:125

> Good and evil are not alike. Repel evil with what is good. Then you will find your erstwhile enemy like a close and affectionate friend. And no one will be granted such goodness except those who exercise patience and self-restraint, – none but persons of the greatest good fortune.
>
> – *Fussilat,* 41: 34-35

In his speeches, Sheikh Nadwi frequently referred to examples such as the conversation between Prophet Moses and Pharaoh and between Prophet Yusuf (Joseph) and his co-prisoner who wanted him (Yusuf) to interpret his dream. He took cues from these examples in conveying his message to the people in power and authority.

Since Sheikh Nadwi lived in a country (India) which is mostly populated and governed by non-Muslims, he felt the need of working among that segment of population as well. Thus in order to reach non-Muslims (of India), he adopted methods which were appropriate for their temperament, thinking, and ability. He was careful not to do things in a way that might make them feel that he was trying to impose his ideas on them. He wanted them to feel comfortable so that they could listen to the message with an open mind. While addressing them, he mainly talked about the common issues which were of concern and interest to all the communities.

With the goal of reaching the non-Muslim population of India, he started a movement known as Payam-e-Insaniyat (Message of Humanity) in 1974. From that platform, he mainly talked about common issues that concerned the entire mankind, but also mentioned virtues of Islam in a passing way and cited examples of the efforts of Khawaja Moinuddin Chishti, Khawaja Fariduddin Ganj Shakar, and Khawaja Nizamuddin Aulia. This effort yielded positive results.

With respect to the educated class, he understood it very well that the mindset of those who were modern educated (in secular institutions) was different from that of those who were the product of traditional religious institutions. This understanding enabled him to tailor his speeches and writings to the needs and temperament of the audience. He had developed this understanding because he was exposed to both the traditional and modern systems of education. He had studied *tafseer* of Quran, *hadith* (traditions of Prophet Muhammad), and related subjects from eminent scholars. He had studied secular subjects through vast study of books of modern literature and social sciences, mostly in their original languages.

Sheikh Nadwi's exposure to both types of knowledge (Islamic and secular) had enabled him to objectively analyze and compare the two systems – old and new – and understand the strengths and weaknesses of the modern culture and civilization. This is the approach which he used in his masterpiece *Ma Dha Khasar al-'Alam bi Inhitat-i-Muslimin* (published in English as *Islam and the World: The Rise and Decline of Muslims and Its Effect on Mankind*). He always tailored his talks and presentations to suit the ability and caliber of the audience. That is why people of different walks of life and viewpoints were affected by his speeches and writings.

Due to his vast and thorough study of a wide range of subjects, he did not feel overwhelmed by the outward charm of modern advancements, did not fall victim to inferiority complex and did not feel at a loss in any assembly of learned people. He firmly believed that Islam offered the most suitable and comprehensive system for the mankind and thus he tirelessly strove to articulate this viewpoint through his literary and scholarly abilities.

With respect to modern advancements and experiences, there are two extreme viewpoints. On one extreme, there are those who deny and condemn everything – good or bad – which is the product of modern innovation and progress; most of those who fall in this category are generally unaware of modern education and its accomplishments as their studies and observations are confined to the Eastern know-how and environment only. On the other extreme, there are those who adore everything that appears modern and are so impressed with the outward charm of the Western culture and achievements that they devalue their own religion and Eastern values; their exposure and study are usually limited to Western sources and that too in a very shallow way.

Sheikh Nadwi stayed clear of both these extremes and pursued a middle-of-the-road path which was also the mandate of Nadwatul 'Ulama. He believed that in order to present Islam as the savior of humanity, one should be well versed in both branches of knowledge – traditional and modern. That is why he felt it necessary for the educational institutions to design a curriculum which could equip students with both of these types of knowledge.

Broad-mindedness, vast study, exposure to multitude of viewpoints, and interaction with wide range of people had created in Sheikh Nadwi a high degree of tolerance. He appreciated constructive effort of any person if it was based on sincerity and well wishing. If he noticed some weakness somewhere, he did not rush to correct it and waited for an appropriate opportunity to do the same. This approach sometimes brought upon him the wrath of condemnation and criticism from those who espoused extremism and absolute rigidity and they blamed him for not standing up against the wrongdoers. On some occasions, they even started an organized campaign to defame and discredit him.

On one hand, he was very firm in matters pertaining to the core beliefs and fundamental tenants of Islam. On the other hand, he was quite flexible and accommodating in matters that were trivial and secondary. As a result, he was able to get along with many diverse groups and enjoyed a position of love and respect in the entire Muslim *ummah*. He was loved and respected by eminent scholars and elders of all rightful denominations and they considered him one of their own despite having differences among themselves.

As mentioned earlier, Sheikh Nadwi had divided his effort of *d'awah* in three segments of population: (1) common Muslims, (2) modern educated Muslims, and (3) people of power and influence. His efforts proved very beneficial, saved *ummah* (Muslims) from many disasters and prevented numerous unhealthy trends from becoming widespread in the society. His writings, speeches, and guidance helped in preparing a generation which could think and act in a balanced and rational way. He left behind a rich legacy from which the new generation could benefit in nurturing minds which could think correctly and rationally.

Sheikh Nadwi was educated at Nadwatul 'Ulama where

he studied traditional subjects of religion as well as history, languages, social sciences, and other contemporary subjects. He also benefitted from eminent scholars of other religious institutions of higher learning. After finishing education, he began his career in academia and service to *deen*.

At that very time, Sheik Syed Abul A'ala Maududi had published his collection of articles in the form of a book entitled *Tanqihaat aur Tafhimaat* (Urdu) in which he had very eruditely criticized the Western civilization and philosophy. Sheikh Nadwi and Shiekh Manzoor N'umani were very impressed by it. Consequently when they later met Sheikh Maududi, they decided to form a full-fledged organization for the purpose of demystifying effects of the Western culture which was gripping the minds of modern educated Muslims. As a result, Jama'at-e-Islami was founded and an organized effort was launched to reach out to the modern educated segment of population with correct teachings of Islam.

However, Shiekh Nadwi and Sheikh Manzoor N'umani developed differences with Sheikh Maududi with respect to certain religious issues and decided to disassociate themselves from him. Since Sheikh Maududi, unlike Sheikh Nadwi and Sheikh Manzoor N'umani, was not educated in a traditional institution with an established curriculum, his opinion in certain matters was quite different from that of those who had strong connection and affiliation with traditional religious institutions. When they realized that the differences were irreconcilable, they parted away from him. They also felt that it was not enough to limit the effort of *deen*, reform, and preaching to the educated class only.

By that time, the benefits of the work of Sheikh Muhammad Ilyas had become well known and Sheikh Nadwi and Sheikh Manzoor N'umani had become heavily involved in it. It was also the time when Sheikh Nadwi was suffering from several health problems including chronic dysentery which had made his older brother Dr. Syed 'Abdul 'Ali very worried though he liked Sheikh Nadwi's *d'awah* activities and gave encouragement for the same. Dr. 'Ali wanted Sheikh Nadwi to cut down his activities so that he could get proper medical treatment, but Sheikh Nadwi was too enthusiastic to slow down at that time. Dr. 'Ali once commented to Sheikh Nadwi, "Are you longing for martyrdom?" That was the period when Sheikh Nadwi was putting himself through a lot of hardship for the sake of *deen*.

Sheikh Nadwi's command of the Arabic language was as good as that of Urdu (his mother tongue). This made him stand out among his contemporaries who were engaged in the effort of *d'awah* and enabled him to reach beyond the shores of the subcontinent to the Arab world. When he went on a tour of Arab countries, his famous book *Ma Dha Khasar . . .* (*Islam and the World . . .*) had already earned him immense recognition there.

Taking advantage of his ability to fluently speak and write in Arabic, Sheikh Nadwi targeted the modern educated Arabs who had become greatly influenced by the Western culture and thinking. In Arab countries also, he divided his effort of *d'awah* in three segments of population. He addressed common people in mosques, educated people in their clubs and meeting places, and powerful people through letters and individual meetings.

While working in Arab countries, Sheikh Nadwi remained in constant touch with the elders from whom he used to seek spiritual guidance, especially Sheikh 'Abdul Qadir Raipuri who strongly supported and encouraged him in these endeavors. After Sheikh Raipuri passed away, he frequently consulted Shaikhul Hadith Muhammad Zakariya Kandhlawi and sought his advice. When Sheikh Nadwi's effort of *d'awah* expanded and progressed, he was able to involve in it many of his associates and students as well.

To expand the work of *d'awah* among educated people, an organization known as the Academy of Islamic Research and Publications was established in Lucknow, India, in 1959. It facilitated publication and distribution of the writings of Sheikh Nadwi and his associates. It also enabled Nadwatul 'Ulama to launch journals and magazines in Arabic and Urdu.

To protect Muslim children who attended government schools [in Uttar Pradesh, India] and were driven away from *deen* (Islam) under the influence of secular education, an organization known as Deeni T'alimi Council was founded in 1960 under Sheikh Nadwi's supervision. This outfit provided an alternative to the government-sponsored secular education for Muslim children.

Despite his involvement in various academic and educational endeavors, Sheikh Nadwi continued full participation in the work of *d'awah, islah,* and *tabligh* of Sheikh Ilyas. After Sheikh Muhammad Ilyas Kandhlawi passed away in 1944, Sheikh Nadwi continued supporting Sheikh Muhammad Yusuf Kandhlawi (d. 1965) and Sheikh Inamul Hasan Kandhlawi (d. 1995), subsequent *ameer* (head) of Jama'at Tabligh. In the later part of his life, Sheikh Nadwi was not able to personally participate in this effort due to heavy engagements in other activities. But he always encouraged his associates and acquaintances to take part in it. He often used to recount the benefits that he received towards his *iman* (faith), *yaqeen* (conviction), and *ikhlas* (sincerity) from his involvement in this effort.

He was also very particular about making *d'ua* for Jama'at Tabligh. After the death of Sheikh Inamul Hasan Kandhlawi in 1995, Sheikh Nadwi felt more responsibility upon himself towards this effort. A few months before Sheikh Nadwi passed away, an important gathering of Jama'at Tabligh was held during 12-14 June 1999 at Nadwatul 'Ulama in which a large number of prominent and responsible members of Jama'at Tabligh were present. Although it was difficult for him to speak due to his ill health, he delivered an important speech on that occasion. His speech was centered on the following Quranic verse:

> O you who believe! If you fear Allah, He will grant you a criterion to judge between right and wrong.
>
> – *Al-Anfal*, 8:29

It was the last public speech[1] of Sheikh Nadwi's life. His advice to Muslims was that wherever they live, they should live an exemplary life. He said:

> Brothers. You go from here with full determination that you will practice Islam in full and live such a life that the entire surrounding and all of those who live around you will be affected. The people will say that Muslims have unique character and personality, when others stumble and fall down, they remain steadfast and they cannot be bought out, be it for position, power, wealth, or beauty. Had this been our character, the entire country would have respected Islam and benefitted from it. Wherever it happened, a revolution took place.

---

1 This speech was published as a booklet entitled *Musalman Ki Shaane Imteyazi* (Distinctive Pride of Muslims) by the Academy of Islamic Research and Publications.

Social Reform

Sheikh Syed Abul Hasan 'Ali Nadwi was a person of multiple dimensions and every aspect of his personality was visible in his life in practical form. Just as he rendered his services to Islam and Muslims, he also strove to fulfill the demands of humanity at large and left an indelible impact on the society. He was carrying so many different types of efforts at the same time that if someone could manage only one or two of them, he would be easily celebrated as a man of prominence.

His study of Islamic history was very deep and thorough. His study of the history of mankind and the rise and fall of nations was also very vast. His study included all facets of human life – political, religious, cultural, and ideological. In the light of those studies, he analyzed the condition and needs of his country – India – which is populated by followers of different religions and Muslims live there as a minority community. He then, as a concerned Muslim who feels obligated to guide people to the right path and improve their condition, dedicated all of his talents and abilities for the service of the *millat* (Muslims and mankind) and the country.

He was born in a family and environment which was well suited for nurturing and strengthening this sense of responsibility. His environment also helped him develop skills of articulation, speaking, and writing which he utilized wisely as Quran has advised:

> Invite (all) to the Way of your Lord with wisdom and beautiful preaching; and argue with them in ways that are best and most gracious. – *Al-Nahl*, 16: 125

Sheikh Nadwi applied this profound advice of Quran to all of his activities including teaching, mentoring, *d'awah*, preaching, character building, protecting *shari'ah* (Islamic code of conduct), internal purification, research, publication, presenting Islamic viewpoint [on various issues], working from the stage of Payam-e-Insaniyat [to convey the message of Islam to non-Muslims], and social reform of the *millat* and the country.

Out of all the above-mentioned activities, those related to Payam-e-Insaniyat and social reform were most sensitive because they involved interaction with the country's administration on one hand and the non-Muslim population on the other, and thus had the potential of being easily turned contentious and confrontational by political parties. That is why Sheikh Nadwi, following the example of Mujaddid Alf Thani (d. 1624), always kept himself away from confrontational methods and presented himself as a non-political and independent leader.

Sheikh Nadwi considered Mujaddid Alf Thani's methodology to be fully derived from the *sunnah* (traditions) of Prophet Muhammad who had set the best example of kindness, good conduct, patience, and wisdom in inviting people towards the right path. Once, while in a journey, Prophet Muhammad was lying down under a tree in midday in a desert with his sword hanging from a branch of the tree and his companions were scattered at a distance taking rest under nearby trees. The Prophet was awakened by the presence of a stranger who was holding the Prophet's sword in his hand. The man asked the Prophet, "Who can now save you from me?" The Prophet said, "Allah" with full faith and conviction. It had such an effect on the man that the sword fell down from his hand. The Prophet immediately picked up the sword and retorted to him, "Now, who can save you?" The man felt subdued and begged the Prophet to pardon him and show mercy to him. The Prophet asked him, "Do you accept Islam?" He said, "I cannot do this. But I promise not do anything against you." The Prophet let him go. The Prophet neither forced him to accept Islam nor did he punish him.

There are numerous instances in which people of Makkah rejected his invitation and treated him rudely, but he did not retaliate.

Keeping such examples [of the Prophet] before him, Sheikh Nadwi adopted the strategy of Mujaddid Alf Thani who had struggled in this very country (India) in the regime of the Mughal emperor Akbar (1556–1605). Akbar, after becoming disgruntled with the prevailing customs and practices of his time, had started promoting un-Islamic practices and had introduced a new religion (Deen-e Ilahi) in his vast empire and put the future of Islam and Muslims of the country in great peril.

Faced with such a dire situation, Mujaddid Alf Thani did not adopt confrontational methods. Instead he used means of counseling, communication, and wisdom. Also, instead of confronting Akbar directly, he approached Akbar's courtiers and advisers and encouraged them to give appropriate advice to Akbar whenever possible. He communicated with them through letters which were full of genuine concern and compassion. His strategy began showing its effect by the time Akbar's son Jehangir (1605-27) became the emperor. Jehangir's thinking was different from Akbar's. The transformation continued and Jehangir's son Shahjehan (1627-58) turned out to be even better than Jehangir. Finally, the transformation reached complete fruition when Shahjehan's son Sultan Mohiuddin Aurangzeb (1658–1707) became the emperor. Thus the final outcome of Mujaddid Alf Thani's efforts appeared in the form of Aurangzeb who established justice and peace on the pattern of *Khulfa Ar Rashideen* (the first four caliphs of Islam) after a gap of about a thousand years.

Perhaps the Prophet's journey to Taif (a town at a short distance from Makkah) was also in front of Mujaddid Alf Thani. In Taif, when the residents responded harshly to the Prophet's call, drove him out of the town and set street urchins to throw stones on him, he sat down in a lonely place and prayed to Allah. In response to his prayers, the divine help of Allah came down and he was given the choice of getting the people of Taif crushed between the mountains. The Prophet said, "If they don't listen, I hope and pray that their progeny will listen". The Prophet did not take revenge on them although he was badly tortured both physically and mentally.

Sheikh Nadwi adapted the strategy of Mujaddid Alf Thani for his own time and situation. He advised leaders, rulers, and government officials of India and Muslim countries through letters and personal meetings to take necessary steps for eradicating vices which had become widespread in their countries. He did it with wisdom and compassion. In case of India, he also reminded the authorities about the rights of minorities and the protection of Islamic *shari'ah*.

In 1975, when the then Indian Prime Minister Mrs. Indira Gandhi imposed the state of emergency in the country, no one dared to talk to her and tell her to stop the brutalities which the government officials were committing against the public. At that time, Sheikh Nadwi met her with courage and *istighna* (expecting nothing from anyone except Allah) and prudently advised her to change her course of action. Since there was a real danger that he might be detained and might not come out of the meeting, he had advised his associates about what to do if that happened.

In 1985, during the regime of Mrs. Gandhi's son Rajiv Gandhi, the Supreme Court of India, in a court case concerning the alimony of a divorced Muslim woman, gave a ruling which infringed upon the Islamic *shari'ah*. Sheikh Nadwi along with Sheikh Syed Minnatullah Rahmani met Rajiv Gandhi several times, explained the *shari'ah* perspective of the issue to him and convinced him to take necessary measures to rectify the situation. He also worked hard to win the support of non-

Muslims and stayed away from confrontational and violent means. The result was that Rajiv Gandhi was able to get a legislation passed in the parliament which nullified the Supreme Court's ruling and upheld the Muslim Personal Law.

In 1991, when the Bharatiya Janata Party (BJP) came to power in Uttar Pradesh, it issued an ordinance requiring every child [of government-run schools] to recite the polytheistic anthem *Vande Mataram*. Sheikh Nadwi opposed the ordinance with a firm voice and warned the government that if it was not rescinded, he would ask all the Muslims parents to withdraw their children from those schools. Ultimately, the government lifted the restriction and the minister who had issued the order was reprimanded and removed.

Whenever a new leader came to power, Sheikh Nadwi wrote a letter of advice to him and met him as well. Thus when Narasimha Rao became the prime minister in 1991, he met Rao and reminded him about the need of improving social and moral condition of the country and emphasized that these issues were more important than political maneuvering.

When H.D. Deve Gowda became the prime minister in 1996, he came to Nadwatul 'Ulama to visit Sheikh Nadwi. Sheikh Nadwi gave him useful advice and urged him to improve the condition of the country and be fair to minorities. Deve Gowda pledged to do justice to the minority communities and weak sections of the society.

When Atal Behari Vajpayee became the prime minister in 1998, he came to Nadwatul 'Ulama to visit Sheikh Nadwi who was sick at that time. Sheikh Nadwi reminded him to work for the welfare of the country.

Sheikh Nadwi's advice used to be very effective and penetrating. It was due to the fact that his way of giving advice was full of sincerity and wisdom and he never allowed any blemish on his character either as a scholar or as a *da'i* (one who calls people towards Allah). He always kept the interest and welfare of the Muslims, country, and humanity in the forefront and did not care about his personal benefit. This was the reason why everyone had a good opinion about him and considered him as a sincere well-wisher of the country and humanity.

He was firmly determined not to seek or demand any benefit for himself or any family member [in return of his services] or solicit anyone for the same and practiced it very strictly. He avoided accepting any favor due to which he had to feel obliged to anyone. This strictness made some of his relatives complain that so much precaution was unnecessary, but he did not change his practice and chose not to become obliged to government officials and authorities.

On the other hand, he always remained obliged to those officials and authorities who had done any favor to help the cause of *millat* (Muslims) and gave them due recognition. In his autobiography *Karwan-e-Zindagi*, he has mentioned a few of them such as Mulayam Singh Yadav (chief minister of Uttar Pradesh) and Prime Minister Rajiv Gandhi who had played an important role in restoring the Muslim Personal Law in the lawsuit involving a Muslim divorcee; Sheikh Nadwi used to often mention it in his conversations.

No other Muslim leader or speaker attracted as many non-Muslim leaders to their speeches as Sheikh Nadwi and the government knew about it. That is why regardless of which political party came to power, it recognized his status and importance and did not ignore his viewpoint. This was true with BJP as well. Thus when BJP came to power in 1999 at the central government, it realized his influence and weight and gave him due recognition. BJP is a political party that is known to be generally unsympathetic to Muslims.

There is a large organization known as Rashtriya Swayamsevak Sangh (RSS) which mainly espouses interests of Hindus. Some of its leaders, after listening to Sheikh Nadwi's speech, remarked that no other leader had as much love and concern for the country as him.

Sheikh Nadwi's commitment to *deen* (Islam) and *millat* was unwavering. He never compromised with those who were opposed to religious values. He avoided doing anything that could undermine *deen* or *millat;* he was so conscientious in this respect that he seldom accepted gifts from anyone.

With respect to political parties, he maintained absolute neutrality. Though he appreciated and acknowledged their constructive accomplishments and reminded them about the common good, he stayed away from their political differences and wranglings.

He used the same approach with respect to the leaders of Islamic countries as well. To the leaders of India, he talked about the problems of the country, people, and minorities. To the leaders of the Islamic countries, he talked about the problems of *deen* and *millat*. He sent letters to the Saudi kings (Shah Saud, Shah Faisal, Shah Khalid, and Shah Fahad) and met them personally. He reminded them about their obligation to preserve *deen*, maintain sanctity of the holy places (Makkah and Medinah) and fulfill the needs of Muslims all over the world. He met them with full *istighna* (selflessness) and sincerity.

He met Shah Hussein of Jordan, Shah 'Abdullah (grandfather of Shah Hussein of Jordan), Shah Hasan of Morocco, the presidents of Yemen and Pakistan, and other heads of state. He reminded them to improve the condition of their countries and give due importance to the Islamic needs and challenges. A review of the letters that he wrote to various leaders give an insight of his style of addressing, understanding of issues, and foresightedness.

In addition to being a distinguished scholar of Islam, he was also a highly skilled writer and effective speaker. His writings and speeches were very stirring, touching, and penetrating. He did not accept any gift from someone whom he intended to advise and correct. He used to say that if you accept a gift from someone, your advice would become ineffective for that person, but since advising is obligatory upon us, we must not neglect it. He used this strategy not only with rulers and authorities, but also with influential persons and leaders of the community.

There was a *seerah* (life of the Prophet) conference in Qatar in 1980 in which many top leaders, intellectuals, and crown princes from all over the Muslim world were present. Sheikh Nadwi had to deliver the inaugural speech there. In his speech, he told the audience with absolute clarity that if there was any theme of this conference, it must be about getting rid of the duplicity that had crept into the Islamic and Arab societies. He said:

> Thanks to Allah that our disease is not *kufr* (rejection of faith) or *shirk* (polytheism). Our disease is *nifaq* (hypocrisy). We proclaim one thing and do something else. This duplicity has made us and our society untrustworthy. As a result, Islam has now become unattractive to others though our character was the main reason for others to appreciate Islam in the past.

He also kept himself fully abreast of current issues, contemporary thinking and what was happening around the world. His book *As Sirau Bainal Fikratil Islamiyyate Wal Fikratil Gharabiyya* (published in English as *Western Civilization, Islam and Muslims*), speeches, writings, and travelogues bear ample testimony to this effect.

Sheikh Nadwi used the platform of public speaking to bring reform in the society at large. He addressed large public gatherings and delivered lectures at conferences to remind people about important issues and possible solutions. With that goal in mind, he used to convene gatherings of people of all religions in large cities [of India] from the platform of Payam-e-Insaniyat. He also used to convene gatherings of Muslims only from the stage of an outfit known as Islah-e-Mo'asherah (Reform of the Society) in which he drew attention of Muslims towards their religious and social problems and obligations.

Due to these efforts, Sheikh Nadwi had become well known among the educated Muslim population and leaders of the Asian and Muslim countries. He was seen as a sincere and selfless scholar and leader who wished well for all and was able to articulate his viewpoint in a pleasant and stimulating manner. His command of the Arabic language was as if it was his mother tongue and he was able to present his viewpoint in Arabic without any difficulty. He also had the working knowledge of English and Persian.

In 1973, the Muslim World League sent a delegation to Afghanistan, Iran, Lebanon, Jordan, Syria, and Iraq under his stewardship for the purpose of introducing the League to Muslims of those countries and also to know their condition.

In Iran, he met prominent religious and political leaders and explained to them the essence of *deen* and how important it was for the survival and prosperity of the country. He also made it clear to them that Prophet Muhammad was the final prophet and a good can come only through this channel. His knowledge of Persian proved very useful there.

In Afghanistan, he met government officials, *'ulama,* and intellectuals. He impressed upon them the need of creating awareness about Islam among common people. He shared with them his own experiences and suggested to them how to guide people.

He also got opportunities to address intellectuals in Europe and America. He delivered lectures at several universities including Oxford, London and Cambridge in UK, and Columbia in USA. In those lectures, he enumerated high points of the Western civilization and Christianity, highlighted the need of social reform and presented the teachings of Islam.

In a speech at an American university, he said,

> Given the current temperament and lifestyle of the people living in Europe and America, Islam offers a better alternative to them because it professes to combine the good of both the material and spiritual aspects of life. Contrary to that, Christianity which they have adopted as their religion requires them to shun the world and thus does not fulfill all the necessities of the life. As a consequence, they have neglected the teachings of Christianity and have become overly engrossed in the worldly pursuits. They should have studied Islam and seen how beautifully it fulfills their spiritual needs without requiring them to abandon the world.

In a speech at Germany's Berlin University, he first acknowledged the extraordinary contributions of German philosophers and then invited the audience to adopt correct means to realize those ideas.

The lectures that he delivered in Europe and USA were in Arabic or Urdu. They have been translated into English and published in the form of books entitled *Speaking Plainly to the West* and *From the Depth of the Heart in America.*

Most of Sheikh Nadwi's travels to Europe and America had resulted from his annual visits to the Islamic Centre of Geneva, Switzerland, of which he was a member. This center was established in Geneva by the Egyptian scholar Dr. Sa'id Ramadan for the purpose of introducing Islam to the people living in the West.

Sheikh Nadwi used to present his viewpoint in a very pleasant way in his speeches and articles. He used to mention unique traits and needs of the nation or community which he was addressing. He also used to identify specific evils and immoralities which were prevalent in the society. When addressing Muslims, he used to remind them about what was expected of them if they claim to be the best nation. When addressing educational institutions, he used to draw their attention to the need of developing a curriculum which could meet both the religious and contemporary needs.

To the Muslims who had migrated to Europe and America and settled there, he emphasized that they should be aware that the Western countries are not like the Eastern countries because the Western educational system espouses and promotes values that are very different from those of Islam. He used to warn them that if they did not do what was needed to nullify the ill effects of the Western education on their children, the children would grow opposite to their parents. He also urged them to appreciate the discipline and outward cleanliness that existed in the Western countries and not to carry over the bad habits which the people of the East had become accustomed to. Otherwise, they would leave a bad impression on the local inhabitants and make them apprehensive and uncomfortable about Islam and Muslims which would be a big loss.

Sheikh Nadwi's message was very broad and comprehensive and it covered all facets of human life. His method of *islah* could serve as a model for those who are in the positions of leadership, especially in the Muslim communities.

There were several aspects of Sheikh Nadwi's life which the readers of his biography should keep in front of them. His life was very clean, he was extremely conscientious, he practiced complete *istighna* (selflessness) in worldly matters and he completely avoided seeking any material benefit for himself. These qualities made his words very effective.

Listeners saw him as a sincere and selfless person and took positive effect from his advice.

Sheikh Nadwi could have confined himself to writing and publishing. Or, he could have dedicated himself to academics and teaching. Or, he could have devoted himself to *tasawwuf* and *sulook* as Dr. Iqbal, the Poet of the East, has mentioned in his couplet:

> *ya khaak ki aaghosh mein tasbeeh-o-manajaat* (Urdu)
>
> Either isolate yourself in a corner of the earth to remember and glorify Him.

Instead, he chose to fulfill the needs and interests of the *millat* and mankind and dedicated himself to the effort of *d'awah* and *islah* although he was by nature more inclined towards writing and publishing. In other words, he chose:

> *ya wusat-e-aflaak mein takbeer-e-musalsal* (Urdu)
>
> Or, continue proclaiming His greatness in the vastness of the universe.

as Dr. Iqbal has advocated in the second part of his couplet and continued striving for this cause until the very end of his life.

Just one day before Sheikh Nadwi passed away, a delicate issue popped up. Some members of the Muslim community did something which gave the impression that it was permissible in Islam to do anything, right or wrong, to achieve an objective and it did not matter if it harmed other communities or fellow human beings. In order to correct that impression, he issued a statement explaining the correct Islamic perspective which was published in the newspapers the very next day – the day on which he departed from this world.

Advice to the Leaders of India and Muslim Countries

Sheikh Syed Abul Hasan 'Ali Nadwi was educated and brought up in an enlightened environment due to which he had developed a very good understanding of the causes and effects of the rise and fall of nations of the world. He had developed the ability to understand and analyze current situation in the light of the past and predict the future. He was very good at predicting the outcome of an outfit by looking at the thinking of its leaders and how much adherence they had in their personal lives to what they were advocating.

He used to closely observe and analyze the events which were unfolding in the subcontinent and Muslim countries and form his own opinion about them in the light of his studies and experiences. He would then approach the leaders and public with his advice and do whatever was within his reach to improve the situation.

To bring *islah* (reform) among the ruling class, he considered Mujaddid Alf Thani's strategy of prudent advising and counseling to be the most effective method. To reform the educational system, he derived guidance from the methods of Shah Waliyullah Dehlavi, Ibn Khaldun, 'Allamah Ibn Taimiyah, and Shaikhul Islam 'Azzuddin bin 'Abdus Salam. To deal with the social and collective issues, he benefitted from the ideas of Ibn Khaldun. To bring *islah* among the masses, he took guidance from the methods of Ibn Jauzi and Hasan Basri.

Among the Muslim countries, Sheikh Nadwi gave topmost priority to the Arab countries and Hejaz.[2] In April 1947, just a few months before the independence of India, the then prime minister Jawaharlal Nehru convened a meeting of the leaders of Asian countries in Delhi. On that occasion, the *ameer* (head) of Jama'at Tabligh, Sheikh Muhammad Yusuf Kandhlawi sent

---

[2] Hejaz – Western part of Saudi Arabia that includes Makkah, Medinah and Jeddah.

a message to Sheikh Nadwi (who was in Lucknow at that time) asking him to come prepared to address delegates from the Arab countries. In response, Sheikh Nadwi prepared a very effective and comprehensive paper *Ila Mumatthil-al-Bilad-al-Islamiyah*[3] (Arabic), traveled to Delhi, met the delegates and conveyed his concern and advice to them through that paper.

That paper was later published as a booklet and Sheikh Nadwi made good use of it in his visit to Hejaz which took place shortly thereafter. It was highly appreciated by Arab scholars and leaders. Sheikh Muhammad 'Ali Al-Harkan who used to teach in Masjid Nabawi (Prophet's Mosque in Medinah) once read out that paper to his students in his class. Sheikh Harkan was a prominent scholar of *hadith* from Najd (central part of Saudi Arabia) and later became the minister of law and justice (in Saudi Arabian government) and the secretary general of the Muslim World League.

In 1947, when Sheikh Nadwi went for *hajj*, he wrote a detailed letter to the Crown Prince Saud bin 'Abdul-'Aziz al-Saud (d. 1969) who was holding a very powerful and influential position in the Saudi government. In that letter, he reminded the crown prince that the primary duty of the Muslim governments should be to bring lives of their people on the orders of Allah and the ways of the Prophet; the responsibilities of improving living condition, running the government, and making worldly progress were of secondary importance. He also emphasized that Hejaz, because of its special position in the Islamic world, deserved special care and attention. He also acknowledged to the crown prince that there were encouraging signs to indicate that the Saudi government would fulfill its obligations with full resolve and determination.

In the letter, Sheikh Nadwi had also mentioned the

---

3 Approximate translation of the title: *A Model for Islamic Countries*.

profound and thoughtful sentence that 'Umar bin 'Abdul 'Aziz (d. 720) had written to one of his governors,

> O slave of Allah! Prophet Muhammad was sent as a *haadi* (guide), not as a tax collector.

The letter was read to Shah 'Abdul-'Aziz bin Saud (d. 1953) by Sheikh 'Umar bin Hasan Al-Sheikh who was the most influential person of the kingdom at that time. It was later published as a booklet entitled *Bainal Jibayah Wal Hidayah*[4] and included in the collection of articles *Ilal Islam Min Jadid*.[5]

Sheikh Nadwi returned to India from Hejaz in 1948. But his heart and mind remained fully occupied with the urge to do *d'awah* among Arabs and awaken their leaders and eminent people. To get a feel of his enthusiasm and concern, it is worthwhile to look at the following excerpt from his autobiography (*Karwan-e-Zindagi*, vol. 1, pp. 351-52):

> After returning from Hejaz in 1948, I was completely overwhelmed by the urge to invite Arabs in their own language to the glory of Islam, to their role as leader of not only the Islamic world, but of the entire mankind and to regain their lost status. This urge had become so intense that I started thinking of making it the sole purpose of my life. One can get some sense of that intensity by looking at the letter that I wrote to my friend Sheikh Mas'ud 'Alam Nadwi on Shawwal 6, 1368 Hijri (3 August 1949) when he was in Iraq. I am presenting here an excerpt of that letter.
>
> "Don't spare any effort in planting the seed of *deen* in this deserted land. Don't leave any stone unturned. Work day and night. Burn your heart. Melt your body. Shed your blood and tears to such an extent that Tigris and Euphrates feel sorry for being too tiny. Catch hold of each and every person

---

[4] Approximate translation of the title: *Between Levy Collection and Guidance*.

[5] Approximate translation of the title: *From the New World to Islam*.

and tell him, "O the lost oryx (a type of antelope found in the Arabian Peninsula) of the Arabian Desert. O the hope of the world. O the wish of Prophet Ibrahim (Abraham). Where are you lost? What about the midnight prayers and the late night cries of Saiyadana 'Umar? What about the blood that was shed in the martyrdom of Mathni bin Haritha? What about the mutilation of the body of Abu 'Ubaid al-Thaqafi? What about the leadership of S'ad ibn Abi Waqqas? What about the torment and anguish of 'Ali bin Abi Talib and his eloquent and stirring speeches? What about the acute thirst and shedding of the blood of the Prophet's dearest grandsons? What about the genius and brilliance of Abu Hanifah? What about the love of Ahmad Bin Hanbal for enduring punishment? What about the unbridled passion of Ibn Jauzi for *sunnah*? What about the compassion of 'Abdul Qadir Jilani? Have all these sacrifices resulted into your becoming a lowly slave of those who are leading a herd of blinds? Have you degraded yourself into an insignificant dust particle of their pathway? Blow a trumpet in the graves of Iraq and set the stage for *qiyamah* (the Doomsday) because

giraftan cheeniyan ihram wa makki khuftah dar batha[6]

"Chinese have come clad in *ihram* and Makkans are still asleep"

Sheikh Nadwi performed his second *hajj* in 1369 Hijri (1950). That trip was very special for him because he was accompanied by his spiritual mentor Sheikh 'Abdul Qadir Raipuri. After *hajj*, Sheikh Raipuri returned to India, but Sheikh Nadwi stayed back in Hejaz for the purpose of *d'awah*. During that stay, Sheikh Nadwi met highly-educated people, journalists, writers, and high-ranking government officials. A number of his speeches were broadcast from the Saudi radio station. In his meetings and speeches, he reminded people about their responsibility to guide and lead humanity.

---

6 It is a Persian couplet by Dr. Muhammad Iqbal.

The speech entitled *Menal 'Alam Ilaiye Jaziratul 'Arab*[7] was extremely touching.

In the same trip, he visited Egypt, Sudan, Syria, Jordan, and Palestine as well. In Syria, he met eminent scholars and political leaders. He went to Baitul Moqaddas Al-Khalil (in Palestine), met Shah 'Abdullah bin al-Hussein of Jordan and advised him about his delicate responsibilities. Unfortunately, the king was assassinated while Sheikh Nadwi was still there.

During his visit to Syria, Sheikh Nadwi was asked to speak on the issue of Palestine. At that time, only a small portion of Palestine was under the occupation of Israel, but there were clear indications that Israel was intent on expanding its occupation. In his speech, Sheikh Nadwi shed light on the root cause of the problem and explained what losses are incurred when nations shun open-mindedness and become insincere in their actions. That speech was later published in the form of a booklet entitled *Karithatu Falesteen Wa Asbabuhal Haqiqiyah.*[8]

Sheikh Nadwi got another opportunity to visit Syria five years later in 1956 when he was invited as a visiting professor. The invitation was for one or two years, but he could accept it only for three months. His visit proved very beneficial for several reasons. His lectures were attended by Syria's learned scholars and prominent citizens some of whom were later appointed to high positions in the government. One of them was Dr. M'arouf al-Dawalibi (d. 2004) who later became the prime minister of Syria. The learned Algerian leader Sheikh Al-Bashir al-Ibrahimi, who had come to Damascus for a visit

---

7 Approximate translation of the title: *From the World to the Arabian Peninsula.*

8 Approximate translation of the title: *Tragedy of Palestine and Its Real Reasons.*

at that time, also attended his lectures. Two of his lectures were broadcast from the Syrian Radio. One of them was published as a booklet entitled *Isma'i Ya Suriya.*[9] From Syria, he went to Lebanon and Turkey where he met prominent scholars, religious leaders, and leaders of various religious movements and gave them useful advice.

In the same year (i.e. 1956), he again traveled to Damascus to attend a conference that was organized by Motamar al-'Alam al-Islami (World Muslim Congress). The former prime minister of Indonesia Muhammad Natsir and leaders of several other Muslim countries had attended the conference. On that occasion, he presented a paper on the issue of Palestine and highlighted its importance and far-reaching consequences.

Several years later, Sheikh Nadwi went to Morocco to attend a conference which was convened by the federation of Muslim universities. The king of Morocco had come to the conference on the last day and Sheikh Nadwi was asked to speak in front of him on behalf of the participants. It was a delicate occasion. A large number of dignitaries had come to meet the king and it was supposed to be a brief speech consisting of just a few congratulatory remarks and words of thanks. But Sheikh Nadwi used that opportunity to deliver a passionate and effective speech to remind the audience to pay attention to improve the country's religious and moral condition in addition to fulfilling the worldly needs; he also alluded to other issues and problems of the country which had been brought to his attention. He conveyed the message with great courage while maintaining the protocol and decency of the royal gathering. His speech was applauded as very successful.

After Sheikh Nadwi's speech, a renowned Arab scholar expressed his desire to speak. He was given the opportunity.

---

9 Approximate translation of the title: *Listen to Me, O Syria!*

But, despite being a native speaker of Arabic, he could not speak in a way that was fitting for the occasion. Later, the scholars and university professors who were present in that event spoke highly of Sheikh Nadwi's speech while they pointed out weaknesses in the other person's speech.

I was present in that speech. I was amazed to hear Sheikh Nadwi deliver such a scholarly and enlightening speech. I felt that it was merely due to Allah's special help which came down due to his sincerity and burning desire for *d'awah*. I have witnessed it happen on so many other occasions also. There were instances when he addressed very powerful people and it appeared that they might feel offended and retaliate. But it never happened so. Instead, his position got further elevated in their eyes as it happened in Morocco. The king came up to the door to see him off and lamented that he was invited to visit Moroco so many times, but did not come. The king asked him to come to Morocco more often.

There was a similar situation with the king of Jordan. Sheikh Nadwi got an opportunity to meet the king. While advising the king, he pointed out the weaknesses that were prevailing in the country. The king listened to Sheikh Nadwi's advice patiently and appreciated it.

In his trip to Kuwait in the beginning of 1962, Sheikh Nadwi delivered a speech entitled *Isma'i Ya Zahratus Sihra*[10] that was broadcast on Kuwait Radio. In that speech, he reminded the people of Kuwait about the kind of character they were supposed to present to the world. He also presented a letter to the Ameer of Kuwait Sheikh 'Abdullah al-Salim al-Sabah in which he advised him about the progress, unity and leadership of the Arabs. He also reminded the Ameer about the responsibility of properly utilizing the wealth.

---

10 Approximate translation of the title: *Listen to Me, O Flower of the Desert!*

Sheikh Nadwi had in his heart a burning desire and deep concern about how the Muslim countries could remain firm in their *deen* (Islam) and *'aqidah* (faith) and still fulfill the needs of today and enjoy position of respect among the community of nations. That is, how they could combine *deen* and *duniya* (worldly matters) together, convey the message of truth to the entire world, and keep their own people on Quran and *hadith* which they have inherited from their ancestors.

Sheikh Nadwi determined his line of action in the light of his deep study of history, sound knowledge of *deen* and *shari'ah*, and clear understanding of the connection between knowledge and practice. His sincerity and selflessness made his words effective. From the leaders and authorities whom he felt obliged to advise, he never sought any material benefit and refused to accept gifts from them.

Sheikh Nadwi was a founding member of the Muslim World League and a member of the Advisory Council of the Islamic University of Madinah. So from 1961 onward, he went to Hejaz almost every year to attend meetings of the Muslim World League and the Islamic University of Madinah. He also started getting opportunities to address and sometimes preside over meetings. Whenever he got an opportunity, he utilized it to convey his message and advice. He delivered numerous speeches and wrote many letters during those visits. The speeches which were broadcast on radio were published as *Bayna al-'Alam wal Jazirat al-'Arab.*[11] The collection of letters which he wrote to the members of the royal family was also published in the form of a book.

Sheikh Nadwi got several opportunities to meet Shah Faisal of Saudi Arabia both when he was the crown prince and later when he became the king. I also happened to be with him in

11 Approximate translation of the title: *Between the World and Arabian Peninsula.*

some of those meetings. On every occasion, he met and advised Shah Faisal with complete *istighna* (selflessness) and cautioned him against possible dangers to the kingdom and the Harmain Sharifain (Makkah and Madinah). The king assured him that he would not allow anything to happen which was contrary to the spirit and status of the center of Islam. Sheikh Nadwi used to write letters to the king and the king used to reply promptly.

In 1984, while returning from Jordan, Yemen, and Hejaz, Sheikh Nadwi stopped in Karachi to meet Pakistan's president General Ziaul Haq. On that occasion, Sheikh Nadwi presented to President Ziaul Haq the souvenir of Masjid al-Aqsa (of Jerusalem) that was presented to him (Sheikh Nadwi) in Amman, Jordan. By this gesture, he in fact wanted to remind the president that he, as the head of a Muslim country, should feel obligated to strive for the liberation of Masjid al-Aqsa.

In all of his visits to the Islamic world, Sheikh Nadwi did his best to fulfill the obligations of *deen* and *d'awah*. When he visited Burma (now Myanmar) in the beginning of 1960, he told the Muslims living there,

> You may feel happy that Allah has blessed you with so much wealth and respect in a big city like Rangoon. But it is very worrisome because there is very little compliance with the teachings of Islam in your character and life. To show gratitude to Allah for His favors, Islamic character and qualities must be inculcated in your lives.

He further warned them:

> I am afraid that you may be afflicted with the same punishment that befell affluent nations of the past as Quran has mentioned in chapter *Hud* (11: 84) – I see you in prosperity, but I fear for you the penalty of a day that will compass (you) all round.

Shortly after his return from Burma, the communist revolution took place and all the prominent Muslim businessmen who were mostly of Indian origin had to flee the country and move to either Indian subcontinent or Europe. They later used to recall Sheikh Nadwi's speeches and acknowledge how profound were his warnings and predictions.

He had given similar warnings in his visit to Syria also where people were living a prosperous and comfortable life before the military coup took over the country. He had told the people of Syria:

> Your condition makes me worried. You should strive to live according to the orders of Allah and His prophet. When Allah bestows His favors on people, He wants them to be thankful to Him.

It is amazing that only a year later, a series of military coups took place there. People were deprived of all the comforts of life, living condition became miserable, and many talented people were forced to leave the country.

Whichever country Sheikh Nadwi went, he closely observed the prevailing conditions and presented his thoughts and advice with a genuine concern. Allah had blessed him with such a foresight that he could look at the condition of a nation and exactly identify the underlying diseases. His diagnoses, in some instances, looked flawed initially, but proved exactly right as time passed by.

When the call for Arab nationalism was made in the Arab countries, Arabs embraced it enthusiastically and told non-Arabs that Arabism and Islam were one and the same and the Arab solidarity should be considered as the Islamic solidarity. But Sheikh Nadwi said very openly and loudly that it was merely a *fitnah* (deception) conspired by anti-Islamic forces to drive a wedge between the Arab and non-Arab Muslims for their own gains.

The result was that Arabs got disconnected from non-

Arabs and Arabs further divided themselves on the regional basis. It destroyed Arab unity and the Arab countries became a fertile hunting ground for the anti-Arab and anti-Islamic forces. In this connection, Sheikh Nadwi wrote two articles entitled *Isma'uha Minni Sarihatan Aiyohal 'Arab*[12] and *Ilai Rayatil Muhammadiyah Aiyohal 'Arab.*[13]

Sheikh Nadwi used to recall the words of Sayyidna 'Umar (the second caliph) which he had spoken to admonish Sayyidna Abu 'Ubaidah (a companion of Prophet Muhammad) at the time of the conquest of Jerusalem. The Patriarch of Jerusalem had insisted that he would surrender the city only if Sayyidna 'Umar came there in person. When Sayyidna 'Umar came to Jerusalem, Sayyidna Abu 'Ubaidah advised him to change his tattered clothes before meeting the Patriarch. Upon hearing that, Sayyidna 'Umar said:

> Allah has given us honor due to Islam and we can remain honorable only through Islam and nothing else.

Sheikh Nadwi used to say that the dignity of Arabs was due to Islam and the more they remained connected to Prophet Muhammad, the more protection and security they would have.

Sheikh Nadwi visited both the Arab and non-Arab countries for the purpose of *d'awah*. He visited Pakistan, Bangladesh, Malaysia, Burma, Turkey and several countries of Europe, and America. In every place, he told the resident Muslims:

> Don't forget your roots. Take care of the wealth of Islam that Allah has given to you. Your dignity and respect depend on it.

---

12 Approximate translation of the title: *O Arabs! Listen to My Frank Talk.*

13 Approximate translation of the title: *O Arabs! Come Under the Banner of Muhammad.*

If he got an opportunity to address Muslim organizations or movements in those countries, he drew their attention to their weak points. His message was:

> Don't forsake your Islamic and cultural values. Don't be influenced by the moral and religious weaknesses of local population. Educate and raise your children in such a way that their connection to Islam is not compromised. Learn the language of the land as best as you can so that you can do the work of *d'awah* effectively. Live a life that becomes a means of introduction of Islam to non-Muslims. Look at your surrounding environment in such a way that you see an evil as an evil. And if you find something good, appreciate and value it as is mentioned in the prophetic advice: "Wisdom is the lost treasure of a *momin* (believer) and he is the most deserving to acquire it wherever it is found."

In his visits to various Muslim countries, Sheikh Nadwi was grieved to notice deficiencies and lack of high moral character in the lives of people. He then wrote detailed letters and essays to express his grief and concern and sent them to the leaders and intellectuals of those countries. He sent the very first such letter to Egypt that was entitled *Isma'i Ya Misr* (Listen to Me, O Egypt!). He then sent letters to Syria (Listen to Me, O Syria), Hejaz (From the World to the Arabian Peninsula), Kuwait (Listen to me, O Flower of the Desert!), and Iran (Listen to Me, O Iran!). The lectures that he delivered during his visit to Pakistan bear the same concern; those lectures were published from Karachi in the form of a booklet entitled *Hadith-e-Pakistan* (Urdu).

These letters and speeches highlight problems and needs of Muslim countries in an objective and balanced manner. They also show how much concern he had for the progress of Muslim communities and countries in *deen*, education, and preservation of Islamic values and practices. Allah blessed him to discharge this duty in an exemplary manner.

Reform of the System of Education and Mentoring

Sheikh Nadwi's vision of education was shaped in a unique environment. His mother was a purely religious person. His father Sheikh Syed 'Abdul Hai Hasani (d. 1923) was an accomplished scholar of religion, history, literature, and poetry; he had several acclaimed publications in Islamic history to his credit. Sheikh Nadwi had thus inherited strong religious and literary aptitude from his parents.

He was also acquainted with the modern education as several of his close relatives were educated in the modern system of education and some of them had gone to America, England, and Germany for higher studies in the beginning of the last century.

Furthermore, he was associated with the environment of Nadwatul 'Ulama from his very childhood. Nadwatul 'Ulama was established in 1893 by Sheikh Muhammad 'Ali Kanpuri-Mongheri with the collaboration of Sheikh Shibli N'umani, Sheikh Nadwi's father Sheikh, 'Abdul Hai, and Nawab Sadar Yaar Jang Sheikh Habibur Rahman Khan Sherwani (head of Religious Affairs of Hyderabad State) with the mission to develop a dynamic and comprehensive educational system by incorporating new ideas and discoveries of education into the traditional religious curriculum. His association with this institution enabled him to understand another dimension of religious education – how to make it versatile to meet contemporary needs and challenges.

Those who were just above Sheikh Nadwi in the family hierarchy[14] were closely connected to Shah Fazlur Rahman

---

[14] One of Sheikh Nadwi's uncles Syed Khaliluddin Ahmad Hasani, who was my paternal grandfather, had taken *bay'ah* (oath of spiritual allegiance) with Sheikh Gangohi. Sheikh Nadwi's father had taken *bay'ah* with Shah Fazlur Rahman Ganj Moradabadi and was also connected with Sheikh Gangohi.

Ganj Moradabadi (d. 1895) and Sheikh Rasheed Ahmad Gangohi (d. 1905). Through this channel, he got exposed to the traditional Islamic educational system that had started in Deoband in 1862.

As a result, Sheikh Nadwi on one hand developed a solid foundation in Quran and *hadith* – two primary sources of Islamic knowledge – by studying them under the tutelage of very distinguished scholars. And on the other hand, he became well versed in secular subjects such as history, literature, and languages as well. Thus he developed expertise in three areas – Quran, *hadith* and secular subjects – and excelled in each one of them.

From the study of history, he understood how important both traditional Islamic and modern knowledge systems were in meeting contemporary needs and challenges. He also understood that the extraordinary progress of the Western nations had resulted mainly from their advancement in empirical knowledge. Thus Muslims, who have fallen very low today, need to examine which aspect of the modern knowledge could fulfill their needs, help them get out of the position of disgrace and enable them regain their lost dignity and power. They also need to look at how their system of religious education should be re-tooled and improved so that it becomes vibrant and meets new challenges – the very purpose for which Sheikh Nadwi's predecessors had launched the mission of Nadwatul 'Ulama.

That is why Sheikh Nadwi, upon entering practical life, put special emphasis on the need of revamping the educational system of Muslims. He proposed that some subjects of the existing curriculum should be re-designed whereas priority of some others should be rearranged. Quran and *hadith* must be used as the primary and direct source for acquiring expertise in religious knowledge. A good command of language and literature should be acquired for discharging the duty of *islah* and *d'awah* which are the primary obligations of the *ummah* (Muslims), especially of *'ulama*. Additionally, one should also acquire essential knowledge of the history of Islam and reformist movements.

A thorough and deep knowledge of Arabic and a working knowledge of the internationally spoken languages are essential for working in academic and religious fields. It is also important to be familiar with contemporary issues and subjects that impact everyday life. These can be achieved by introducing in the curriculum of religious institutions new subjects in place of those which were introduced in the past out of necessity, but have now become obsolete or less relevant.

Through his own study and contact with the relatives who were educated in the modern system, Sheikh Nadwi had become fully aware of the reasons of the progress of the Western nations. He was convinced that the Western nations did not progress because they were genetically superior to other nations. Rather, it was the result of their hard work and advancements in education. He was fully convinced that Islam is the divine religion and the practices of the Prophet Muhammad are most suited for the mankind. He believed that Muslims could accomplish higher levels of success than the Western nations if they could combine Islamic principles with the know-how of the West.

He realized that Muslims, in order to regain their lost power and dignity, must come out of the intellectual and ideological domination of the West. It is useless to be simply apologetic and defensive. Muslims are the custodian of the divine knowledge and guidance that Prophet Muhammad brought for the benefit of mankind. Thus the success and progress of Muslims depend strictly on following that very code of conduct and the real cause of their decline is the failure to adhere to it. Sheikh Nadwi expressed this viewpoint more forcefully in Arab countries than in India.

Sheikh Nadwi had both aspects of education in his mind – secular and religious. With respect to the secular education, we need to see what our current needs – religious, worldly, individual, and collective – are and which disciplines of secular education are required to fulfill those needs and necessary expertise should be acquired in them.

The purpose of religious education is twofold: (1) to instill in students the understanding that Islam is the divine and natural way of life for the mankind, and (2) to develop in students the skills and abilities to properly convey the message of Islam to mankind which is the basic requirement for being called the best nation. Sheikh Nadwi argued that we need to design a curriculum that develops the above-mentioned qualities and capabilities in our young generation.

Regarding the institutions of secular education, he felt that their curricula for humanities and social sciences are not compatible with the needs and temperament of Muslims as they have been developed mainly by people who have been greatly influenced by materialism and aversion to religion. Muslim experts of these disciplines need to make them compatible with the Islamic principles, but it is unfortunate that they have not yet paid attention to it.

Modern knowledge has become a necessity of life, but it must be made compatible with the condition and temperament of the Muslim *ummah*. These subjects by themselves are not to be blamed for turning young generation of Muslims away from Islam. Rather, the real culprits are the materialistic and irreligious twists and interpretations that have been added to them. Thus it is necessary to change the purpose and content of the educational material that is being used in these subjects.

Sheikh Nadwi felt that those who are running Muslim

institutions of secular education have not yet paid enough attention to this problem. In subjects such as philosophy, psychology, geography, and history, they are still using material which is prepared by those who are generally indifferent towards Islam. It is unfortunate that we feel contented and continue using such material without first adapting it to Islamic beliefs and values. It is harmful to use material which is the product of an environment that is opposed to the belief in Allah and Islamic principles. The least harm that it can inflict is that it will devalue Islam and illustrious Muslims of the past in the eyes of students.

Regarding the Islamic education, Sheikh Nadwi held the view that one should try to acquire and understand it from the original sources instead of relying on translations, especially in the case of Quran. Though it may be beneficial and necessary to know opinions of different interpreters in understanding a verse of Quran, one should try to benefit from it in the same way as the Companions of Prophet Muhammad benefitted despite being totally illiterate. To fully understand a Quranic verse, it is also necessary to know the specific condition and environment under which it was revealed. Quran is revealed by Allah not only for those who are learned, but also for those who are unlettered and possess only natural instinct. Also, the effect of Quran is greater (in making a person act upon it) if it is approached directly.

However, in order to benefit from Quran directly, it is essential to know Arabic and its dialect that was prevalent in the early days of Islam. Additionally, all other prerequisites that scholars have identified for understanding Quran must also be fulfilled. A good command of Arabic is very essential for *d'awah* as well.

Sheikh Nadwi held the view that it is very important for students of *madaris* (institutions of Islamic learning) to be well versed in the Arabic language and literature. It greatly helps in getting a better understanding of Quran and *hadith*; it greatly helps in explaining meaning and purport of *deen*; it enables one to discharge the duty of *d'awah* more effectively. That is why he felt that the institutions of religious learning must include and give due importance to Arabic language and literature in their curriculum. Furthermore, it will make the graduates of these institutions more confident and they will not feel inferior and marginalized in the society and in front of those who are educated in the secular system of education.

In addition to being well versed in Arabic and the mother tongue, one must also be familiar with the languages (such as English) which are commonly spoken in the society. It greatly helps in *d'awah* and proves quite useful in everyday life. Thus *madaris* should also include such languages in their curriculum.

These institutions should also make students aware of the ongoing *fitnah* (misguided viewpoints which distract and confuse people) and anti-Islamic efforts so that they can protect themselves as well as others from getting affected by them.

Sheikh Nadwi observed these guidelines in his own personal life and tried to implement them in institutions which were under his supervision. His knowledge of Quran and *hadith* was outstanding and he made good use of it in his academic and *d'awah* works. His study of history was very broad and thorough. He had mastered language and articulation. Though Arabic was not his mother tongue, his proficiency in it was like that of a native Arab; in fact, there were occasions when he even excelled native Arab scholars. He was also familiar with English to the extent that he could use it when needed. Given the importance of English in today's world, he deemed it essential for the Islamic educational institutions to include English in their curriculum.

All the qualifications and expertise that Sheikh Nadwi possessed were the outcome of the balanced and comprehensive education that he received. He had developed keen interest in language and literature which he expeditiously utilized later in his religious, academic, and *d'awah* endeavors. He had studied Quran and *hadith* under the supervision of eminent scholars of his time. He had thoroughly studied world and Islamic history. Thus when he was appointed to Nadwatul 'Ulama as a member of the faculty, he was assigned to teach Quranic studies and Arabic literature. He taught these two subjects for ten years with full dedication. In addition to teaching, he also used to spare time for *d'awah*.

Sheikh Nadwi did not limit his effort of *d'awah* and *islah* to lectures and speeches only. He devoted his time to writing and composition as well which kept on increasing as the time passed by. Ultimately, he resigned from the full-time teaching position and agreed to teach only on volunteer basis so that he could focus more on writing and public speaking for *d'awah* and *islah*. His effort of *d'awah* and *islah* did not merely involve presenting ideas in an eloquent and attractive way. It was based upon solid scholarship and was geared up to nurture human minds. As a result, he was able to produce a number of highly acclaimed books on a variety of topics.

Whenever Sheikh Nadwi was invited by Arab universities and educational institutions for speaking or consultation, he reminded them about the need of developing a balanced and comprehensive curriculum. His advice was welcomed by experts of education. He advocated that a subject should be taught using the principle of progressive approach which was recommended by the eminent Arab philosopher and sociologist Ibn Khaldun (d. 1332) in his famous book *Moqaddimah*. He also advocated that a subject should be taught in depth with its unique flavor and taste without mixing it with other subjects like a hodgepodge. This is exactly how he himself was taught. He also stressed upon developing skills of speaking and articulation which are essential tools not only for *d'awah*, but also for academic and scholarly pursuit.

Sheikh Nadwi held the view that Quran which is the fountainhead of all Islamic knowledge should be taught in its original form so that students get a deep understanding of its message and meaning. This viewpoint was strongly advocated by both Sheikh Syed Sulaiman Nadwi and Sheikh Abul Hasan 'Ali Nadwi and was very conspicuous in their writings and interpretations of Quranic verses.

Sheikh Nadwi did not confine teaching of Quran to classroom only. Rather, he made it a part of his effort of *d'awah* and mentoring as well, as is evident from his speeches and writings. From the very beginning of his career, he conducted Quranic classes in his neighborhood mosque on a weekly basis. These classes were attended mainly by modern educated people and he used to expound upon the guidance that Quran provides with respect to real-life situations and problems.

With the same goal in mind, he established an institute known as Idarah T'alimate Islam in Aminabad, Lucknow, with the co-operation of his friend Sheikh 'Abdus Salam Nadwi. The objective was to provide a facility where people could learn Quranic Arabic and study the entire Quran with translation during a short period of time. It helped the participants learn Arabic and develop affinity with Quran as well. In addition to conducting regular daily programs, the institute also offered weekly Quran and *hadith* classes for highly educated members of the society. Sheikh Nadwi conducted the Quran class and Sheikh Abdus Salam Nadwi conducted the *hadith* class.

Since the Arabic language and literature have very strong connection with Quran and *hadith*, Sheikh Nadwi, in his approach of teaching Arabic, used to emphasize on Quran and *hadith* from the very beginning. After a student had acquired necessary level of competency in the Arabic language and literature, he could then move on to *tafseer* of Quran, *hadith*, *fiqh* (jurisprudence), and other branches of Islamic *shari'ah* (code of conduct) for specialization according to his ability and interest.

In Arabic language and literature classes, Sheikh Nadwi used to put more responsibility on students. He believed that a student should be helped only when it became impossible for him to understand the material on his own. He made students read the text (in Arabic), translate it (into Urdu) and derive the underlying meaning on their own by using a dictionary and their prior knowledge. He did not tolerate their slackness or inattentiveness and strongly admonished them for the same. This forced them to work harder which in turn developed in them the ability to read the Arabic text correctly and extract the underlying meaning.

In *tafseer* (of Quran) classes, though he allowed students to consult existing interpretations so that they did not err in determining the real meaning, he required them to translate the text [from Arabic to Urdu] on their own. This was his strategy for the beginners. But for those who were in the advanced class (*Fadhil* level which is equivalent to M.A.), his strategy was different and the goal was to develop in them the ability to interpret on their own.

What has been described above is the standard mode of teaching at Nadwatul 'Ulama. But Sheikh Nadwi also taught some students on one-to-one basis without adhering to the formal structure of a classroom. He taught his nephew Syed Muhammad Al-Hasani (son of Sheikh Nadwi's elder brother Dr. Syed 'Abdul 'Ali Hasani) using this approach.

In teaching *hadith*, if a *fiqh* (jurisprudential) issue was encountered, Sheikh Nadwi went in detail only to the extent which was necessary for that particular *hadith*. But in case of issues which dealt with manners, character, and social life, he discussed them in great detail because of their impact and application in everyday life.

For the teachers of *tafseer*, Sheikh Nadwi's recommendation was that they should themselves study books of *tafseer* before teaching the text of Quran to students. He recommended students also to consult books of *tafseer* on their own. He preferred to interpret Quranic verses in such a way that it transformed the life of an individual and developed (in student) the ability to appreciate the beauty of Quran.

Whenever he had an opportunity to develop or revise a curriculum at Nadwatul 'Ulama or any other institution, he tried to incorporate the above-mentioned ideas in it. He strongly felt that the curriculum should be designed with contemporary needs and challenges in mind and it should include commonly spoken languages and other subjects which were deemed essential for survival in the society. That is why he deemed it necessary to include subjects such as social sciences, humanities, history, geography, and mathematics in the curriculum to make it comprehensive and meaningful.

In Sheikh Nadwi's opinion, the main objective of the curriculum of a religious institution is to prepare students to carry out the work of *d'awah* and *tarbiyah*, disseminate Islamic knowledge, lead the Muslim *ummah*, and represent Islam to the world correctly. Graduates of these institutions should also possess manners and qualities of a pious Muslim and sincere *d'ai*. Thus it is not enough for these institutions to simply teach students subject matter and make them mere depository of knowledge. They must also strive to inculcate Islamic character and values in students and provide them with opportunities for practical training so that they can apply their knowledge to real-life situations.

With that goal in mind, Sheikh Nadwi, in the beginning years of his teaching, used to take his students every Thursday evening to nearby villages where they could do the work of *d'awah* and practice conversation in Arabic. He also used to involve students (who had the potential to excel in research) in research projects, polish their research skills, and train them as researchers.

More details about Sheikh Nadwi's vision of education and curriculum can be found in the educational policy statement of the catalog of Nadwatul 'Ulama. It can also be found in the book *Nahw al-Tarbiyyat al-Islamiyyat al-Hirrat*[15] (Arabic) which is a collection of his essays on curriculum and education.

Sheikh Nadwi agreed with the modern concept that education does not merely entail acquisition of knowledge, but it also means *tarbiyah* – nurturing of character and personality. Thus the purpose of education should be to equip new generation with both sound knowledge and high moral ethics and this should be kept in mind at the time of designing an educational system and its curriculum. The curriculum should have proper mix of subjects and it should develop in students the ability to make theoretical knowledge applicable and beneficial to real-life situations.

---

15 An approximate translation of title: *Towards a Complete Islamic Educational System.*

4

Movements and Institutions

Academy of Islamic Research and Publications

Sheikh Abul Hasan 'Ali Nadwi, in the very beginning of his academic and professional career, thoroughly studied lives and works of those who had carried out revivalist and reformist movements at various times in the history of Islam. He understood under which circumstances 'Umar bin 'Abdul 'Aziz (d. 720) became the *khalifah* (caliph) and how he utilized his *khilafah* (caliphate) to bring revolutionary transformation in his regime. He understood what kind of hardship Imam Ahmad bin Hanbal (d. 855) had to endure and what kind of determination, patience, and perseverance he had exhibited.

Sheikh Nadwi became well acquainted with the struggles of Imam Ghazali (d. 1111), Imam Ibn Taimiyah (d. 1328), Imam Ibn Qaiyam (d. 1350), and Abdur Rahman Ibn Jauzi (d. 1200). He also became familiar with the efforts of those who had struggled in the Indian subcontinent during thirteenth to nineteenth centuries. This list includes illustrious personalities such as Khawaja Moinuddin Chishti (d. 1230), Sharfuddin Yahya Maneri (d. 1291), Khawaja Nizamuddin Aulia (d. 1325), Syed 'Ali Hamdani Kashmeri (d. 1384), Mujaddid Alf Thani (d. 1624), Shah Waliyullah Dehlavi (d. 1762), and Syed Ahmad Shaheed (d. 1831). Each of them had set an example of how to struggle in a certain situation.

During the course of this study, Sheikh Nadwi was fortunate to have the supervision of distinguished teachers and mentors who greatly helped him develop an excellent understanding of the above-mentioned struggles. His brother, Dr. Syed 'Abdul 'Ali Hasani, played the most instrumental role in this regard. This study enabled Sheikh Nadwi to understand how important it was for a reform effort to be diverse and broad-based. His first book *Seerat Syed Ahmad Shaheed*[1] (Urdu) was the result of this enlightenment. Conscientious Muslims and enlightened *'ulama* of the Indian subcontinent highly appreciated this book and considered it to be a special reminder for carrying out the effort of guiding the Muslim *ummah*.

Sheikh Nadwi was educated at Nadwatul 'Ulama where differences in various schools of jurisprudence were not considered as rigid and irreconcilable as in some other institutions and collective needs and challenges of the *ummah* (Muslims) were viewed on a much broader and larger scale. That is why he did not limit his efforts to the subcontinent only and extended it to Arab and other countries as well. His elder brother Dr. 'Ali had the same thinking. Not only was he concerned about the condition of Muslims of the subcontinent, but he was also concerned about Muslims of North Africa, Middle East, and Arab countries which were colonized by the European imperialist powers during the last two centuries.

Sheikh Nadwi kept in front of him the famous *hadith* in which the Prophet has said: "He who does not care about our affairs or the affairs of Muslims is not from us". He was concerned about what kind of difficulties Muslims of Nepal were facing, what were the impending dangers for Harmain Sharifain (Makkah and Madinah), what kind of injustices and atrocities France and Italy were inflicting in Morocco and Libiya, what kind of hardship Muslim countries in Africa were facing, what was the condition of Muslims in Spain and in

---

[1] It is a biography of Syed Ahmad Shaheed (d. 1831).

which countries British imperialism was hurting Muslims and Islam. Sheikh Nadwi inherited this feeling and concern from his brother, family, teachers, and mentors.

Sheikh Nadwi was also fortunate to have excellent teachers such as Sheikh Khalil bin Muhammad Arab of Yemen and Sheikh Taqiuddin Hilali of Morocco. He also had the love and affection of his uncle (husband of his father's sister) Sheikh Syed Talha Hasani who was a professor at Lahore Oriental College. Since Sheikh Nadwi's father had passed away while he (Sheikh Nadwi) was still very young, his uncle Sheikh Syed Talha Hasani gave him some special attention. He introduced Sheikh Nadwi to several prominent persons (in Lahore and Punjab) from both the modern and religious education circles. The purpose of those encounters was to broaden Sheikh Nadwi's vision and widen the circle of his acquaintances. One such meeting was with Dr. Muhammad Iqbal, the Poet of the East.

These were the concerns which inspired Sheikh Nadwi to write the famous book *Ma Dha Khasar al-'Alam bi Inhitat-i-Muslimin* (published in English as *Islam and the World: The Rise and Decline of Muslims and Its Effect on Mankind*) in which he presented a critical analysis of the history of Islamic culture and civilization and addressed questions such as how the Muslims became the leader of the world, how they remained in that position for several centuries, how they started drifting away from that position, how they fell behind others, what kind of injustices others brought when they gained power, and what the Muslims need to do to regain their lost glory and honor.

Writing such a book required an in-depth knowledge about both Muslims and non-Muslims. It was also important to know about non-Muslims through their own media and sources. It was also needed to know both the past and the present. Due to his familiarity with some of the modern languages and superb command of both the classical and modern dialects of Arabic, he did not encounter difficulties in writing this book which he would have faced otherwise. The book gained extraordinary popularity in the entire Muslim world. It provided readers with a clear picture of the history and cause of the rise and fall of Muslims and a blueprint for regaining the lost heritage.

Sheikh Nadwi had not yet traveled outside the subcontinent. But when he was very close to finishing the manuscript of this book, he got an opportunity to go for *hajj* in 1947. There, he met important people from different parts of the world, exchanged views with them and gathered more information which helped him further augment the content of the book. The book was published after his return from *hajj*.

Three years later, in 1950, he got another opportunity for *hajj* after which he visited several Arab countries as well. That was the period when many of those who had stood against the colonial powers in North Africa and the Middle East were forced to leave their respective countries and live in exile in Egypt. He met many of them in his visit to Egypt and came to know first hand about their experiences and aspirations. Many of them already knew about him through his book *Ma Dha Khasar. . . .* Those encounters and experiences helped him solidify his thinking and vision about the problems and challenges of the Muslim world.

It was also the period during which many countries, shortly after gaining independence from the colonial powers, had succumbed to the pressures of superpowers and become their pawns. Widespread suffering, dissatisfaction, and unrest had become the order of the day. The military had taken over in many countries due to which conditions had further deteriorated. Sheikh Nadwi keenly observed those developments.

A few years later, Sheikh Nadwi visited Syria and Turkey.

In Turkey, he closely witnessed the deplorable conditions of the country that had resulted from over forty years of anti-Islamic military rule of Mustafa Kemal Ata Turk (Ata Turk means father of Turkey). Though Mustafa Kemal was initially hailed as a savior, he later became anti-Islamic and used all of his talents and resources to decimate Islam and establish an atheist form of government in Turkey with the blessing of colonial powers.

All these tumultuous events of the Islamic world created in Sheikh Nadwi a certain kind of restlessness which he expressed in the form of the book *As Sirau Bainal Fikratil Islamiyyate Wal Fikratil Gharabiyya* (published in English as *Western Civilization, Islam and Muslims*). In this book, he first highlighted the difficulties that the Islamic world was facing due to the conflict between the Islamic and Western ideologies and then presented a possible solution to it. He explained that the West had gained dominance over the East due to its know-how and military power and Muslims, despite possessing the truth, had become victim of the West's oppression and atrocity. It was as if Muslims were being punished for falling behind in acquiring knowledge and power.

These two books *Ma Dha Khasar* . . . and *As Sirau Bainal* . . . fully represent Sheikh Nadwi's thinking and vision. But he also deemed it necessary to present history of the efforts that Muslims had made in the past to overcome difficulties and regain the position of honor and prestige. Such a treatise might serve as a source of inspiration to the current generation in improving its condition and reviving its standing in the world. For that very purpose, he wrote the book *Taarikhe Dawat wa Azimat* (published in English as *Saviours of Islamic Spirit*).

He had great concern for the *ummah* and used to remain very restless for the same. He used to meet leaders and write letters to them to express his concerns. He used to warn masses through public speaking of the impending dangers which could be caused by misguided leaders or movements.

There were occasions when his statements, at the time he made them, did not make much sense, especially to those who did not fully understand the condition of the Islamic world. As a result, he was opposed and condemned by leaders who were considered very influential in their respective countries. But as the time passed by and the reality came to light, the world witnessed that his statements were profoundly right.

After returning to India from Turkey, Sheikh Nadwi strongly criticized Mustafa Kemal Ata Turk for his deep animosity towards Islam. Until that time, Muslim leaders and *'ulama* of India had the impression that Mustafa Kemal was a savior of Islam and thus they were very surprised and angered by Sheikh Nadwi's statements and complained that he had branded a hero as an enemy of Islam.

Similar was the case when he, after returning to India from Egypt, praised Ikhwanul Muslimeen for its Islamic character and aspirations and criticized the Egyptian military leader Gamal Abdel Nasser for his anti-Islamic attitude. Muslim leaders and *'ulama* of India were infuriated by his statements, but he did not change his stance because he knew the reality that Gamal Nasser was with Ikhwanul in the beginning, but when Ikhwanul demanded him to implement the Islamic policies, he refused to go along and turned against Ikhwanul, maybe on his own or under external pressure.

What transpired later proved that Ikhwanul's demands were justified, its members were living a righteous life, and they were subjected to excessive torture and brutality by the military rulers. Consequently, influenced by Nasser's ideology, Egypt as well as the entire Arab world started drifting away from Islam towards communism and atheism and became agents of the imperialist powers who dictated policies of those countries. All of this was happening as part of the Cold War between USSR and USA and consequently Egypt had to endure two wars and suffer huge losses.

Syria went through similar kind of turmoil. The military revolution brought to power the people of Druze sect who were vehemently opposed to Islam and caused immeasurable hardship to Muslims of Syria.

Iraq also witnessed a number of military coups which were instigated by Gamal Abdel Nasser. As a result, first Ahmad Hassan al-Bakr and then Saddam Hussein came to power. The kind of oppression and suffering that the people of Iraq had to face in their regimes in practicing Islam and securing democratic rights is no more a secret.

Sheikh Nadwi has argued in his book (*As Sirau Bainal . . .*) that all these conditions have basically resulted from the clash between the Islamic and Western ideologies. He emphasized that we must untangle ourselves from the conspiracy whose primary objective is to divide Muslims and promote anti-Islamic sentiments in Muslim countries. Not only did he highlight these issues in his book, but he also conveyed them to the leaders of Muslim countries whenever he met them. It shows his deep concern and commitment for *islah* (reform) of Muslims. It is rare to find such a leader and reformer at this time. His views can be further understood by studying his travelogues.

The most insidious ideology that was ever introduced by the colonial powers in the Arab world was the Arab nationalism which looked attractive from outside, but was very deadly from inside. It was the brainchild of Michel Aflaq who was a pro-Western Christian ideologue from Syria. He floated the idea that all the virtues and grandeur that Arabs possessed came from their Arab heritage and thus they should be proud of their Arab origin and adopt the ancient Arab traditions in all of their political and cultural affairs. The movement became extremely menacing when the influential military leader Gamal Abdel Nasser of Egypt embraced it. The result was that the entire Arab world started drifting towards a system in which Islam had only a marginal role both in terms of ideology and practice. Thus the Arabs who were able to reach the pinnacle of success and glory due to Islam were about to endanger their very basic identity of being Muslim.

History bears testimony to the fact that there had been in the past many nations who had perished after they had confined themselves to their own racial, tribal, or linguistic boundaries. Arab nationalism was pushing the Arabs towards the same danger – the danger of extinction. But their biggest loss would be the severance of their relationship with Islam – the main source of their pride and honor. Thus Arab nationalism was in reality a conspiracy to deprive Arabs of Islam.

Sheikh Nadwi vehemently opposed the call for Arab nationalism. He said:

> I myself come from Arab origin, but I consider Arab nationalism as an enemy of Islam. Any prejudice that is based upon language or race is divisive and destroys basic human values.

On this issue, he wrote two very powerful articles *Isma'uha Minni Sarihatan Aiyohal 'Arab*[2] (Arabic) and *Ilai Rayatil Muhammadiyah Aiyohal 'Arab*[3] (Arabic).

Sheikh Nadwi quoted the following couplet of Dr. Muhammad Iqbal, the Poet of the East, in one of his articles and recited it once in a large public gathering in Delhi.

---

2 Approximate translation of the title: *O Arabs! Listen to My Frank Talk.*

3 Approximate translation of the title: *O Arabs! Come Under the Banner of Muhammad.*

Nahin wujood hudood-o-saghoor se is kaa
Muhammad-e-arabi se hai 'alam-e-arabi!

Its existence does not rest on borders and seashores
Arabian land exists because of Muhammad Arabi.

Sheikh Nadwi once got an opportunity to speak in a meeting of Muslim World League in which the Palestinian leader Yasser Arafat was also present. Sheikh Nadwi very openly and strongly said that the issue of Palestine belonged to the entire Muslim world and it would be improper and unwise to treat it as an Arab issue. This issue must be tackled with Islamic spirit like our predecessors did. He said:

> If you take this approach, you will be remembered in the same way as Salahuddin Ayubi (d. 1193) is remembered. Otherwise, it will become a game of imperialist powers and many innocent lives will be lost for no reason. So treat it as an Islamic issue and try to resolve it in the light of Islamic principles. If you do so, the entire Islamic world will be with you.

He had said the same thing in a speech at Damascus University a decade ago. He had written a detailed article *Kaarithatu Falesteen wa Asbabuhal Haqiqiyah*[4] in which he had outlined ways of resolving the Palestinian issue and what were the possible pitfalls which could further complicate it. Those Arabs who had looked at the Arab nationalism only superficially did not like his views at that time. But when they started seeing its ill effects, they appreciated what he had said.

His stand had always been the same. In Bangladesh, when the linguistic prejudice was openly patronized and it gave rise to conflict between Bengalis and Biharis (non-Bengalis), he warned against its dire consequences and emphasized that it (linguistic prejudice) was inhumane and anti-Islamic and it

---

4 Approximate tanslation of the title: *Tragedy of Palestine and Its Real Reasons.*

would only strengthen the hands of atheist forces. He wrote the article[5] *Lisani 'Asbiyat Kaa Almiyah.*

Shiekh Nadwi, in his writings and speeches, highlighted the damaging effects of linguistic prejudice and Western hostility towards Islam. He considered them to be extremely harmful and dangerous to the unity of Muslims. He took cues from the following verse of Quran:

> And hold fast, all together, by the rope which Allah stretches out for you, and be not divided among yourselves; and remember with gratitude Allah's favor on you; for you were enemies and He joined your hearts in love, so that by His Grace, you became brethren; and you were on the brink of the pit of fire, and He saved you from it. – *Al 'Imran,* 3:103

In this verse, Allah's favor refers to the spirit and feeling of brotherhood that binds believers together under the banner of divine guidance.

In Sheikh Nadwi's opinion, the dangers of Western ideology were not limited to politics only. In fact, politics was only a vehicle whereas the real danger of Western ideology came from its deep-rooted aversion to religion. The rebellious attitude that developed in Europe against religion in the last few centuries forced religion to be separated from politics. Politics dictated cultural and social issues while religion became limited to the rituals which were performed within the walls of a church. Thus everyday life became disconnected from religion in the lives of European nations and religion became confined to church only. But in Islam, religion encompasses all aspects of human life and anything that is done according to the orders of Allah and His Prophet is part of religion. Thus religion in Islam cannot be separated from everyday activities of life.

---

5 Approximate translation of the title: *Tragedy of the Linguistic Prejudice.*

Western thinkers and those who are the product of Western education try to promote the idea that Islam is an outdated religion and an obsolete way of life. At the top of that, the imperialist powers adopt and promote policies which are geared towards continuing their dominance on the East which comprises mostly of Muslim countries. That is why what they present to Muslim countries in the name of reform or democracy is actually aimed at destroying Islamic spirit and feeling in the hearts of Muslims and Arab nationalism is one of such arsenals.

The restrictions that Islam places on human conduct are in fact good for the human society as well as for individuals and are aimed at preserving basic human values. Thus any ideology that seeks to disconnect religion from everyday life will never be acceptable to the followers of Islam though it may be acceptable to others. Not only will such an ideology remove Islam from the lives of Muslims, but it will also deprive them of the basic human qualities. That is why Sheikh Nadwi considered the Western philosophy of separating religion from everyday life to be very dangerous and harmful. Since this attitude was becoming very pervasive due to the popularity of Western education, he condemned it very forcefully.

In some of his speeches, Sheikh Nadwi bluntly said that the situation had become so grave that there might be people who were buried in Muslim graveyards, but a little investigation would reveal that they did not fall within the precincts of Islam. If a person did not have faith in the basic tenets of Islam, how he could be counted as a Muslim even though he had a Muslim name or was born in a Muslim family. Thus we must pay attention to make ourselves true Muslims. In this connection, he wrote a very important paper *Raddatun wa la Ababakr laha* (published in English as *The New Menace and Its Answer*) which was published by the Academy of Islamic Research and Publications. On his initiation, it was also decided to prepare more literature on this topic and make more effort on curbing this disease which was becoming rampant among modern educated Muslims. The following is an excerpt from that article:

> Today's *jihad* (struggle), obligation, and most important religious need is to fight the wave of atheism which is sweeping through the entire Islamic world. The need is to launch an all-out assault on the very root of this menace. The need of the hour is to revive in young and educated Muslims their trust in Islam, its belief system, and the prophethood of Muhammad as they have lost connection with these fundamental tenets. Today's greatest worship is to remove intellectual and ideological confusion from the minds of young educated Muslims and fully satisfy their rational and logical queries about Islam. Today's greatest *jihad* is to fight ignorance (which has fully captured the hearts and minds of people) with knowledge and reasoning until it is completely replaced by correct Islamic faith and practice.
>
> It has been a full century since Europe started preying on our young and talented minds. It has created a storm of skepticism, doubt, hypocrisy, and godlessness in our hearts and minds. Our belief in *ghaib* (unseen) has been shaken and materialistic views of politics and economy have taken its place. Though we have been in the state of defeat and destruction for a century, we did not do anything to fight it. We did not care to replenish the knowledge (that we had inherited) to make it vibrant and capable of facing new challenges.
>
> We had no interest in understanding, analyzing, and evaluating European philosophy. We should have dissected it like surgeons. Instead, we spent all of our time in debating only peripheral issues so much so that we, at the end of the century, were caught off-guard in a state where the very foundation of our *iman* (faith) and *yaqeen* (conviction) was terribly shaken and there had grown a whole new generation which neither believed in the principles of Islam nor had any feeling or concern for Islam. Nor did it have

> any connection with the rest of the *ummah* (Muslims) except that it was counted as Muslims for statistical or political purposes.
>
> Furthermore, through literature, politics, and culture, the epidemic of indifference towards Islam has afflicted majority of Muslims and they are faced with the danger of forsaking Islam. May Allah forbid, but the time seems to be nearing when Islam may be completely driven out of the lives of Muslims.

For the very purpose of combating the unhealthy trend that was pervading the new generation, the Academy of Islamic Research and Publications was established in 1959 under Sheikh Nadwi's guidance. The Academy had already published more than 200 items (books and booklets) in Sheikh Nadwi's lifetime. It publishes literature in Urdu, Arabic, English, and Hindi. Sheikh Ishaq Jalees Nadwi and Dr. Ishteyaq Hussain Quraishi played a key role in establishing the Academy – Sheikh Ishaq Jalees in administration and management and Dr. Quraishi in publicity and finance.

Sheikh Nadwi cared much about the Academy and gave a lot of importance to the work it was doing. He also wanted to get his writings translated into other languages. As his fame and reputation grew around the world, more of his writings got translated into other languages, especially in Turkish.

By the grace of Allah, the Academy has produced more than 300 publications so far. There are several books whose multiple editions have been published. The work has started in Bengali as well as in other regional Indian languages.

From the very inception of the Academy, its objective has been to serve the humanity and carry on the effort of *d'awah* and *islah*. That is why it has sent books to many parts of the world on its own expense and has widely distributed books among students so that they can be guided properly.

World Forum of Islamic Literature

By the time Sheikh Syed Abul Hasan 'Ali Nadwi finished his formal education, he had fully understood that the current decline of Muslims started only about five or six centuries ago and it was nearly the same time when Europe started coming out of darkness and its bright minds started getting inspiration for knowledge from the Muslim institutions of learning. Europe took advantage of the negligence of Muslims and raced ahead of them. About 300 years ago, the West, by virtue of its superior resources and power, started dominating the East which included many Muslim countries. The Eastern countries were too weak to stop the onslaught and suffered defeat, mainly on two fronts – education and governance (i.e. public administration). The East remained engulfed in turmoil during that period and gave ample opportunity to Western educators and administrators to exert their influence on the East.

That was also the period during which a tussle between religion and politics, and between religious and worldly pursuits erupted in the minds of Western intellectuals and they completely separated these two (religion and politics) from each other. According to this separation, individuals had complete freedom in their private lives while government regulated their social and public lives. As a result, thinking and morality of people became quite unregulated and godlessness thrived freely in the society.

This kind of separation may be acceptable to others, but there is absolutely no place for it in Islam. Islam does not differentiate between religion and worldly pursuits; politics and morality cannot be separated. Islam does not leave human beings to live a life that is driven solely by lust and desires. It gives a code of conduct that encompasses all aspects of human life.

Literature that was produced in the West during that

period was also heavily influenced by this separation. So wherever the Western powers went, their literature also followed which in turn incited local population to become free from all religious constrains.

Muslim intellectuals became very concerned that it would be catastrophic if the new generation of Muslims, under the influence of Western education and culture, shunned their Islamic beliefs and values. But the question was: How to combat that danger? Sheikh Nadwi believed that the solution laid in providing right kind of literature which could replace Western literature and counterbalance its negative influence, and it could be done only if the material produced for that purpose was of high quality and appealed to the psyche and taste of the new generation.

Many of our elders, because of the brutal and oppressive treatment that they had received at the hands of the colonial powers, had developed such a bitterness and distaste towards the West that they did not even bother to look at what made the Western nations advance so much in knowledge and power. Instead, they fully concentrated on preserving their old heritage and spent all of their resources in defending it against the onslaught of modern thinking and literature. As a result, they remained confined to their own age-old methodology and thinking.

Contrary to that approach, the founders of Nadwatul 'Ulama felt that the aforementioned danger could be countered more effectively by providing a competing curriculum and education that could stand face-to-face with the opposing forces. So they focused on developing an educational system which could become a viable alternative to the one promoted by the West. Sheikh Nadwi had fully subscribed to this approach.

Instead of being apologetic and defensive about the

allegation that Islamic teachings have become outdated, the objective of this approach is to prove that they (Islamic teachings) are the most versatile and comprehensive, both logically and theoretically. In fact, it is needed to show through intelligent reasoning and historical facts that emancipation and survival of mankind lie only in Islamic teachings. It is also needed to show that the Western philosophy and system are fraught with great dangers of destroying humanity.

Institutions of secular education proved to be a fertile ground for nurturing Western thinking and attitude in the new generation which was exposed to books and literature which were prepared according to the Western doctrine and philosophy. As a result, many graduates of those institutions developed aversion to Islam and affinity for Western values and thinking.

On the other hand, the traditional *'ulama* and religious institutions remained tied to their age-old methodology and curriculum in languages, literature and other subjects which did not appeal to the mindset of new generation. However, Sheikh Nadwi, under the purview of Nadwatul 'Ulama, adopted and advocated strategies which were more effective, both academically and psychologically. He put special emphasis on the Arabic language and literature and involved his students and associates also in developing curricular material in these areas.

The Arabic language and literature are the real treasures of Islamic knowledge and cultural heritage, and thus a good acquaintance with them is essential for any religious undertaking. Yet, the religious institutions lacked a suitable curriculum in these areas. That is why Nadwatul 'Ulama, mostly on the pattern of what was done in Arab countries, especially Egypt, took initiative to develop a curriculum with the goal of preparing students with high proficiency in Arabic – both modern and classical. Special attention was given to ensure that a strong connection remained with the language and dialect of the early periods of Islam. With these objectives in mind, a concerted effort was launched to develop educational material and books in these areas.

The first book that resulted from that effort was an elementary book *Durusul Loghatul Arabia* (Arabic) on language by Sheikh Syed Sulaiman Nadwi. Then came his (Sheikh Syed Sulaiman Nadwi's) thesaurus *Loghat Jadidah* (Arabic) which comprised of Arabic words commonly used in modern dialect. Thereafter, Sheikh Syed Abul Hasan 'Ali Nadwi prepared books which were substituted for the Egyptian books. These books were of high quality in both style and content and were also aimed at fostering proper Islamic attitude and character among students. This series included two books on Arabic language and a book on Arabic literature. The first book *Qasas-al-Nabiyyin* (published in English as *Stories of the Prophets*) on language had five volumes and the second one *Al-Qara at-ur-Rashidah* (Arabic) had three volumes. The book *Mukhtaarat Min Adab-al-Arab* (Arabic) on Arabic literature consisted of two volumes.

These books proved very effective in fulfilling the curriculur needs of the Arabic language and literature at Nadwatul 'Ulama and earned high recognition from reputed scholars of Egypt and Syria for their style and content.

Sheikh Nadwi also guided his students in preparing several books on Arabic language, grammar, composition, and literature such as *M'oal-li-mul Inshaa* (in three volumes), *Tamrinus Sarf*, *'Ilmul Tasrif*, *Tamrihun Nahw*, *Mansurat min Adabul Arab*, and *Al Adab Al Arabi Bain Ardh wa Naqad*.

Sheikh Nadwi believed that our literature must conform to Islamic teachings and temperament in both style and content and it should serve as a better alternative to the Western literature which conflicts with Islamic thought and spirit. With this goal in mind, he and others under his supervision developed substantial amount of literature in which he highlighted differences between the Islamic and Western ideologies and objectives.

He lamented that though concerned Muslim educators and intellectuals have opened their own educational institutions for the purpose of combating challenges of the Western thinking and culture, they have adopted the same Western curriculum which espouses non-Islamic principles and values. Furthermore, Muslim educators, despite being well qualified and plenty in number, have not yet paid attention to this problem. In his articles and books, Sheikh Nadwi often urged Muslim scholars and educators to develop literature that may foster Islamic spirit and attitude among students.

Sheikh Nadwi presented his vision and concern [of using literature to foster correct Islamic attitude and thinking] to Arabs also. He did so in the form of a paper that he presented to experts of the Arabic language and literature at the time of his nomination in 1985 to the international literary academy known as al-Majm'a al-'Ilmi al-'Arabi (Academy of Arabic Learning) of Damascus, Syria. He found many who concurred with his vision and were eager to work for it.

Encouraged by favorable response which he received for his idea in Damascus, Sheikh Nadwi convened a conference at Nadwatul 'Ulama on the topic of Islamic literature. It was the first such conference on this subject and was very successful. To follow up what had transpired in that conference, two more conferences were held, first at the Islamic University of Madinah, and second at the Imam Muhammad Bin Saud Islamic University, Riyadh. The proposals, which were drafted at the Nadwatul 'Ulama conference, were ratified at the Madinah and Riyadh conferences.

Gradually, the above-mentioned idea about Islamic literature gained momentum and took shape of a strong movement. Several professors of Arabic literature from Arab universities met Sheikh Nadwi during his stay in Makkah and proposed to establish a central organization to carry out efforts in an organized manner. They also proposed to convene a conference in which such an organization could be formed.

Consequently, a conference was convened in the beginning of 1986 and an international organization known as the Rabita al-Adab al-Islami al-'Alami (World Forum of Islamic Literature) was founded. The conference was attended by experts of literature from all over the Islamic world and the organization's constitution was ratified. Sheikh Nadwi was unanimously appointed its president and Nadwatul 'Ulama was established as its head office.

Prof. 'Abdur Rahman Rafat al-Basha of the Imam Muhammad Bin Saud Islamic University, Riyadh, Saudi Arabia, was very instrumental in the establishment and progress of the World Forum of Islamic Literature. After Prof. al-Basha passed away, Dr. 'Abdul Quddus Abu Saleh took extraordinary interest in continuing the work. After Sheikh Nadwi passed away, Dr. Abu Saleh was appointed as the president of the World Forum of Islamic Literature and the head office was moved to Riyadh.

The World Forum of Islamic Literature has grown considerably over the years. In the beginning, there was some skepticism about its worthiness, but gradually its importance and need became widely recognized. Its branches have opened in several countries. Now it has branches in about a dozen countries. These branches arrange meetings and seminars, work to promote Islamic literature and prepare literary material as needed. In order to co-ordinate efforts in various countries, two regional offices have been opened, one in Lucknow and the other in Riyadh. Each regional office guides activities in nearby countries and has a vice-president.

The officers of the organization are appointed or their term is renewed every third year in a conference. There is a central board of trustees which has one or two representatives from each participating country. The president and the vice-presidents are members of this board. The board of trustees serves as the advisory council. The board meets every year to review and discuss policies and incomplete/unattended issues. The organization publishes literary material. It has so far published several valuable books. The central as well as the regional offices publish monthly and quarterly magazines and newsletters which contain news and articles pertaining to Islamic literature.

In his writings, Sheikh Nadwi argued that the thinking and attitude of Muslims should be endowed with the spirit and motive of Islam, and Islamic literature should be geared towards that goal. He clearly articulated this role of Islamic literature and satisfied many skeptics. As the work of the World Forum of Islamic Literature progressed and gained recognition, his pioneering contribution was widely acknowledged.

Sheikh Nadwi emphasized in his writings that literature has a profound connection with the feelings and convictions of a person and affects all aspects of the human life. It is very shortsighted to limit literature to entertainment purposes only. Islamic spirit makes literature sublime and beneficial and does not curtail its scope. His views on this subject are represented in the books *Nazrat fil Adab* (by Shekh Nadwi), *Rawaye min Ada-bud D'awah* (by Sheikh Nadwi), and *Deen aur Adab* (by Rabey Hasani) and in the preface of the book *Mukhtaarat Min Adab-al-Arab* (mentioned earlier).

The following is an excerpt from the speech that Sheikh Nadwi delivered at the end of the inaugural seminar of the World Forum of Islamic Literature that was held at Nadwatul 'Ulama in 1985:

This is a gathering of literary people. All of you have been students of literature and now you are its spokesmen and interpreters. You know that if something is abbreviated, it reduces to a dot and if it is enlarged, it becomes a line, a page, a book, and a huge depository of books. This is exactly what literature is and this is exactly why this seminar has been convened. Since I am in a literary gathering at this moment, I will take a cue from the following couplet of the renowned Urdu poet Mirza Ghalib:

> *faryad ki koi lai nahi*
> *naalah pabande naiy nahi hai*
>
> A lament has no format
> A cry knows no tune

Crying and laughing know no boundary – national or tribal. Nor do they need any skill. In fact, true crying and laughing must be free from all kinds of artistry. Provided there is no pretense, one cries only when the pain becomes unbearable and one laughs only when the joy becomes overpowering. These are expressions of emotions. Thus they (crying and laughing) require inner feelings. A cry is not real if it is not triggered by an internal feeling, pain, or distress. A laugh is not real if it requires an external inducement.

The same applies to literature also. It does not belong to any nation or country. It has no gender. It does not have any specific terminology. It is not bound by any protocol. Yet, strangely enough, many of those who have dedicated their lives to literature and given their best to it view the vast ocean of literature only as a small vessel. A piece of literature is valuable whether it comes from a religious person, a prophet, or a divine scripture. The criteria is that it must be articulated in such a way that it affects the heart, its composer feels that he has fully conveyed the message, and the audience enjoys and accepts it.

Yesterday, in the Arabic seminar,[6] I had mentioned that the

---

6 In that session, papers were submitted in Arabic and the audience consisted of Arab scholars and journalists.

appreciation of beauty was that it (beauty) must be admired regardless of which form it came in. You cannot restrict a nightingale to perch on this flower and not on the other. What kind of appreciation and justice is this if a flower is recognized and enjoyed as a rose if it blooms under the shade of a tavern and is considered unattractive if it blooms in the courtyard of a *masjid*. Is it a crime for the rose to grow in a *masjid*? I could not recite Dr. Iqbal's couplet there [because it was in Urdu], but I am reciting it here:

> *husn-e-beparwa ko apni be-naqabi ke liye*
> *hun agar shehron se bann payare to shehar achche ke bann*
>
> To the reckless beauty, for her unveiling
> If woodland is lovelier than town, is town better or woodland?

Are we concerned about the reckless beauty, city or desert? We have dealt literature the same treatment. If you permit, let me recite the following Persian couplet:

> *dile 'abs lab pe shikwah dana kunad*
> *shisha taa na shikand sadaa na kunad*
>
> A heart does not complain until it gets hurt
> A glass does not make noise until it breaks

If you hear the rattling noise of glass, you know that it has broken. Thus it is the cry and protest of a broken heart and broken goblet about the restrictions which have been imposed on literature that it must wear certain attire. Literature is most independent of formalities. Restrictions of coming in a certain outfit and speaking a certain language are totally unacceptable to it. If it is literature, it deserves to be seated on throne and given recognition even though it may come in torn and old clothes. If it comes in the robe of a king, but does not know how to express itself properly, it is not literature. Something does not become literature simply because it has come from a person who speaks English, is so-called progressive, is a professor or chairman of the department of literature or is a president. A genuine piece of literature may be heard in the call of a beggar, lullaby of a mother who is lulling her baby to sleep or the midnight supplication of a godly person who wants only his Lord to listen to him. Thus real literature may come from any person, in any form or in any language.

Unfortunately, it has happened, especially in the recent past, that certain frivolous conditions have been imposed on literature, such as it must make fun of religion or it must include some joke and humor. But let me ask you what these things (joke and humor) have to do with literature. It is possible that the joker may be a literary person, but literature does not require him to joke. It all depends upon his taste, attitude, and upbringing. A man of literature, like any other human being, may say something which may be right or wrong. It is his individual act and has nothing to do with literature.

Nowadays, it is argued that a piece of literature is not genuine unless it talks about progressiveness, makes fun of old traditions, and criticizes religious scriptures. As a humble student of literature, let me tell you quite frankly that literature did in fact originate from divine scriptures. Literature was non-existent. When God sent His messengers to guide people, He gave them language and words with their meaning. This is where literature came from. History has no trace of literature prior to the coming of divine scriptures. If someone claims contrary to this, I challenge him to come forward to tell us when did literature begin and when did the world come to know about it?

Literature began with divine scriptures and the holy Quran inscribed the everlasting seal of perfection on it. Allah has revealed in Quran:

> Which the trusted spirit descended with. To (communicate) to your heart that you may be a warner. In eloquent Arabic.
> – *Ash-Shu'ara*, 26: 193-95

How high Allah has elevated literature by praising it together with His scripture! Quran is a miracle and is in clear Arabic tongue. No one is more self-sufficing (*as-samad*) than Allah. Yet, He has used the best possible form of expression to explain His message to humans.

Not only did Sheikh Nadwi verbally advocate these ideas and invite others to them, but he fully embodied them in his writings and speeches in both Urdu and Arabic. He was an accomplished writer with extraordinary literary skills. His unique accomplishment was that he excelled simultaneously in three areas of literature – pure academic, literature for children, and perceptive writing (dealing with intellectual and ideological issues). He was widely acclaimed for his diversity and was recognized as a thinker, a *da'i* and a man of literature at the same time.

Sheikh Nadwi's contributions to Islamic literature in clarifying its role and purpose and in advancing its cause were highly appreciated all over the Islamic world. Several major conferences have been held on Islamic literature in various parts of the world and prominent writers and experts of language and literature have participated in them representing their countries and regions. International seminars on Islamic literature have been held in Turkey, Morocco, Egypt, India, Pakistan, Bangladesh, Europe, and USA. In India alone, more than 20 such seminars have been held on the national level.

Sheikh Nadwi was very particular about attending these seminars and conferences. In addition to presiding over these events, he often presented his own papers. Under his supervision, the Riyadh and Lucknow branches of the World Forum of Islamic Literature started publishing *Majal-latul Adab al-Islami* (Arabic) and *Karwan-e-Adab* (Urdu) respectively. These two journals are published every three months. The journal *Qaflaye Adab Islami* (Urdu) is published from Lahore, Pakistan. These branches regularly publish articles and books on important topics due to which a good collection of material has come into existence.

Payam-e-Insaniyat

The grandeur and prestige of a nation is built upon the sacrifices that its worthy sons give for its establishment and progress. The history of a nation and civilization is made from such accomplishments which also determine the standing of a nation in the world.

Sheikh Abul Hasan 'Ali Nadwi worked tirelessly on three fronts – educational, social, and religious. His services to mankind, especially to Muslims in improving their educational and religious condition, were widely recognized both inside and outside India. In the academic world, he distinguished himself as an outstanding scholar and accomplished writer. In the social arena, he was seen as a reformer and guide. In religious circles, he was revered as a spiritual mentor and gifted speaker.

He was very patriotic towards his country (India), was always eager for its prosperity and progress and was always mindful of fulfilling his obligations towards it. In his books, he has lavishly praised India for the progress that it has made in education and culture and introduced India to the world in a glowing way. It can be seen in his speeches and books such as *Al-Muslimoon fil Hind* (published in English as *Muslims in India*) and *Ad Dawatul Islamiyah wa Tataw-wura-tuha fil Hind*[7] through which he introduced to the Arab world great Islamic personalities and movements of India and their contributions in the field of education and culture. His father Sheikh Hakim Syed 'Abdul Hai Hasani had done the same before him.

Sheikh Nadwi consistently reminded his fellow countrymen to live by high moral standards and whenever he noticed a failing in the society, he made a concerted effort

---

7 Approximate translation of the title: *Islamic D'awah and Its Growth in India.*

to eradicate it. For this very purpose, he started the movement known as Payam-e-Insaniyat (Message of Humanity) in 1974. From this platform, he used to convene large public gatherings in major cities of India and remind people about moral values which were universally espoused by all religions and societies. He also used to mention teachings of Islam and cite examples of illustrious Muslims of the past. This movement created very positive effect in the society and helped in promoting mutual understanding among different communities. Its accomplishments were recognized by the leaders of different religions, prominent judges, university professors, etc. The speeches that he delivered on different events of this movement are available in the form of booklets. In these speeches, he also pointed out moral vices and inhumane practices that had become pervasive in the Indian society.

Sheikh Nadwi was very distressed to see rapid decline in the moral character and behavior of people in the country. He often lamented that there had been a sharp decline in the number of individuals who were actively engaged in reminding others about good character and high moral values – a great loss to the country. The strength and greatness of a nation come from its character. If the character of a nation deteriorates, it means that the nation is heading towards its downfall and demise.

Sheikh Nadwi had studied history with great dedication. He had studied the history of India, Europe, Arabs, Muslims, and other religions. From those studies, he had understood causes of the rise and fall of nations and developed a burning desire in his heart to see the glorious periods of history revived – a theme that he expressed very passionately in his writings. He considered the era during which the Islamic culture and civilization ware thriving and the entire humanity was benefitting from Muslims as the most coveted period of human history.

In his writings and speeches, Sheikh Nadwi used to emphatically remind Muslims that since Allah has made them the benefactor for the entire mankind, they ought to do their best to bring humanity towards good character and virtuous living. He stressed that Islam is a religion of peace and compassion and Muslims have been enjoined by Quran and *hadith* (traditions of Prophet Muhammad) to strive for these noble and lofty goals. Thus Muslims should be more eager to benefit others than to receive benefit from others.

Whenever he met Indian political leaders or influential people, he encouraged them to adopt high moral values and serve the country. When Prime Minister Mrs. Indira Gandhi was in power, he advised her to be lenient to people instead of being oppressive. Later, when she came to visit him at his home after failing to win the re-election in 1977, he again reminded her that she as a leader should adopt the policy of justice and fairness for all.

Regarding the Hindu–Muslim communal riots, he explained to the political leaders that the riots were like fire which, upon not getting any more fuel, would consume itself and harm everyone. This example of Sheikh Nadwi was highly appreciated by Prime Minister V.P. Singh whom Sheikh Nadwi often counseled.

During the regime of Prime Minister Narasimha Rao, Sheikh Nadwi met him and reminded him that those who had fought for the independence of the country were very concerned about building the moral character of people, but that concern had now disappeared. Now everyone is running after power and wealth which is a very bad omen for the country. He advised Narasimha Rao to take necessary measures to stop this decline. He also advised him to reach common people and remind them about the importance of high moral values so that we could grow into a great nation.

During Sheikh Nadwi's last sickness, Prime Minister Atal Behari Vajpayee came to visit him. It was quite difficult for Sheikh Nadwi to speak because of weakness. Yet, he spoke to Vajpayee, expressed his concern that the country was in great danger because the lust for power and wealth had overcome all other aspirations and implored him to rescue the country from this peril.

Whenever a new prime minister came in power in India, Sheikh Nadwi met him and advised him about the moral and human responsibilities. He wrote letters of advice to those whom he could not meet personally.

In the conventions of Payam-e-Insaniyat also, Sheikh Nadwi reminded people to rise above the greed of power and wealth and live by high moral standards. He used to bemoan that people had stopped differentiating between right and wrong and everyone was only concerned about his own personal benefits without any feeling or concern for the country.

Sheikh Nadwi's concern for eradicating evils and promoting goods was not limited to India only. As a scholar of Islam, he was especially concerned about the condition of Muslims all over the world and reform among them. Through his speeches and writings, he used to admonish Muslims that they were abandoning Islamic values and character and they needed to wake up because they, in addition to taking care of themselves, were also responsible for protecting the entire mankind from going astray. He used to explain it by means of the examples of history that whenever Muslims drifted away from virtuous life, they were afflicted with humility and disgrace and whenever they adopted the right path, they gained respect and saved other nations from destruction as well.

Muslims should be the torchbearers of morality and high character. This is what Prophet Muhammad taught and this is what Quran has commanded again and again. Allah is the Master of everyone and everything that we possess belongs to Him. It is thus incumbent upon everyone to recognize his Creator and Master, have love and affection for fellow human beings and live an obedient, prosperous, and happy life. It is the responsibility of community leaders and men of understanding to strive to establish these values among people.

He spread his message and mission to people through books, speeches, and dialogs. He wanted both Muslims and non-Muslims to live as good neighbors and care for each other. To make people aware of this need, he used to arrange large public gatherings, invite leaders of different communities, and religions and allow them to express their views. It enabled leaders of different religions to come to a common platform and understand each other. It also helped ease communal tension between Hindus and Muslims. Such effort is still continuing from the stage of Payam-e-Insaniyat.

There were several individuals who fully co-operated with Sheikh Nadwi in these efforts. Sheikh 'Abdul Karim Parikh was the most prominent among them. Sheikh Parikh was well acquainted with the temperament of different communities and Sheikh Nadwi had full faith in him. The other notables were Sheikh Ishaq Jalees Nadwi, Qazi 'Abdul Hameed Indori and Prof. Anees Chishti of Pune. Prof. Chishti is still carrying on this effort.

Sheikh Nadwi was so accommodating and eager to patch differences with others that people of different viewpoints saw him as a well-wisher and conciliator and accepted him as their common leader and representative. This perception about him was more widespread among non-Muslims (of India) than Muslims. Not only did most of the community leaders of India have good opinion about him, but they also looked at him with great respect and reverence. The government officials also kept him in high esteem and paid attention to his opinion. Despite being so accommodating, he was very strict in his religious beliefs and practices and never compromised in matters pertaining to the core Islamic principles.

Sheikh Nadwi always preferred negotiation and mutual dialog to confrontation which he considered counter-productive. This approach enabled him to get a number of difficult and complicated issues resolved amicably. Due to his non-confrontational and non-controversial nature, he had emerged as a leader who was acceptable to all factions of Indian Muslims. If there was an issue that concerned Muslims at large, all the factions used to agree on him as their representative and the government also gave due recognition to his representation.

Sheikh Nadwi's vision about the welfare and progress of the country was very clear. He viewed the country as a common garden whose protection and prosperity was the responsibility of every citizen. The country does not belong to the majority community only. The minority communities also have equal stake in it as has been guaranteed by the Constitution of India. The progress and strength of the country lie only in adhering to these principles and people must co-operate with each other for the common good of the country. It will be disastrous if individual communities become selfish and care only about themselves with no concern for others and the country. Unless both the majority and minority communities co-operate with each other, the country will be weakened and devastated.

Not only did Sheikh Nadwi fully understand the importance of mutual co-operation and understanding, but he also presented it with full force to leaders, intellectuals, and government authorities of the country. He told them that they should not be concerned only about getting votes and gaining power. Corruption had become rampant and everyone was looking for his own interest without any concern for the country. He asked leaders and authorities to go out and work among masses to stop corruption and promote good moral character. Otherwise, the country would be destroyed. The leaders who had fought for the independence of the country had worked very hard on social reforms of the country also. It is sad that their efforts had been abandoned today.

Sheikh Nadwi had started the work of Payam-e-Insaniyat as early as 1954, although it was formally launched in 1974 in the city of Allahabad. He used to convene large gatherings and deliver stirring speeches urging people to strive for the welfare and reform of the mankind and society. Some of those speeches have already been published. The following excerpt from the speech that he delivered in Mau, Uttar Pradesh, India, on 24 January 1954 may help in understanding the message and purpose of the movement of Payam-e-Insaniyat:

> We consider this message to be essential for every [political] party. Our existence is more essential than that of any party because if we succeed, the beautiful bouquet of humanity will come into existence. Thorns are coming up everywhere but humans are rare. We came here to call you to revive and beautify humanity. Today, thorns and bitter fruits are coming out of the human tree. We call you to make this tree bear sweet fruits of humanity. We did not come here to create obstacles for you. We came here to remind you that you need to take care of the humanity. We came here to create in your hearts the concern and pain for this spoiled world. May this feeling of empathy develop in you! This was the message and mission of prophets and we have come here to revive their mission. Some of us limit our efforts to intellectual debates, some

> to tackling hunger, and some to securing cloth and shelter. Religion fosters faith and love for the Creator in hearts and removes deception of eyes. It was the work of prophets to remove the curtain of darkness from eyes and bring peace and tranquility to hearts.
>
> We tell Muslims that you have devalued the message and work of prophets. You are guilty of being negligent. You have abandoned this treasure and become an agent of the greedy people of the world. You have become a mere bargainer and developed the mentality of a selfish businessman. You were not supposed to be a mere trader. You had come here as a *da'i* (one who calls people towards Allah and His divine religion). But you forgot your position and purpose for which you had come. Had you been living with the message of *d'awah* and love, you would have enjoyed a life of respect and success. Now your success lies in regaining your lost position. Your success of this world lies in valuing the work of prophets. Political parties and other outfits, instead of fighting for power and control, should strive to mend the broken structure of humanity. Instead of working only for their own interests and those of their friends and relatives, they should work for the welfare of the entire mankind. Without this reform, no one can attain peace and success.

Sheikh Nadwi's concern and worry was such that Muslim as well as Hindu intellectuals looked at him with great respect and reverence. Thus when he passed away, people of all religions and political affiliations expressed deep grief, love and affection for him and felt that it was a great loss to the nation and country.

Deeni T'alimi Council

India is a country where people of different faiths, colors, and backgrounds live. When India gained Independence in 1947, every citizen of the country was given full and equal right to benefit from independence. The Constitution of India explicitly recognized that every citizen will have full freedom to follow the religion and way of life of his choice and no one will be allowed to impose his values and traditions on others.

It thus became incumbent upon the government (regardless of its political affiliation) and its officials (regardless of which religion or class they belonged to) to run the country properly, maintain peace and order, protect rights of every citizen irrespective of their religion and race, and insure that every citizen got its democratic rights which had been granted by the constitution. But it is unfortunate that all of those who came to power, no matter which political party or religion they came from, failed to fully live up to these promises. Discrimination took place on the basis of religion and Muslims suffered most in this respect. As a result, Muslims faced difficulties in preserving their Islamic identity and that of their younger generation. Conscientious Muslims realized the severity of the problem and took initiatives at different levels to combat it. Qazi 'Adeel 'Abbasi of Basti, Uttar Pradesh, India, a respected freedom fighter and devoted Muslim leader, was one of those who spearheaded such efforts.

Qazi 'Abbasi started an after-school program for the Muslim children who were attending daytime government-run primary schools so that basic Islamic education could be provided to them. In addition, he also came up with the idea of establishing a network of full-time independent schools which would be fully funded by Muslims. He presented this idea to the Muslim community and solicited support for it.

Sheikh Mahmoodul Hassan 'Uthmani, a close relative of Qazi 'Abbasi, was among those who fervently supported this idea from the very beginning. Sheikh Syed Abul Hasan 'Ali Nadwi and Sheikh Muhammad Manzoor N'umani also endorsed and supported his idea.

In order to bring Qazi 'Abbasi's dream into reality, a conference was convened in Basti during 30-31 December 1959 and an organization known as Deeni T'alimi Council was founded. Sheikh Nadwi and Qazi 'Abbasi were appointed the founding president and the general secretary, respectively. Sheikh Nadwi remained its president until he passed away on 31 December 1999.

Prominent among the patrons of Deeni T'alimi Council were attorney Zafar Ahmad Siddiqui, Principal Riazuddin Ahmad, and Dr. Ishteyaq Hussain Quraishi. The Council worked in a very organized manner, opened schools in villages all over the State of Uttar Pradesh and provided basic religious education to hundreds of thousands of Muslim children. These schools proved essential for the religious and cultural survival of Muslims. In order to make educated and concerned Muslims aware of the need and importance of such schools, several conferences were held. More can be learned about the purpose and mission of the council from the speeches of the Council's president and secretary.

As the time passed by, more people joined the Council's efforts. After Qazi 'Abbasi passed away, Dr. Ishteyaq Hussain Quraishi became the general secretary. Currently, Sheikh Sa'yidur Rahman 'Azami Nadwi (Vice-Chancellor of Nadwatul 'Ulama) is the president, Prof. Nafees Ahmad Siddiqui of Aligarh is the vice-president, and Dr. Mas'udul Hasan 'Uthmani is the general secretary. Over the years, the Council has expanded its work significantly.

Qazi 'Adeel 'Abbasi had actively fought for the freedom of India and had supported the secular form of political structure of the country. But he, as a conscientious Muslim, was very concerned about the Islamic and religious identity of the Muslims of India. Thus when he saw political leaders discriminating against Muslims after Independence, his feelings were deeply hurt. As a result, he dedicated himself entirely to the cause of preserving and protecting the rights of Muslims and worked tirelessly for this cause.

Sheikh Nadwi also had become very apprehensive about this issue [of possible discrimination against Muslims] since the very beginning of India's Independence. To highlight this issue, he delivered several speeches at different places and wrote numerous letters to government officials. For this very reason, he fully supported Deeni T'alimi Council from its very inception. His presidential addresses fully reflect this concern.

Sheikh Nadwi was so distressed by the prevailing condition of Muslims in the country that he often recited with great pain the words which Prophet Yakoob (Jacob) had spoken to his children at the time of his death. As mentioned in Quran, Prophet Yakoob, while on his deathbed, asked his children: "Whom will you worship after me?" (*Al-Baqarah*, 2:133). Reciting this verse, Sheikh Nadwi used to tell Muslims:

> O Muslims. Protect *iman* (faith) and *tawheed* (belief in the oneness of Allah) of your new generation. See how much effort Prophet Yakoob made to insure that his children (who, despite being believers, were living as a minority in Egypt which was ruled by Pharaoh) remained steadfast on *iman* and *tawheed* after him. See how concerned and restless Prophet Yakoob was for this at the end of his life. O Muslims! It is thus incumbent upon each one of you to make necessary arrangement before you die to insure that your children remain steadfast on *iman* and *tawheed*.

To help understand Sheikh Nadwi's vision of basic religious

education, the following excerpt from the speech that he delivered in the regional conference of Deeni T'alimi Council held in Allahabad on 17 February 1985 is being presented here:

> Religious education and basic awareness of *deen* (Islam) are as essentials to a Muslim as are air and water to a human being. In order for a Muslim to live like a Muslim, to be counted as a Muslim, to face Allah and His Prophet in the hereafter and to seek ultimate emancipation, he needs to have basic knowledge of *deen* in the same way as a human being needs to have air and water to survive. Muslim is not the name of a tribe, sect, nation, or culture; culture is in fact a part of Islam and helps in fulfilling its demands. If a child is born in a Brahmin family, he always remains a Brahmin whether he accepts it or not and he does not need to do anything to remain so. Among Muslims also, there are many families who take pride in their lineage and they are considered respectable in society due to their pedigree. But the real pride lies in correct *'aqidah* (faith) and submission to Allah which can be acquired only through knowledge. This is what Prophet Yakoob wanted to ascertain at the time of his departure from this world. That is why he at the time of his death gathered all of his children and grandchildren (who were large in number) and asked them: "Whom will you worship after me?" – *Al-Baqarah*, 2:133
>
> If I am consulted by someone who wants to make a banner for the *millat* (Muslims) and the banner has space for only one sentence, I will tell him to write on it "Whom will you worship after me?" I will also tell him to write beneath it: Every Muslim should question his children before he dies, take account of himself and ask himself whether or not this matter is important to him; he should ask himself if he considers it necessary to prepare his children and future generation to satisfactorily answer the question "Whom will you worship after me?
>
> We should search our hearts to see if this matter is important

> to us or not. We should check whether or not these questions are taken seriously at all levels – individual, family, tribal, village, town, and community. In which direction will our future generation go after we die? Which group or trend will they follow? Whom will they worship? What will be their belief? Will they worship the one God or hundreds, thousands, millions and billions of deities and gods? Whom will they see as the controller and sustainer of this huge universe and their lives?"

Sheikh Nadwi's feelings in this matter were very strong from the very beginning. Even before Deeni T'alimi Council was established, he had strongly opposed the campaign of *Hindu-Pooruj* according to which a person was not considered an Indian unless he recognized and revered Hindu saints of the ancient India as his guide and ancestor. When Sampurnanand (chief minister of Uttar Pradesh) and Purushottam Das Tandon (speaker of the Uttar Pradesh Legislative Assembly) wanted to impose *Hindu-Pooruj* in Uttar Pradesh, Sheikh Nadwi wrote strong letters to condemn their actions. Those letters were later published in Hindi and English as booklets.

To protect Muslims from the influence of ideas such as *Hindu-Pooruj*, an organization known as Majlis-e-Isha'at was established in Lucknow and Sheikh Muhammad Ishaq Sandelvi was appointed its secretary. Sheikh Sandelvi was the Vice-Chancellor and Shaikhul-hadith of Nadwatul 'Ulama at that time. Majlis-e-Isha'at published a number of Sheikh Nadwi's articles and booklets on this topic. These publications were sent to leaders of the majority community and it was conveyed to them that Muslims could not consider seers and saints of the Hindu religion as their guides and spiritual leaders. It was also emphasized that being an Indian did not mean that members of the minority communities would have to subscribe to the faith and traditions of the majority community. India is a secular country and everyone has full right to profess and practice his own faith and religion. Sheikh Nadwi continued reiterating this message from the platforms of Deeni T'alimi Council and Payam-e-Insaniyat as well.

The educational system which is generally available to the new generation in India tends to promote values and traditions of the majority community and portray its religious figures as the ideals to follow. It thus conflicts with religious beliefs and traditions of Muslims and dampens their enthusiasm for Islam. As a consequence, Muslim children, because of not knowing their own elders and ideals, might become more inclined to follow non-Islamic values and leaders of other religions in their adult life. This poses a great danger as it may eventually change the religious direction of India's Muslim community which believes in the oneness of Allah.

Sheikh Nadwi took this matter very seriously and constantly fought for it. Thus when the Government of Uttar Pradesh made it mandatory for school children in government-run schools to recite *Vande Mataram* (a hymn to praise the Hindu goddess Durga) and pay homage to the Hindu goddess Sarasvati, he vehemently opposed it. The government took note of it and retracted its position. This was considered a huge victory for Muslims. Muslims felt emboldened and started keeping a vigilant eye on the school curriculum – a task that Deeni T'alimi Council is currently carrying.

In response to Sheikh Nadwi's opposition to mandatory recitation of *Vande Mataram* in schools, some extremist factions of the Hindu community reacted very sharply. Not only did they harshly criticize him, but they also orchestrated a raid on his residence in Rae Bareli in the night of 22 November 1998 and conducted a house search. Perhaps, it was done to intimidate him so that he would stop his opposition to *Vande Mataram*. But it did not work and he remained steadfast in his opposition. Ultimately, they received condemnation from all corners for their action. The incident also created an awareness among Muslims that if they did not stand up to defend their values and traditions, they would be gradually cajoled to accept anti-Islamic practices and lifestyle which would prove disastrous to their religious and communal identity.

Sheikh Nadwi's stand [on the issue of *Vande Mataram*] was firm and clear. Extremist Hindu factions' action drew national and international condemnation. These were widely reported in national newspapers and media and served as a deterrent to the extremist Hindu factions. The government apologized for the raid and rescinded the order of *Vande Mataram* and *Sarasvati Puja* (worship of the Hindu goddess Sarasvati). The state's education minister was discharged from his duties. On the other hand, unprecedented level of Support poured in for Sheikh Nadwi.

How important was this issue to Sheikh Nadwi? To enable the reader understand it, the following excerpt from the speech that he delivered in a gathering of Deeni T'alimi Council in Moradabad, India, is being presented below.

> Muslims will have to make necessary arrangements to fight against these challenges [like that of *Vande Mataram*] in the same way as they do in building mosques and places of worship to perform prayers and maintain relationship between their soul and body. They must not wait for any assistance from the government in this regard. They will have to arrange sermons and lectures in mosques, properly raise their children in homes and provide religious education in *madaris* and schools. They will have to establish in the entire country a network of before-school and after-school learning places so that not even a single village or locality is left out.
>
> In this regard, there are three things which are essential.

> (1) Development of a curriculum that provides the children knowledge which they need for religious and basic needs of everyday life. It must be based upon sound pedagogical methods which are best suited for young children and must be acceptable to majority of Muslims. (2) Preparation of a pool of teachers who are adequately trained to implement the curriculum and are willing to teach children with passion and devotion. (3) Teaching Urdu as it is the easiest medium to impart Islamic knowledge to children (in India).
>
> If a nation makes a collective decision with unity of mind, it can change the fate and destiny of that nation. Today what we need most to overcome all of our difficulties and sway the condition in our favor is our decision to give priority to religious education of our children over all other types of education. We will consider it a sin and betrayal against our religion if we give to our children worldly education before giving them the knowledge that enables them to recognize their Creator, Prophet, fundamental beliefs, and obligations. If this is our decision and we remain faithful to it, no power, persuasion or threat will take us away from the straight path and deprive our future generations from the wealth of Islam.

With regards to Sheikh Nadwi's services to Deeni T'alimi Council and basic religious education, Dr. Mas'udul Hasan 'Uthmani, general secretary of Deeni T'alimi Council, has prepared a valuable book *Takbeer-e-Musalsal* (Urdu) which includes Sheikh Nadwi's speeches and articles. It gives a comprehensive view of Sheikh Nadwi's vision of Deeni T'alimi Council and the basic religious education.

All India Muslim Majlis-e-Mushawarat and AIMPLB

Both Hindus and Muslims fought against British for several decades for the Independence of India. Among Muslims, *'ulama* (Islamic scholars) were in the forefront of the struggle and gave tremendous amount of sacrifice. Though Pakistan was formed in response to the demand by a segment of Muslim population for a separate homeland for Muslims, *'ulama*'s participation in the mainstream struggle for independence played an important role in establishing India as a country of multiple religions and communities.

Since people of all religions had fought shoulder to shoulder to secure Independence, it was hoped that they all would be able to enjoy the same degree of privilege and protection in Independent India. But the wave of Hindu–Muslim communal riots made the future of Muslims uncertain and they suffered huge loss of life and property. The riots of Jamshedpur (an industrial city in the State of Jharkhand, India) and Rourkela (an industrial city in the State of Orissa, India) were extremely horrifying and devastating.

Muslim leaders became very alarmed by these riots. To deliberate on this issue, a convention was held at Nadwatul 'Ulama in August 1964. It was attended by prominent Muslim leaders, scholars and representatives of various Muslim organizations. Sheikh Syed Abul Hasan 'Ali Nadwi and Sheikh Muhammad Manzoor N'umani were the main sponsors of this convention.

An organization known as the All India Muslim Majlis-e-Mushawarat (AIMMM) was founded at the convention. The immediate goal of AIMMM was to re-build confidence and optimism among Muslims, create an environment of mutual understanding between various communities, and develop sense of responsibility towards protecting life and property of each other. Groups of responsible and influential people toured different parts of the country and attempted to reassure Muslims and alleviate their fears. Leaders and influential people of the majority community were also urged to work towards building an atmosphere of peace and harmony and many of them fully co-operated in these efforts. The result was very positive and Muslims were able to overcome the state of uncertainty and pessimism.

Since all those communal riots had taken place during the regime of the Congress party, Muslims lost faith in its government. Muslims also felt that it was necessary to make the Congress party realize that mere lip service would not suffice and Muslims were electorally powerful enough to affect the outcome of an election. Thus Muslims did not support the Congress party in the next election. The result was that the Congress party was defeated and the parties which had been sympathetic to Muslims came to power in its place; these parties, after coming to power, remained helpful to Muslims. In this way, the message got around the entire country that regardless of which political party it was, it could remain in power only if it looked after the democratic rights of people of all religions and affiliations.

AIMMM has been working effectively for several decades and Sheikh Nadwi was fully involved in it. Prominent among those who worked with him for AIMMM were Sheikh Muhammad Manzoor N'umani and Dr. Ishteyaq Hussain Quraishi.

Dr. Syed Mahmood was the first president of AIMMM. Due to his long association with the Congress party, his presidency had very good effect on the organization. After Dr. Mahmood passed away, Mufti 'Atiqur Rahman 'Uthmani became the president. He also served AIMMM diligently. But after his death, AIMMM became weak. Though Sheikh Nadwi remained associated with it and lent his support to it, he felt that its utility had significantly diminished and the task for which it was founded was no more a priority.

In the meantime, a new issue – protection of Islamic *shari'ah* (code of conduct) – had emerged which was more pressing and time consuming. It also required a new approach and strategy because of the unique situation of India – a country that is inhabited by followers of many religions. Though Hindus are in majority, there are many other communities which live there and practice their own religion and customs. Muslims are the largest minority community and they have their own complete code of conduct.

Given the huge diversity of religions, languages, and cultures that exist in India, the framers of the Constitution of India did not make laws favoring any specific segment of population. Instead, they left the power of deciding religious matters in the hands of religious leaders of each community and each community was granted full freedom to follow its own religious edicts. However, the Constitution also subtly indicated that it would be desirable to achieve some sort of uniformity in dealing with social issues.

Thus shortly after India gained Independence, some factions of the majority community wanted to take undue advantage of the above-mentioned subtlety of the Constitution. Since Muslims were the largest minority community and had their own comprehensive code of conduct to govern their social and religious issues, they were most vulnerable to such a move. The conscientious Muslim leaders and *'ulama* sensed the danger and strongly opposed the concept of uniform civil code – code that applies to everyone regardless of the person's religion.

To counter such intrusions in an organized manner, a large conference was held in Mumbai at the end of 1972 and an organization known as All India Muslim Personal Law Board

(AIMPLB) was founded which included representatives of all segments of the Muslim population. Qari Muhammad Taiyab Qasmi (of Darul 'Uloom, Deoband) and Sheikh Syed Minnatullah Rahmani (of Imarat Shari'at of Bihar and Orissa) were appointed as the founding president and general secretary, respectively. AIMPLB organized meetings all over the country and made Muslims aware of the potential injustice and harm that could be caused to the minority communities by the introduction of the uniform civil code. Muslims became united in their stand which both the government and majority community took note of.

Eleven years after the formation of AIMPLB, Qari Muhammad Taiyab Qasmi passed away in 1983. Thereafter, Sheikh Nadwi who was the Rector of Nadwatul 'Ulama was appointed as the new president. Due to his upbringing, education, and studies, Sheikh Nadwi had a very good understanding of both the traditional and modern ways of thinking. He was an eminent scholar. He was a gifted speaker, and writer. He was blessed with the ability to present his viewpoint in an eloquent and scholarly way to both Muslims and non-Muslims. Thus he persuasively argued that since Islamic *shari'ah* was a divine code of conduct, it could not be tampered with. He also argued that, as per the Indian Constitution, Muslims were well within their right to demand that their religious matters be governed by the laws of Islamic *shari'ah*. He continued this effort tirelessly for sixteen years until he passed away in 1999.

Only two years after Sheikh Nadwi became the president of AIMPLB, Muslims of India were plunged into a crisis by a Supreme Court ruling in a lawsuit involving a Muslim divorcee. The ruling emboldened the Hindu factions who were demanding a uniform civil code and Muslims felt threatened that their right to follow Islamic *shari'ah* might be severely jeopardized. Thus AIMPLB, under the guidance of Sheikh Nadwi and using the means which were permitted by the Constitution of India, launched a concerted effort to nullify the Supreme Court's ruling.

Consequently, the Parliament passed the legislation known as the Muslim Women's Protection of Rights on Divorce Act, 1986 which nullified the Supreme Court's ruling and upheld the Muslim Personal Law.

The passage of the above-mentioned legislation was an extraordinary event in India's political history and was hailed as a great accomplishment of AIMPLB. It raised the stature of AIMPLB and the board's weight was felt in all corners. It also silenced the calls for a uniform civil code. Though the advocates of the uniform civil code had claimed that the goal was to eliminate the confusion that the presence of so many different sets of code (one for each religious group) could create, it was in fact aimed at depriving Muslims of their right to follow Islamic *shari'ah*. It was being done in disguise of pursuing the subtle hint that the framers of the constitution had given for such a code.

From the very inception of AIMPLB, General Secretary Sheikh Syed Minnatullah Rahmani had played a very prominent role in its operation and had given full support to Sheikh Nadwi. They fully trusted each other and gave utmost respect to each other. There was a complete cohesion between them with respect to their thinking and approach. This enabled AIMPLB to resolve many difficult issues. After Sheikh Rahmani passed away in 1991, Sheikh Syed Nizamuddin (of Imarat Shari'at of Bihar and Orissa) was appointed in his place as the general secretary of AIMPLB. Sheikh Nizamuddin also gave his full support to Sheikh Nadwi.

It had not been long since AIMPLB achieved a huge success in restoring the status of Islamic *shari'ah* that the explosive issue of Babri Masjid raised its ugly head as a flashpoint for igniting serious confrontation between Muslims and Hindus all over the country. That is, shortly after securing a victory on a social issue, Muslims were faced with a dire situation involving a place of worship.

Since other Muslims organizations had already taken initiative to tackle the Babri Masjid issue, AIMPLB did not involve itself in it. As a general policy, AIMPLB does not get involved in an issue if other Muslim organizations are attending to it although its members do offer their support in their individual capacity in whichever way they deem appropriate.

The Muslim committees which were working on the issue of Babri Masjid issue were mainly employing methods of political maneuvering, confrontation, and public agitation. The result was that several Hindu organizations also jumped into the fray and since they outwitted Muslim organizations in both number and resources, Muslim organizations soon realized that they were losing the battle.

On the other hand, Sheikh Nadwi worked on this issue in his individual capacity and directed his efforts on two fronts. On the political front, he personally met the then Prime Minister Narasimha Rao and urged him to use all means to protect the *masjid* from any physical damage and adopt firm policies to insure its safety. I happened to be present in one of the meetings and saw Sheikh Nadwi stressing upon the prime minister that the government must act promptly and do whatever was necessary to insure that the *masjid* was protected from any destruction. He also warned Narasimha Rao that any delay might further complicate the issue and the danger to the *masjid* might increase. Rao did not give any firm commitment, but it appeared that he might do something positive. However, as days passed by, it became clear that he did not do anything to help resolve the issue. Instead, he sided with those who were opposed to the *masjid*.

On the other front, Sheikh Nadwi met the Hindu Shankaracharya (a high ranking priest) and urged him to use his influence to resolve the dispute. He explained to the Shankaracharya that it was better for the country to maintain *status quo* with respect to all places of worship and every community should be allowed to handle its religious matters in its own way.

The meeting with the Shankaracharya went very well and the Shankaracharya promised to work on the issue of protecting the *masjid* from any damage. The Shankaracharya proposed a formula which could protect the *masjid* from any damage, establish congregational prayers there and move the idols from there to some other temple. Those who were actively involved with Sheikh Nadwi in this effort included Sheikh 'Abdul Karim Parikh, Yunus Saleem (former governor of Bihar) and Krishan Kant (former Vice-President of India). When the Muslim committees which were working on this issue were approached so that Shankaracharya's formula could be presented to them, they did not even agree to look at it saying that they did not approve individual effort of anyone. At this, Sheikh Nadwi decided not to go any further and the issue remained in the hands of those committees.

Later, when the Hindu extremists demolished Babri Masjid in December 1992, the situation became extremely volatile and chances of resolving the dispute became very bleak. At that time, the Muslim committees which were handling the case until then approached AIMPLB and handed over the case to it.

At that time, Sheikh Nadwi, as the AIMPLB president, did not take any stand of his own on this issue. Instead, he left it to the entire board to decide what to do. Thus a special committee known as the Committee on Babri Masjid was formed for this purpose on behalf of AIMPLB. This committee, instead of using provocative and confrontational means, is pursuing legal and democratic means to resolve the dispute. Temperature has cooled down since then and legal fights and deliberations are continuing in the courtrooms. It is hoped that the case will be finally resolved in an amicable way.

Sheikh Nadwi's strategy for solving any problem had always been to present and argue the case in an appropriate manner and to do whatever was permissible within the boundaries of law and Constitution. He believed that problems could be solved more effectively through these means provided we demonstrate prudence, determination, and unity. He also believed that it would be more beneficial if we engage in these endeavors without expecting any material or financial gain for ourselves.

He considered it very harmful to ask for any personal or material favor from the government or its officials while talking to them in connection with a community problem or need. That is why when it was proposed that the government might pay salary to *imams* (those who lead congregational prayers in mosques) of mosques, he opposed it arguing that it would force *imams* to compromise in matters of *deen* (religion) with the government. Given their high position and status in the community, if *imams* yield to any external pressure, it would be like inviting interference in *deen* from others. In one of the meetings, when some members of AIMPLB were pushing hard for this proposal, Sheikh Nadwi firmly said that he would not allow it to happen as long as he was associated with AIMPLB. His stand was widely acclaimed and the proposal was withdrawn.

The main focus of AIMPLB's efforts has been the protection of Islamic *shari'ah*. In order to accomplish this objective,

AIMPLB gave priority to establishing Darul Qadha (Islamic judicial court) and institutions of social reform so that Muslims could themselves implement Islamic *shari'ah* in their lives without becoming dependent on the government. These institutions facilitate implementation of Islamic *shari'ah* rules in social matters and dealings such as marriage and distribution of inheritance. To work in these two areas – judicial and social – AIMPLB has formed separate committees which are constantly working to expand and improve. Thus AIMPLB is moving forward in pursuing its goals and tackling new problems as they come.

Today Sheikh Nadwi is not with us. But his speeches and writings are still present from which we can benefit and get guidance. Sheikh Nadhrul Hafeez Nadwi Azhari, who teaches at Nadwatul 'Ulama, has compiled Sheikh Nadwi's speeches and writings in the form a book entitled *Juhd Musalsal* (Urdu) which was published by the current general secretary of AIMPLB Sheikh Syed Waliyur Rahmani. This book was presented to the members at the seventeenth AIMPLB conference that was held at Monghyr, Bihar, in 2003.

How much concern did Sheikh Nadwi have for the country and *millat* (Muslims) and how much worry did he have for the protection of Islamic *shari'ah* and the identity of Muslims? To help understand that concern and worry, the following excerpt from his presidential speech that was read in the thirteenth AIMPLB conference (held on 28-30 October 1999 in Mumbai) is being presented here; he could not attend the conference due to illness:

> We Muslims have made the decision to live in our homeland India only after thorough deliberation and with full determination. Nothing except the decree of Allah can change this decision. We did not make this decision under

any pressure or duress. Nor did we do so out of helplessness or because of lack of choice. We made this decision only willfully.

The second decision that we made – which is no less important than the first one in firmness and determination – is that we will live in this country with full Islamic faith, identity, values, principles and practices, and will not forsake even the smallest part of it.

As the citizens of this country, we have full right to live a life of freedom and dignity – a right that has been guaranteed by the democratic Constitution of the country. It thus does not mean for a moment that we, in order to live here, will have to sacrifice what is dear to us such as our identity, *shari'ah,* faith, tradition, language, and culture. If we are forced to give up these things, we are no more living in our home country and it will become like a prison where the entire community is being punished by denying freedom, respect, and amenities of life.

It is true that we are sons of this soil and this land is very dear to us. But we belong to the Abrahamic tradition. Wherever he lives and whatever is his nationality, a Muslim's heritage will be Abrahamic. We want to live here as a vibrant and dignified community. We are free in this country. We have been full participants in its founding, construction, and progress. Thus there is no question that we should live here like second-class citizens. It is the innate, moral, and legal right of every citizen to live a free life in his country. Whenever an attempt has been made to take away this right, the consequences have been very grievious.

We will live and die on Islam. Allah has demanded from Muslims that they must strive to remain steadfast on Islam and *iman,* live by Islam and *iman,* and die on Islam and *iman*- Die not except in the state of Islam. – *Al 'Imran,* 3: 102

Nadwatul 'Ulama

Sheikh Syed Abul Hasan 'Ali Hasani Nadwi began his teaching career when he was only about seventeen or eighteen years old. It happened in the scholarly and literary atmosphere of Nadwatul 'Ulama. It was also the period during which Nadwatul 'Ulama was flourishing under the stewardship of 'Allaamah Syed Sulaiman Nadwi and was studded with distinguished faculty like Dr. Sheikh Taqiuddin Hilali, a renowned scholar of Arabic literature from Morocco. Thus Sheikh Abul Hasan 'Ali Nadwi and a number of his peers (who were of approximately the same age) were energizing and brightening the academic atmosphere of Nadwatul 'Ulama under the guidance of 'Allaamah Syed Sulaiman Nadwi and Dr. Sheikh Tqiuddin Hilali.

Notable among Sheikh Nadwi's peers were Sheikh Muhammad Nazim Nadwi, Sheikh Mas'ud 'Alam Nadwi, Sheikh Abul Lais Islahi Nadwi, Sheikh Muhammad 'Imran Khan Nadwi, and Sheikh 'Abdus Salam Qidwai Nadwi.

Sheikh Muhammad Nazim Nadwi became the Vice-Chancellor of Nadwatul 'Ulama. He then became the head of Jamiyatul Abbasiyah of Bhawalpur, Pakistan. Later he taught at the Islamic University of Madinah, Saudi Arabia. After retiring from Madinah, he settled in Karachi, Pakistan, where he passed away a few years ago.

Sheikh Mas'ud 'Alam Nadwi was the chief editor of Nadwatul 'Ulama's Arabic magazine *Al- Dhiya*. He later became the head of Darul Arubatul Islamiyah, Jalandhar, India, and passed away in 1954 at the young age of 44.

Sheikh Abul Lais Islahi Nadwi was the first *ameer* (head) of Jama'at-e-Islami Hind. He led many religious and social projects in his lifetime. He passed away in 1990.

Sheikh Muhammad 'Imran Khan Nadwi became the Vice-Chancellor of Nadwatul 'Ulama. In 1958, he moved from

Nadwatul 'Ulama to Bhopal to work on the expansion project of Tajul Masajid (a historical mosque in Bhopal, India). He also established a *darul uloom* (religious school) there. He passed away in 1986.

Sheikh Abdus Salam Qidwai Nadwi was the head of the department of Religious Studies at Jamia Millia Islamia, Delhi. He was also the dean of education at Nadwatul 'Ulama. He passed away in 1980.

Sheikh Nadwi was appointed as a teacher of *tafseer* (exegesis of Quran) and literature at Nadwatul 'Ulama in 1934. He continued teaching there on a full-time basis for 10 years. But the *d'awah* (calling people towards Allah and His divine religion) engagements required him to travel extensively which made him uneasy about receiving salary from Nadwatul 'Ulama. Thus he got himself excused from being a salaried employee in 1944 and instead continued teaching on a volunteer basis.

Nadwatul 'Ulama administrators knew his caliber and potential. Thus the then dean of education 'Allaamah Syed Sulaiman Nadwi appointed him as his assistant. After 'Allaamah Syed Sulaiman Nadwi migrated to Pakistan and passed away in 1953, Sheikh Nadwi was appointed as the permanent dean of education which significantly increased his responsibilities at Nadwatul 'Ulama.

In the meantime, his masterpiece book *Ma Dha Khasar al-'Alam bi Inhitat-i-Muslimin* (published in English as *Islam and the World: The Rise and Decline of Muslims and Its Effect on Mankind*) which was published in 1950 gained immense recognition in the Arab world and made him hugely popular there. The book gave a tremendous boost to Nadwatul 'Ulama also as people felt that the institution which had produced such an extraordinary thinker and writer must also be of very high caliber. This attracted intellectuals and influential people of the Islamic world to Nadwatul 'Ulama. Sheikh Nadwi himself was also very eager to raise academic standard and stature of Nadwatul 'Ulama. So he used his contacts in the Arab world and regularly invited renowned scholars and academicians for lectures, seminars, and conferences at Nadwatul 'Ulama.

Sheikh Nadwi was appointed as the rector of Nadwatul 'Ulama in 1961 when it was a little known institution with a small student population. But it gradually started gaining prominence due to its recognition in the Arab world and Sheikh Nadwi's efforts. He also received substantial co-operation from his close associates, especially the Vice-Chancellor Sheikh Muhammad 'Imran Khan Nadwi and Sheikh Qazi Muhammad Moinullah Indori Nadwi.

Sheikh Qazi Muhammad Moinullah Indori Nadwi later became the Chancellor of Nadwatul 'Ulama. He worked very diligently to bring Sheikh Nadwi's dream into reality and remained Sheikh Nadwi's right hand until the very end. Due to the efforts of Sheikh Indori, Nadwatul 'Ulama was able to accomplish most of what Sheikh Nadwi had envisioned for it in education, research, publication, and *d'awah*.

Sheikh Indori possessed exceptional management capacity and was uniquely talented in overseeing building projects. At the time of his appointment as the Chancellor, there was only one single storey building which was used as a dormitory for students. Now that building has expanded into two storeys and there are five new multistoreyed buildings in addition to that. In the beginning, there were only 150-200 students. By the year 2000, the student population had grown to about 4,500 which included 2,000 on the main campus and 2,500 in the satellite campuses which were located in different parts of the city of Lucknow. Now Nadwatul 'Ulama has about 150 branches spread all over India and there are a few in foreign countries as well. The current total student enrollment (of main campus, satellite campuses, and branches) is more than 15,000.

At the beginning of Sheikh Nadwi's tenure as the rector, there were only four levels/years in the primary curriculum and nine levels/years in the Arabic curriculum and there was only one section in each level. However, over a period of time, it gradually expanded into six years of primary, two years of secondary, three years of higher secondary, four years of graduate (*'Aliyah*) and two years of postgraduate (*Fazilat*) – a curriculum that is spread over seventeen years. For graduate and post-graduate studies, there are two possible tracks: (1) Theology, and (2) Language and literature. Each track is further divided into several branches. For example, theology is divided into *tafseer* (exegesis of Quran), *hadith* (traditions of Prophet Muhammad), and *fiqh* (Islamic jurisprudence); language and literature are divided into classical literature, modern literature, speech, and criticism. In the postgraduate studies, students are given a choice to specialize in an area of their interest.

Graduate students in the theology track are required to complete a one-year course in Islamic law and jurisprudence. All students (in both tracks) are required to complete a one-year course in Islamic thought and propagation so that they can get practical training and acquire necessary skills. Since the number of students in the theology track has grown significantly, multiple sections are being run in it.

Nadwatul 'Ulama was not able to publish any journal or magazine for a long time. The Arabic magazine *Al-Dhiya* was discontinued only after two-three years due to lack of funds. Similar was the fate of the Urdu magazine *An-Nadwah*. However, mainly due to Sheikh Nadwi's interest, two Arabic magazines *Al B'ath Islami* (monthly) and *Ar Raaed* (fortnightly) were launched in 1960 and they are still continuing. These magazines are quite popular in the Arab world and the number of subscriptions is reasonably high. At the end of 1963, the Urdu fortnightly magazine *T'amir-e-Heyat* was launched which has carved its own place in the Indian subcontinent literary circles. Last year, a quarterly magazine in English (*Fragrance of the East*) and a monthly magazine in Hindi (*Saccha Raahi*) were also launched and they are being well received. The main office of the World Forum of Islamic Literature, which is located in Nadwatul 'Ulama, publishes a quarterly magazine known as *Karwan-e-Adab* (Urdu).

During Sheikh Nadwi's tenure as the rector, four international conferences were held at Nadwatul 'Ulama. The attendees included the Sheikh of Al-Azhar University and several ministers, university vice-chancellors and dignitaries from Arab countries.

The first conference[8] was on religious education. It was a historic conference being the largest of its kind at any religious institution in India. It helped Nadwatul 'Ulama gain immense international recognition and stature. The second conference[9] was on Islamic literature which was attended by eminent scholars, men of literature, and thinkers from the entire Arab world as well as from the subcontinent.

The third conference which was held in 1986 was on Islamic literature as well and the World Forum of Islamic Literature was founded on that occasion. The fourth conference was held on Qadianism in 1997 which was attended by Sheikh Saud ibn Ibrahim al-Shuraim (the *imam* of the Grand Mosque, Makkah) and Sheikh Muhammad bin 'Abdullah al-Subayyal and other eminent scholars and dignitaries from the Arab countries and the subcontinent. All of these conferences received widespread acclamation from religious scholars and learned people.

---

8 Its proceedings can be found in *Roodade Chaman* (Urdu) by Sheikh Syed Muhammad Al-Hasani.

9 Its proceedings can be found in *Deen wa Adab* (Urdu) and *Al-Adab Al-Islami Fikratahu Was Minhahah* (Arabic) by Sheikh Syed Muhammad Rabey Hasani Nadwi.

The library of Nadwatul 'Ulama was located in the same hall where classes were held. During Sheikh Nadwi's tenure, a separate five-storeyed building was constructed for the library. Also, a separate building was constructed for administrative offices. A number of residential quarters were constructed for faculty. Since the number of students has increased significantly, more facilities are being acquired in the outskirts of the city of Lucknow. Due to these facilities and diverse programs that Nadwatul 'Ulama offers, it has now emerged into a major Islamic institution of higher learning.

Sheikh Nadwi constantly kept himself busy in research and writing and involved many others as well in these endeavors. The Academy of Islamic Research and Publications was established mainly for this purpose. The Academy has so far published more than 200 books and publishes material in four major languages – Arabic, Urdu, English, and Hindi.

Due to these accomplishments, Nadwatul 'Ulama has gained wide recognition in the entire Islamic world. It is as diverse as a university. Its curriculum is as comprehensive and broad as that of any major institution. It offers courses in both traditional and contemporary disciplines.

Sheikh Nadwi fully understood and embraced the purpose and academic standard that the founders of Nadwatul 'Ulama had envisioned for this institution. In their mind, it was supposed to be a place where young generation of Muslims could be nurtured and groomed. It thus required a rigorous evaluation of both the system of education and its curriculum to determine if it was fulfilling the desired objective and producing the desired kind of graduates.

Muslims need to know and understand what responsibilities Allah has placed on them, what are the challenges of the community, and which skills and qualities are needed to fulfill them. In Sheikh Nadwi's eyes, an educated person should be a *mard-e-momin* (a true believer) who understands the challenges of the hour and is fully prepared to meet them.

Regarding the curriculum, Sheikh Nadwi's vision was that it should embody good of both the old and the new. That is why one of the fundamental principles which govern the curriculum of Nadwatul 'Ulama is that it must incorporate classical (Quran, *hadith,* and authentic and perennial works of the past scholars) as well as modern and contemporary knowledge which are necessary and beneficial in everyday life. With these goals in mind, the curricula at Nadwatul 'Ulama is reviewed and updated on a regular basis.

Sheikh Nadwi had the opportunity to closely observe and listen to the founders of Nadwatul 'Ulama from his very childhood. His father Sheikh Syed 'Abdul Hai Hasani was the rector of Nadwatul 'Ulama until he died in 1923. Thereafter, his elder brother Dr. Syed 'Abdul 'Ali Hasani served in that capacity until his death in 1961. Thus Sheikh Nadwi constantly remained in close association with Nadwatul 'Ulama. He also understood the dynamics of the needs and challenges of the Muslims and Islamic world. Guided by these experiences and observations, he chalked out his plan of action and continued serving the *millat* through Nadwatul 'Ulama.

Sheikh Nadwi firmly believed and remained committed throughout his life that the system of education and its curriculum must be geared towards producing people who could fulfill needs – current as well as future – of the community, were not inferior to their contemporaries in any respect (such as knowledge and thinking), and possessed necessary skills to serve the *ummah* (Muslims and mankind). They must be well versed in authentic Islamic knowledge and traditions so that they do not wither away while presenting

Islam to others. Furthermore, they must also master the skill of speech and articulation so that they can effectively discharge the duty of *d'awah*. To achieve all these goals, Sheikh Nadwi constantly refined and revised the curriculum of Nadwatul 'Ulama. The outcome is quite encouraging as has been demonstrated by the caliber of recent graduates.

Sheikh Nadwi felt that such a curriculum was needed not only by Nadwatul 'Ulama, but by every institution of Islamic learning – a theme that he often repeated in speeches at Nadwatul 'Ulama and wherever he got a chance to speak. He was of the opinion that the books which are included in the curriculum must contain material that fulfills the desired objectives of education. That is why he greatly emphasized upon the development of high-quality books and personally took active part in preparing them.

With that goal in mind, he, with the assistance of his students, prepared textbooks for courses in the Arabic language and literature. These books ultimately replaced the books which Nadwatul 'Ulama had to import from Egypt. Such efforts made Nadwatul 'Ulama self-sufficient with its own in-house developed textbooks in several areas including Arabic language and literature. These textbooks are now fulfilling the needs of other institutions as well and they have been adopted by several government and parochial institutions both inside and outside India.

Sheikh Nadwi held the view that a curriculum that was purely abstract and theoretical was not so beneficial. So he emphasized on incorporating practical training and real-life experiences in the curriculum and included them in the curriculum of Nadwatul 'Ulama.

Though the resources of Nadwatul 'Ulama are limited, efforts are being consistently made to accomplish the goals that were set by Sheikh Nadwi. A lot has already being achieved and the outcome has received acclamation from all over the world. But we are still far away from where Sheikh Nadwi wanted us to be. However, his students and associates are earnestly following the path that he has shown and they are committed to continuing the mission.

Sheikh Nadwi received strong support from many of his associates and patrons such as Sheikh Muhammad 'Imran Khan Nadwi, Sheikh 'Abdus Salam Qidwai Nadwi (as the dean of education), Sheikh Mohibullah Laari Nadwi (as the Vice-Chancellor), and Sheikh Muhammad Manzoor N'umani. Among the faculty, the contributions of Sheikh Muhammad Owais Nagrami Nadwi, Sheikh Muhammad Ishaq Sandelvi, and Shah Halim 'Ata Ceyloni are worth mentioning.

Among Sheikh Nadwi's students, Sheikh Qazi Muhammad Moinullah Indori Nadwi, who later became the Chancellor of Nadwatul 'Ulama, was most supportive. He understood Sheikh Nadwi's vision and fully co-operated with him in its execution. He played a key role in expanding Nadwatul 'Ulama's building facilities and making it financially stable. Since Sheikh Indori had spent a considerable amount of time in the effort of *d'awah* after completing his education, he was also very instrumental and effective in inculcating importance of *d'awah* among the students of Nadwatul 'Ulama.

After Sheikh 'Abdus Salam Qidwai Nadwi passed away in 1980, Dr. 'Abdullah 'Abbas Nadwi who was a former student of Sheikh Nadwi was appointed as the dean of education in his place. Since Dr. 'Abdullah 'Abbas Nadwi was an alumnus of Nadwatul 'Ulama, he took special interest in the affairs of his *alma mater* and did whatever was within his reach to serve it. Although he was living in Makkah, he often used to come to Nadwatul 'Ulama on his own expenses to look after the affairs of Nadwatul 'Ulama.

When Sheikh Muhammad 'Imran Khan Nadwi moved to

Bhopal in 1958, Sheikh Abul 'Irfan Khan was appointed as the Vice-Chancellor in his place. Sheikh Abul 'Irfan Khan Nadwi, through his able administration, gave full co-operation to Sheikh Nadwi. All these individuals gave their full support to Sheikh Nadwi in moving Nadwatul 'Ulama forward.

There are many among Sheikh Nadwi's junior students as well whose contributions are worth mentioning. The two who stand out most are his renowned nephew Sheikh Syed Muhammad Al-Hasani and Sheikh Ishaq Jalees Nadwi. Sheikh Al-Hasani fully assisted Sheikh Nadwi through his writings which were in complete congruence with Sheikh Nadwi's thinking and vision. Sheikh Jalees was heavily involved in the operation of the Academy of Islamic Research and Publications and the publication of the fortnightly Urdu magazine *Tameer-e-Hayat*. It is sad that both of them passed away at an early age and did not get opportunity to serve for long. Both of them had also played significant role in making the first international conference successful that was held at Nadwatul 'Ulama.

In addition to the above-mentioned individuals, there are many who deserve acknowledgement for their services. The list includes Dr. Ishteyaq Hussain Quraishi, Sheikh Sa'idur Rahman 'Azami Nadwi, and Sheikh Nadwi's nephew Sheikh Syed Muhammad Wazeh Rasheed Hasani Nadwi. Dr. Ishteyaq Hussain Quraishi, in particular, was very helpful in supporting Sheikh Nadwi in his *d'awah* and other activities. I also happen to be among those whom Sheikh Nadwi provided opportunities to assist him in his academic, *d'awah,* and administrative works.

The following excerpt from Sheikh Nadwi's autobiography *Karwan-e-Zindagi* (vol. 1, pp. 141-43) about Nadwatul 'Ulama's work and mission is being presented here. It will enable readers to know and understand the soul, spirit and fabric of

Nadwatul 'Ulama. It is a part of the speech that Sheikh Nadwi delivered in November 1975 on the occasion of Nadwatul 'Ulama's eighty-fifth anniversary which was attended by distinguished guests from India and abroad.

> In matters of *deen* (religion) and *'aqaaid* (faith), Nadwatul 'Ulama's policies are based upon pure *deen* which is free from all types of adulterations, altercations, fabrications, and deceptions and is fully preserved in its original form in all respects.
>
> In interpreting and explicating *deen*, we rely upon the sources which are pure and pristine, come from of the earliest period of Islam, and seek to reach the very core of *deen*.
>
> In actions and morals, we aspire to capture the essence of *deen*, remain steadfast in it, follow the rules of *shari'ah*, stay close to the spirit and reality of *deen*, and acquire *taqwa* (piety) and *salah batin* (internal purification).
>
> With regards to history, we believe that the best period of human history is the one in which Islam came and reached its zenith and the best generation of humans is the one which was taught and trained by Prophet Muhammad and had graduated from the school of Quran and *iman* (firm faith in Allah). They are the best examples to follow. Our success, salvation, and progress depend upon how much we benefit from them and how much we strive to follow their footsteps.
>
> Our philosophy of knowledge and education is that knowledge is a single unit that cannot be divided into old, new, Eastern, or Western. If at all possible, it can be divided only into right and wrong, beneficial and harmful, or means and end. We are guided by the prophetic command "Wisdom is the lost treasure of a *momin* (believer). Wherever it is found, you deserve most to acquire it." We are also guided by the old saying: Take what is clean and pure and leave what is dirty and impure.
>
> Our strategy to defend Islam and fight against irreligious forces is based upon Allah's command:

> Against them make ready your strength to the utmost of your power. –*Al-Anfal*, 8:60

Our effort of *d'awah*, explaining the beauty and virtues of Islam, and preparing the hearts and minds of people to accept the truthfulness of Islam is based upon the advice:

> Talk to people in a way that is appropriate to their level of understanding. Do you want them to reject Allah and His Prophet (due to faulty presentation)?

In matters of *'aqaaid* (tenets of Islam) and fundamental principles, we adhere to the majority opinion of *ah-lul-sunnah* (followers of the traditions of Prophet Muhammad) and stay within the boundaries set by the scholars of earlier times. With respect to the issues that are non-essential and jurisprudential, our position is that we stay away from those matters which are controversial and are likely to cause further division and misunderstanding in the *ummah* (Muslims). We inculcate good opinion about our past elders and try to find a good excuse for them (for their mistakes, if there is any). We consider the collective good more important than anything else.

In short, we are closely aligned with the school of thought – in knowledge, vision, theology, and jurisprudence – of Hakimul Islam Shah Waliyullah Dehlavi (d. 1762). Thus Nadwatul 'Ulama, instead of being a center of education with limited scope, is an institution with a broad and diverse set of goals.

5

Travels to Foreign Countries

To Arab Countries

SHEIKH Syed Abul Hasan 'Ali Hasani Nadwi, from his study of the mission, *d'awah,* and struggles of Mujaddid Alf Thani (d. 1624) and Hakimul Islam Shah Waliyullah Dehlavi (d. 1762), concluded that the downfall of Muslims was caused mainly by their political missteps and impious living. He also became aware of the horrible atrocities which the colonial powers had afflicted on Muslims in the Middle East and felt that the Muslim leaders had failed in assessing the damage and understanding the ramifications. All of these had created in him an earnest desire to remind Arabs that their dignity and progress depended solely on their true allegiance to the Prophet and in following the Prophet's ways with love and pride. Their success and honor lie only in uniting under the banner of the Prophet and in following the footsteps of the illustrious elders of the past.

Sheikh Nadwi's elder brother Sheikh Dr. Syed 'Abdul 'Ali Hasani had played a key role in ingraining this feeling and concern in Sheikh Nadwi. Dr. 'Ali used to take deep interest in the affairs of Muslims from all over the world and was always eager to improve their condition. Not only did he plant the seed of this concern in Sheikh Nadwi, but he also nourished it. As a result, Sheikh Nadwi became overwhelmed with this concern. Once when he was visiting Mumbai (probably in 1935), he gathered employees of the Arab embassies and reminded them that they must come under the banner of Prophet Muhammad. That speech was later published as a booklet[1] entitled *Ilai Rayatil Muhammadiyah Aiyohal 'Arab* (Arabic).

Consequently, Sheikh Nadwi chalked out a plan to work among Arabs by making *d'awah* and the life of the Prophet as the focal point of his strategy. Thus when he went for *hajj* in 1947, he took stock of the situation and exchanged views with the learned people there. What he found useful in those discussions, he later added those to his renowned book *Ma Dha Khasar al-'Alam bi Inhitat-i-Muslimin.*

That trip to Hejaz was very fruitful in many respects. Abundance of wealth and modern advancements which appeared later had not surfaced yet and Hejaz was still living in its unique old traditions. *'Ulama* were enjoying special status in the society and they were usually teaching in the premises of the *Haram* (the Grand Mosque of Makkah) which was like an independent university. Most prominent among those who were teaching there included Sheikh Hasanul Masat, Sheikh 'Abdur Razzaq Hamzah, Sheikh Muhammad 'Ali Al-Maghrabi, and Sheikh 'Alvi Maliki. Each of them was considered an expert in his subject.

Since Sheikh Nadwi was quite fluent in Arabic, in both speaking and writing, and his study was very broad, he developed good rapport with those scholars and engaged in scholarly discussions with them. He became especially close to Sheikh Hamzah who was also the *imam* of *Haram*. Sheikh Hamzah was from Egypt and was a distinguished scholar with very broad study. Impressed by Sheikh Hamzah's eminence and caliber, Sheikh Nadwi presented a manuscript of his book *Ma Dha Khasar . . .* to him. Sheikh Hamzah highly appreciated it and exchanged his views with Sheikh Nadwi on some topics.

---

1 Approximate translation of the title: *O Arabs! Come Under the Banner of Muhammad.*

Sheikh Nadwi benefited so much from his conversations with Sheikh Hamzah that he felt that he had been to some extent compensated for not visiting Syria and other Arab countries in that trip.

Sheikh Nadwi stayed in Hejaz for about six months. He had taken his mother, wife, and a sister with him. He had also taken his nephew Sheikh Syed Muhammad Thani Hasani to assist him in taking care of the family members. Since Sheikh Syed Muhammad Thani Hasani was a graduate of Nadwatul 'Ulama and was well versed in Islamic knowledge, he was able to assist Sheikh Nadwi in his scholarly pursuits as well. Thus Sheikh Nadwi had the opportunity of benefitting from scholars of international repute without much distraction.

The observations and experiences in Hejaz benefitted Sheikh Nadwi greatly in *d'awah,* academic and research efforts, and enabled him to broaden and diversify the effort of *d'awah* after returning to India. That was also the time when India had just gained Independence and Indian Muslims were experiencing great difficulty and uncertainty with respect to their life and property – an issue that also played an important role in shaping Sheikh Nadwi's future strategy.

The other important aspect of that trip[2] was that he was able to introduce the work of Jama'at Tabligh to the learned and educated people of Hejaz. It had been several years since the founder of Jama'at Tabligh, Sheikh Muhammad Ilyas Kandhlawi had passed away and his son Sheikh Muhammad Yusuf Kandhlawi was leading the effort now. Sheikh Yusuf was very anxious to introduce the work in Hejaz and had sent Sheikh 'Ubaidullah Balyawi there for that very purpose.

---

2 Details of that trip can be found in (1) the first volume of Sheikh Nadwi's autobiography *Karwan-e-Zindagi,* and (2) the biography of Sheikh Muhammad Yusuf by Sheikh Syed Muhammad Thani Hasani.

Sheikh Balyawi was constantly writing to Sheikh Yusuf that someone who could effectively communicate with Arab scholars was needed to make any headway and Sheikh Nadwi would be very suitable for that purpose. Both Sheikh Yusuf and Sheikhul Hadith Muhammad Zakariya Kandhlawi agreed with Sheikh Balyawi's request and asked Sheikh Nadwi to lend his support to Sheikh Balyawi in his effort in Hejaz. In this way, the effort of Jama'at Tabligh which had initially started among common people started gaining ground among the learned and influential people of Hejaz.

Sheikh Nadwi's second trip to Hejaz and other Arab countries came in 1950. The primary purpose of the trip was *d'awah* and conveying message to the concerned people of the region. Sheikh 'Ubaidullah Balyawi and Sheikh Sa'yeed Ahmad Khan Saharanpuri were already carrying on the work of Jama'at Tabligh in Hejaz with full dedication. On Sheikh Nadwi's recommendation, they were joined by two graduates of Nadwatul 'Ulama, Qazi Muhammad Moinullah Indori Nadwi (who later became Chancellor of Nadwatul 'Ulama) and Sheikh 'Abdur Rasheed 'Azmi a year ago. Thus at the time Sheikh Nadwi reached Hejaz, an active group was already in place there.

The main purpose of sending Sheikh Indori and Sheikh 'Azmi was to reach the elite Arabs, especially of Hejaz, and provide them with literature that could wake them up from the state of apathy, enable them to understand prevailing condition, and make them realize the position and responsibility of the Muslim *ummah*. To approach them, some literature was produced in preparation of which Shiekh Nadwi had himself actively participated.

Sheikh Nadwi's book *Ma Dha Khasar . . .* (Islam *and the World . . .*) was not published yet. But a few articles had already been published. One of them was the article *Ila Mumthili al-*

Bilad al-Islamiyah[3] that he had prepared for the Muslim delegates who had come to Delhi to attend a conference of Asian countries in 1947. In that article, leaders of the Muslim countries were reminded of their obligations and how to fulfill them. The other article *Bainal Jibayah wal Hidayah*[4] was also prepared by Sheikh Nadwi; it was aimed at reminding rulers and leaders of the sacred region of Hejaz that their obligation of rendering proper Islamic leadership was more critical than that of providing political and material benefits.

Though Najd (central part of Saudi Arabia), due to having the capital (Riyadh) of the kingdom, is more important from the administrative point of view, Hejaz, due to being the home of Harmain Sharifain (Makkah and Madinah), enjoys greater importance from the religious point of view. Thus Sheikh Nadwi wanted to make the leaders of Hejaz and other Arab countries understand the special responsibility that fell upon their shoulders because of the importance and sanctity of their countries. He felt that scholarly and inspiring literature could be very effective in this regard, especially if its language was eloquent.

Sheikh Nadwi had also taken four of his students – the author (Rabey Hasani), Sheikh 'Abdullah 'Abbas Nadwi (who was teaching Arabic at Nadwatul 'Ulama), Sheikh Syed Rizwan 'Ali Nadwi, and Sheikh Syed Muhammad Tahir Mansoorpuri Mazahari – with him in that trip. His intention was that they would continue working in Hejaz after he had left for other Arab countries.

One of the special features of that trip was that it was taking place in the blessed company of Sheikh Nadwi's spiritual mentor and guide Sheikh 'Abdul Qadir Raipuri. Sheikh Raipuri

---

3 Approximate translation of the title: *A Model for Muslim Countries.*

4 Approximate translation of the title: *Between Levy Collection and Divine Guidance.*

was not only leading the *hajj* rituals, but was also giving inspiration and encouragement to Sheikh Nadwi in all of his *d'awah* efforts.

There was something very special that happened in that trip. Sheikh Shaibi, one of the high-ranking officials of Baitullah (cube-shaped structure in Makkah which is known as the House of Allah) himself made an offer to Sheikh Nadwi that he could go inside Baitullah and take with him whomever he wished. Sheikh Nadwi used to say that he got that opportunity only due to the auspicious company of Sheikh Raipuri because he did not get such an offer either before or after although he used to make frequent visits to Makkah. However, later in 1996, he was offered the key of Baitullah and had the privilege of opening its door.

That trip (to *hajj* in 1950) had a very interesting background which Sheikh Nadwi himself used to recount. In 1949, two years after he performed his first hajj, an opportunity came by to go for *hajj* again. Based upon his experience of the first *hajj*, he was very eager to avail that opportunity. But, from the very childhood, he had the habit of not doing anything without the consent and permission of his elders – his mother, elder brother Dr. 'Ali, and Sheikh 'Abdul Qadir Raipuri.

When Sheikh Nadwi approached Sheikh Raipuri to get permission for the trip, Sheikh Raipuri looked at him and asked, "How about if I say no to you?" Sheikh Nadwi replied, "Whatever you decide, I shall accept it wholeheartedly". At this, Sheikh Nadwi dropped the idea of undertaking that trip. That left a very good impression upon Sheikh Raipuri who greatly valued Sheikh Nadwi's sincerity and humility and rewarded him for the same by offering to go with him for *hajj* the following year. Sheikh Raipuri told Sheikh Nadwi, "I am undertaking this journey just for you because you had forsaken the opportunity last year upon my saying".

The journey for *hajj* by itself is very blessed and auspicious. But it becomes doubly blessed if it happens under the tutelage of an eminent *sheikh* (pious elder) and one can easily feel the special spiritual blessings of such a company. Thus that trip proved very fruitful in enriching Sheikh Nadwi's intellectual and scholarly capabilities and in widening his recognition in the Islamic world – something which proved very useful later. There were many benefits and blessings of that trip which we saw right away. But there were many more the seeds of which were planted in that trip and their fruits continued appearing for years to come. Sheikh Nadwi did the work of *d'awah* in such a way that a solid foundation was laid down for the future effort.

We traveled from Mumbai to Jeddah by ship. The ship stopped on the port of Makalla, Hadramout, Yemen, for passengers to board from there. The sight of land after continuously sailing for four or five days on water gave special happiness to the passengers on board. The passengers who boarded the ship at Makalla included the son of the *qazi* (judge) of the town and several other learned *'ulama*. When they came to know that the group from India also included *'ulama*, they came to meet us and we developed good relationship with them. Three days later, the ship reached Jeddah and we met those who had arrived there earlier. Since we were very close to the days of *hajj*, we became very busy with the rites of *hajj*.

After completing the rites of *hajj*, Sheikh Nadwi started contacting *'ulama* and learned people of Hejaz. There were two persons who proved very helpful in that respect. One of them was Sheikh Syed Mahmood Hafiz who was the director of the government press. Since Sheikh Hafiz's mother was from the Indian subcontinent, he was familiar with Urdu and had good relationship with people of the subcontinent. He also felt quite close to Sheikh Nadwi. So Sheikh Nadwi asked him if he could arrange a meeting with the journalists and intellectuals of Hejaz so that he could talk to them about how to make their (literary) expertise and talent useful for *deen* (Islam) and *millat* (Muslims). Sheikh Hafiz then introduced Sheikh Nadwi to Sheikh Ahmad 'Abdul Ghafoor 'Attar who was a very respectable figure in the literary circle of Hejaz and had very good connection with the intellectuals of Hejaz; he felt close to Sheikh Nadwi and became quite friendly with him.

Due to Sheikh 'Attar's efforts, a number of prominent journalists, poets, and intellectuals were invited to a dinner in a resort. Conversations took place between Sheikh Nadwi and the invitees before and after the dinner on topics ranging from literature to current issues. One of the invitees was Syed 'Ali Hasan Fad'aq. He was a man of progressive thinking and was very popular among his peers, but his religious views were shaky and wobbly. He posed questions to Sheikh Nadwi as if he was probing Sheikh Nadwi's knowledge and acquaintance with the Western literature and thinking. But he and others were extremely impressed with how Sheikh Nadwi responded to his queries and Sheikh Nadwi's command of the Arabic language.

It was a big test for Sheikh Nadwi as he himself used to recount, but the final outcome was very positive and the meeting left a very positive impact on the hearts and minds of the progressive-minded journalists, poets, and literary people of Hejaz. All of the invitees became life-long admirers of Sheikh Nadwi and in turn became deeply committed to Islam in their lives.

On that occasion, Sheikh Nadwi proposed to them that they all should come out of their respective environments, spend some time together, and freely exchange their views. They all agreed to do so. Wadi Fatima, a village about 15km from Makkah, was chosen as the venue. It was decided to stay in a mosque so that a religious environment could be experienced.

So an entourage of learned individuals came out of Makkah

and headed towards the village of Wadi Fatima to spend a day and night together. They got an opportunity to discuss and exchange their views about *d'awah* and related issues. Since they were new to this kind of environment and more geared towards amusement and fun, one of them had brought a radio with him. In those days, radio was considered a vice in religious circles, but Sheikh Nadwi tolerated it for the sake of *d'awah*.

The overall effect was very positive. They all got connected to Sheikh Nadwi and the effort of *d'awah* and remained so for life. In this way, a foundation was laid down for the effort of *d'awah* among the modern educated population of the holy land of Hejaz. Besides Syed 'Ali Hasan Fad'aq, there were a few other journalists who were very influential among youth groups. They became very close to Sheikh Nadwi. They were 'Abdul Quddus Ansari, Muhammad Mohsin Baarom, Sa'yeedul 'Aamoodi, and Ahmad 'Abdul Ghafoor 'Attar.

Some of the above-mentioned journalists and poets had good connection with Sheikh Muhammad Suroor al-Sabban who was the second-most influential persons in the Saudi government and was also well respected in the literary circle. Their acquaintance with Sheikh al-Sabban became a means of introducing Sheikh Nadwi to him. Sheikh al-Sabban later arranged a five-day trip of Sheikh Nadwi to Taif where Sheikh Nadwi met local scholars and learned people and presented his views to them. Those who accompanied Sheikh Nadwi to Taif included me, Qazi Muhammad Moinullah Indori Nadwi, and Sheikh Ahmad 'Abdul Ghafoor 'Attar. Sheikh 'Attar was very helpful in reaching the educated people of Taif. After returning from Taif, meetings with local scholars continued in Makkah and Sheikh Nadwi's speeches were broadcast on Saudi Radio as well.

Education and journalism had not yet made any significant progress in Saudi Arabia. In the entire country, there were hardly three or four institutions up to high school level and most schools were up to the primary level only. Students, after finishing education in Saudi Arabia, used to go mostly to Egypt to complete their education.

In Makkah, there were two traditional institutions, namely Madrasah Saulatiyah and Madrasah al-Falah. Madrasah Saulatiyah was a private institution which was run on the pattern of *madaris* (institutions of Islamic learning) of the Indian subcontinent. Madrasah al-Falah was a government institution which was run according to the old traditions of Hejaz.

In Madinah, there was an institution known as Madrasah Uloom Shari'ah which was established by Sheikh Syed Ahmad Faizabadi (older brother of Sheikh Syed Hussain Ahmad Madni) and run by his brother Sheikh Syed Mahmood Madni. It was run on the same pattern as that of Madrasah Saulatiyah. In fact, both Madrasah Saulatiyah (Makkah) and Madrasah Uloom Shari'ah (Madinah) were established on the behest of prominent scholars (such as Sheikh Rahmatullah Kairanawi) of the subcontinent to counter the influence of Christianity. In the past, these institutions had produced many distinguished scholars. But, after the modern educational system was introduced in Saudi Arabia, they started losing ground and their influence has significantly diminished.

After having developed a circle of acquaintances in Hejaz, Sheikh Nadwi wanted to visit Egypt, Syria, and Sudan. These countries, especially Egypt, had made significant progress both educationally and intellectually and were influencing the entire Arab world. Egypt had in fact emerged as the educational and ideological leader of the Arab world. A serious effort was being made in Egypt to revive Islam under the leadership of Sheikh Hasan al-Banna. Young and common people were getting inspired and Islam was coming back into their lives. But when Sheikh Hasan al-Banna was martyred, those who were eager to revive Islam were greatly hurt and needed to be consoled and comforted to continue their struggle. At that moment, Sheikh Nadwi's book *Ma Dha Khasar . . .* played an important role in healing their wounds and everyone found in it a kind and caring companion.

Sheikh Nadwi had stayed in Hejaz for four months (September 1950 to January 1951) in that trip. During that stay, he felt that Egypt enjoyed central position in the Arab world, both educationally and intellectually. Though it was producing illicit, harmful, and immoral kind of literature, it was also producing healthy, robust, and stimulating literature. Sheikh Nadwi also felt that if an idea, change or revolution had to gain currency in the Arab world, it was more likely to succeed if it came from Egypt. He thus became fully convinced of the importance and benefit of visiting Egypt and finally made up his mind to go there.

His book *Ma Dha Khasar . . .* had already reached Egypt and gained widespread popularity. As a result, he felt at home as soon as he arrived there. In his meetings, discourses, and speeches, he explained to people that it would be best to adopt the strategy of Mujaddid Alf Thani in the situation that was prevailing in the Islamic world at the moment. Mujaddid Alf Thani, in order to counter ill effects of the anti-Islamic attitude of Emperor Akbar on the country and people of India, had adopted the path of negotiation and persuasion (instead of confrontation) for his *d'awah* and his strategy had proven very successful in changing the attitude of future rulers.

The trip gave Sheikh Nadwi a good understanding of the condition of the Arab world – its complexity, dangers, potentials, and expectations. He also got opportunities to meet many leaders who were spearheading efforts of *d'awah* and *jihad* in the Arab world and Middle East. He met Sheikh Shamil of Qafqaz of Azerbaijan, Sheikh 'Abdul Karim Refi of Morocco, Ameer 'Abdul Qadir of Algeria, and Mufti Aminul Hussaini of Palestine. All of them were living in Egypt in exile. They were leading the efforts of *d'awah* and *islah* in their respective countries before being forced to take refuge in Cairo. He also met Sheikh Amin Siraj and other Turkish *'ulama* living in exile in Cairo. Those encounters and experiences gave Sheikh Nadwi a better understanding of the intent, politics, and diplomacy of the imperialist powers.

He also got an opportunity to visit Syria and Sudan and met important personalities there. These experiences and exposures created in him a kind of restlessness, feeling, and pain which set him apart from other *'ulama* of his time. It also gave him special understanding and insight of the dynamics of the ups and downs of the Islamic world.

After returning from that trip, Sheikh Nadwi started focusing more on the Islamic world in his speeches, writings, and *d'awah* efforts. He also found that what he had written in his book *Ma Dha Khasar . . .* was quite appropriate to the need of time and accurately represented his viewpoint. The book continued making the same impact that it had made when it first came out.

For the next ten years, Sheikh Nadwi did not get any opportunity to visit Hejaz. However, after five years, he was invited in 1956 for a lecture series by the Shari'ah College of Damascus University. He stayed in Syria for two months on that occasion. During that stay, he got opportunities to meet many prominent scholars, intellectuals, and spiritual elders and benefit from them. He became very close to Sheikh Ahmad Haroon al-'Asal al-Hajjar who was a prominent *sheikh* of the al-Ghazaliyah tradition.

Those who attended Sheikh Nadwi's lectures regularly in Damascus included many distinguished scholars and academicians of Damascus such as Sheikh Mustafa al-Sabai, Dr. M'arouf al-Dawalibi, 'Allamah Bahjatul Bitar, Sheikh Mustafa Zarqa, and Muhammad al-Mubarak. Dr. al-Dawalibi later became the prime minister of Syria.

During the stay in Syria, he made a side trip to Turkey and became intimately familiar with the conditions there. The visits to the Arab countries and Turkey allowed him to get a true understanding of the two issues about which the *'ulama* of India were either totally unaware of or fully relied upon hearsay and formed a misleading opinion. One of those issues was the military revolution of Egypt.

Col. Gamal Abdel Nasser had led the military coup and ended the monarchy in Egypt. Since the support of Ikhwanul Muslimeen, the strongest pro-Islamic group, had played an important role in making the coup successful, it was generally believed that the coup was a victory for the pro-Islamic forces and Col. Nasser was sympathetic to the cause of Islam. But, soon thereafter, he distanced himself from the pro-Islamic groups, consolidated his power and started pursuing his own agenda. As a result, a rift erupted between Col. Nasser and Ikhwanul Muslimeen.

Since Ikhwanul Muslimeen was very strong and popular movement in Egypt, it was not easy to wipe it out. So Gamal Nasser, in an attempt to dismantle Ikhwanul Muslimeen, adopted the slogan of Arab nationalism so that he could mute the Islamic sentiments of people. To accomplish this, he instituted very harsh policies, resorted to all kinds of brutalities and sought the assistance of foreign powers. Even the *'ulama* of the country got carried away by the idea of Arab nationalism and started supporting Gamal Nasser instead of Ikhwanul Muslimeen. They failed to recognize that Arab nationalism, despite its outward pro-Islamic face, was in fact anti-Islamic and deeply rooted in anti-religious sentiments.

Thus when Sheikh Nadwi, upon his return from Egypt to India, made statements explaining the noble mission of Ikhwan and anti-Islamic attitude of the secular government of Gamal Nasser, many Indian *'ulama* strongly rebuffed him and rejected his assessment. Because of not knowing the facts, they adored

Gamal Nasser as an Islamic hero and condemned Ikhwanul as a rebel group leader.

The other issue about which Sheikh Nadwi made statements after his return to India was the condition of Turkey which had witnessed demolition of the Islamic *khilafah* (caliphate) at the hands of Mustafa Kemal Ata Turk in the beginning of the last century.

Before Ata Turk started dismantling the *khilafah,* he had played a heroic role in defeating Greeks in the Greco-Turkish War (1919-22) and thus was hailed as a hero. But, soon after his spectacular success in the battleground, he embraced anti-Islamic ideas of secularism, decimated the *khilafah,* and banned all Islamic traditions and practices including the use of Arabic script, calling of *azan* (call for prayer) in Arabic and display of any Islamic identity.

All Islamic practices were banned and declared unpatriotic. Any Islamic act that was contrary to secularism was declared illegal and punishable by the Turkish constitution. Thus Turkey was driven out of Islam and Ata Turk imposed his anti-Islamic ideology with full force. According to the new constitution, even the judiciary was banned from hearing complaints against anti-Islamic moves.

In other words, Mustafa Kemal Ata Turk took Turkey out of Islam and flung it back into the days of ignorance. After Ata Turk's death in 1938, his confidant Ismet Inonu continued his policies and kept Turkey on the same path of hostility towards Islam for more than a half century.

Sheikh Nadwi, after returning from Turkey, gave statements explaining in detail that Ata Turk was in fact an enemy of Islam and was the root cause of the destruction of Islam in Turkey. Many Indian *'ulama,* based upon their knowledge of Ata Turk's early accomplishments, still considered him a hero and thus rejected Sheikh Nadwi's assessment. However, what transpired later confirmed Sheikh Nadwi's appraisal and views.

Sheikh Nadwi felt that the main culprits for the problems and hardships of the Islamic world were the Muslim leaders who were serving as puppets of the Western powers. While keeping their own public in dark, they were implementing policies which were aimed at continuing the political and ideological domination of the West over Muslim countries.

Thus whenever Sheikh Nadwi got an opportunity to meet leaders of the Islamic world, he advised them to pay attention to rectify the situation. To those whom he could not meet personally, he wrote letters reminding them of the same. In his books and articles also, he highlighted reasons for the sad plight of the Islamic world and the destructive role that the Western politics and diplomacy had played in it.

The colonial powers have been constantly working to brainwash the bright and intelligent minds (potential future rulers) of the Islamic world. As a result, Muslim rulers have failed miserably in implementing policies which were appropriate for their own countries – main cause for the deplorable condition which they are in today.

In Sheikh Nadwi's travels to Muslim countries, Europe and America, I often had the opportunity to accompany him. In those trips, I always witnessed how concerned he was about the condition [of Muslims] in those countries and how anxious he was to make the intelligent and talented individuals concerned and motivated about Islam.

Given that Hejaz is the heart of the entire Islamic world, Sheikh Nadwi took great pains to impress upon the rulers and influential people of that land of the very special responsibility that falls on their shoulders. Since he was blessed with the ability to speak and write Arabic like a native, whenever he spoke, people listened to him very attentively.

After he visited Hejaz in 1950, he did not get an opportunity to go there again for the next ten years. But based upon what he had observed and learned in the last two visits (1947 and 1950), he continued conveying his message to the people of Hejaz through his writings – letters and articles – until the time came in 1962 for the establishment of the Islamic University in Madinah. He was appointed to the Higher Council of the university and thereafter he went to Madinah every year to attend the annual meeting of the council.

Then came the founding of Muslim World League of which Sheikh Nadwi was appointed as one of the founding members. The main person responsible for that appointment was Sheikh Muhammad Suroor al-Sabban. In 1950, when Sheikh Nadwi was visiting Hejaz, Sheikh al-Sabban had become very close to him. He was the finance minister of Saudi Arabia at that time. He was also a respected poet and literary man and had participated in the event that was arranged in Taif during Sheikh Nadwi's trip.

When the Saudi Arabian government approved the formation of Muslim World League, Sheikh al-Sabban was given the responsibility of putting it together and he included Sheikh Nadwi as one of the founding members – a position of great distinction. Thereafter, Sheikh Nadwi started visiting Hejaz frequently to attend meetings of the Islamic University of Madinah and Muslim World League. During those visits, he always kept *d'awah* before him and whenever there was an opportunity, he did not hesitate in presenting his views. There were occasions when he was presiding over meetings and had to deliver concluding remarks. He fully utilized those opportunities to remind the audience about the problems which Muslims were facing in the world and how to set them right. His talks and style of presentation were so touching and penetrating that many in the audience would find tears in their eyes and leave the gathering with a genuine concern and message.

In connection with Muslim World League, Sheikh Nadwi got an opportunity to meet Shah Faisal, the ruler of Saudi Arabia. He reminded the king of his responsibilities as the ruler of his country, special position of Saudi Arabia in the Islamic world, and the need for Saudi Arab to be a role model for other Muslim countries. He also brought to the king's attention other administrative and social issues which deemed appropriate to him.

Sheikh Nadwi gave his impression about Shah Faisal that he was a very intelligent and experienced ruler. As soon as Sheikh Nadwi started talking about an issue, the king himself began explaining what was the intention and plan of the government in that regard. In other words, the king was very quick in sensing what Sheikh Nadwi wanted to know and genuinely replied to his queries.

In later years, Shah Faisal spearheaded the effort of bringing unity among Muslim countries although Europe and America were not willing to give any chance to such an effort. At that time, there were only two leaders – Ahmadu Bello of Nigeria and Shah Faisal – who were bold enough to fully embrace that mission. Though the king could not fulfill this dream in his lifetime, he laid its foundation by establishing Muslim World League. The king also played a leading role in establishing Motamar al-'Alam al-Islami (World Muslim Congress) which is still actively functional. The European powers could not tolerate Ahmadu Bello and ultimately got him martyred by the Masonic forces.

From his visits to Arab countries, Sheikh Nadwi had concluded that Hejaz and thus Saudi Arabia held special place in the Islamic world. If Hejaz truly assumed the mantle of leadership, it could serve as a catalyst for bringing positive changes in the entire Muslim world and in bringing Muslims out of the state of desperation, uncertainty, and disgrace.

Similar was his impression about Egypt. Due to the

progress that Egypt had made in education and culture, it enjoyed a position of eminence among Arab countries. Its educational system was most advanced in the Arab world; its people were very spirited; it was the most populous country in the Arab world. Thus Egypt also had the potential of assuming the mantle of leadership of the entire Arab world and if a reform effort was launched from there, it would affect the entire region as was demonstrated by the movement of Ikhwanul Muslimeen. Ikhwanul Muslimeen under the leadership of Sheikh Hasan al-Banna had spread all over Egypt and was significantly changing the lives of people and influencing other Arab countries as well.

He also got opportunities to address people – common as well as elite – of Syria, Jordan, UAE, Qatar, Kuwait, Yemen, and Morocco. In Yemen, he spoke to the army also. In every place and on every occasion, he reminded people of their Islamic and moral obligations. For that purpose, he had prepared a series of lectures which were published in the form of booklets known as the *ism'ai* series: *Isma'i Ya Misr*, *Isma'i Ya Suriya*, *Isma'i Ya Zahratus Sihr*, and *Bayna al-'Alam wal Jazirat al-'Arab*.

People were impressed with Sheikh Nadwi's knowledge, vision, wisdom, farsightedness, and understanding of the problems of the Islamic world. They felt that he wanted to unshackle the message of Islam from the regional, linguistic, racial, and cultural constraints and revive it as a universal message that was beneficial for the entire mankind. Also, he was very particular and cautious in avoiding anything which could undermine the message of Islam. That is why he, during his travels to Arab countries, was extremely careful in protecting himself and his associates from being affected by the wealth and material riches of the Arab world. He resorted to *zuhd* (asceticism) and *istighna* (expecting nothing from anyone except Allah) on every occasion. Details of these travels can be found in his travelogues.

To Europe and North America

Dr. Sa'id Ramadan (1926-95), son-in-law of Sheikh Hasan al-Banna, had emerged as a promising young lawyer in Egypt. When the rift between Ikhwanul Muslimeen and the Egyptian government became intense, many who were associated with Ikhwanul left the country for fear of persecution by the government. Dr. Ramadan was one of them. He was young, charismatic and had a lot of influence on the youth. He had a strong Islamic upbringing and was fully committed to the cause of Islam. He moved to Geneva, Switzerland and established an Islamic Centre there.

While Sheikh Nadwi was visiting Egypt in 1950, Dr. Ramadan had become very close to him. Thus when Dr. Ramadan founded the Islamic Centre in Geneva, he wanted Sheikh Nadwi to be one of the Centre's trustees. He also took firm commitment from Sheikh Nadwi to attend the annual meetings of the centre. Keeping in view that it could provide opportunities for *d'awah* in Europe, Sheikh Nadwi agreed to become a trustee of the Islamic Centre of Geneva.

Thus Sheikh Nadwi's first trip to Europe took place in 1962 when he went to Switzerland to attend the meeting of the Islamic Centre of Geneva. Dr. Ishteyaq Hussain Quraishi, a long time friend and associate of Sheikh Nadwi in his efforts among modern educated people, had accompanied him in that trip. Since Sheikh Nadwi was experiencing constant trouble with his eyes and Dr. Quraishi was a physician, his company proved very helpful in that journey.

After attending the Islamic Centre's meeting in Geneva, Sheikh Nadwi went to London, Germany, and Spain. The trip to Spain could be inspiring to any Muslim. At that time, Muslims in Spain did not have much support from the government. Muslims living there were either employees of the Arab embassies or students who had come there for studies. When Sheikh Nadwi met those students, he encouraged them to collect all the Muslims who were living there and start performing *salat* (prayer) in congregation. They started doing so right away. Later, there was an influx of Muslim immigrants and the government also became lenient. As a result, *d'awah* and some other religious activities started there. Now Muslims have grown in number and become more visible.

Sheikh Nadwi visited several cities and archeological sites in Spain. The tourist guides were usually a bit rude to the Muslim tourists. For example, when a guide would talk about a monument of the Muslim era, he would say, "This belongs to the period before we drove Muslims out of Spain". Sheikh Nadwi, through an associate, politely told his guide not to use such words as they were hurtful to Muslim tourists. The guide then changed his tone. Sheikh Nadwi came back from Spain with a lot of memories which he penned down in the form of an essay.

Sheikh Nadwi's association with the Islamic Centre of Geneva paved the way for his frequent visits to Europe. Thus starting in 1962, he went there almost every year. The following year he took me as well with him. Dr. Ramadan was very keen to have Sheikh Nadwi visit other European cities also and introduce Islam and its teachings to the intellectuals living in those places. As a result, Sheikh Nadwi visited London and several other cities of Europe. He addressed students and professors at a number of universities in those cities. Though others accompanied him in those trips from time to time, I was fortunate to accompany him most of the time.

Sheikh Nadwi used to deliver lectures mostly in Arabic because the audience was mainly comprised of Arab students who had come to Europe for higher studies. For the local people who did not understand Arabic, someone from among the Arab students was assigned to translate the speech into English. Sheikh Nadwi gave opportunity to me or others also to speak to those students.

In the speeches that Sheikh Nadwi delivered in Europe, he presented the virtues and importance of Islam in a very prudent and effective way without offending the religious feelings and sentiments of Europeans. When addressing the Muslims who had come to Europe from the East for study or work, he reminded them of what were their religious and *d'awah* responsibilities in a non-Islamic country and what kind of moral character and behavior they were supposed to display.

Those visits continued on a yearly basis without fail and he always used them for the cause of *d'awah*. In the meantime, an invitation came in 1977 from the Muslim Students Association (MSA) of USA to attend its annual convention which was expected to be attended by prominent scholars and leaders of the Islamic world as well. Keeping in view that USA was the leader of the Western world and anything that was said there had a far greater impact on the entire world, he accepted that invitation. It was also thought that he could possibly get his eyes examined there as he had been suffering from a chronic eye disease for several years.

After attending the MSA convention, Sheikh Nadwi visited several cities of USA and Canada in a span of about twenty days. In each place, he delivered a very effective, inspiring and thoughtful speech. By 1970s, a reasonably large number of Muslims had already migrated to North America. They included students and immigrants from Arab countries, Indian subcontinent, and other Asian countries and most of them were highly-educated professionals. The Muslim population of North America was quite different from that of Europe as most of those who came to Europe were uneducated factory workers. Thus the audience in North America was mostly well educated and enlightened – a promising sign for future. At the end of the trip, he also got his eyes successfully operated.

There was something special about Sheikh Nadwi's addresses in those trips. He used to point out those deficiencies and shortcomings which he had noticed in the Muslim community or organization which he was addressing, but were usually brushed aside as unimportant. He used to do so out of sincerity and well wishing. For example, during his visits to several British cities, he noticed certain deficiencies in the lifestyle and habits of the Muslims who had migrated from the subcontinent and had now become British citizens. When he addressed them, he drew their attention to those deficiencies.

In some neighborhoods, as the migrant population (Muslims and non-Muslims) was growing, the original British residents were moving away from there because they (people from the subcontinent) were not able to maintain cleanliness and decency and it was quite obvious from the very sight of those neighborhoods that the residents were mostly from the subcontinent. While addressing those Muslims, he reminded them that their lifestyle, habits, and manners should not give a negative impression about Islam and they should live a cultured and civilized life.

In case of organizations and institutions, he appreciated their efforts and services, gave them appropriate advice and made them aware of their weaknesses if he noticed any. He happened to visit a respectable *madrasah* (institution of Islamic learning) which was very strictly following the pattern of traditional old *madaris* (plural of *madrasah*) of the subcontinent without paying any attention to the local conditions and needs. In his speech at that *madrasah*, he first explained the uniqueness of *madaris* of India, their responsibilities and accomplishments, and then emphasized that the local needs of *d'awah* and other Islamic obligations should not be overlooked.

He argued that it is important to understand the psyche and temperament of people and know the language they speak. Thus an *'alim* (Islamic scholar) who has to live and work in this environment (i.e. Western countries) must pay attention to these matters so that he can present Islam effectively and clarify misunderstandings about Islam. To accomplish this, it may be required to modify the existing curriculum and educational system. If a *madrasah* in the West is run purely on the pattern of the *madaris* in the subcontinent, it will be inadequate and cannot fulfill the real need.

Sheikh Nadwi visited an organization which was engaged in *d'awah* and other Islamic efforts utilizing a certain method. But it considered its own method as the only one that was feasible for serving Islam. While addressing members of that organization, he appreciated what they were doing, but reminded them that it would be wrong to think that there was only one way to serve Islam; one should be broad minded, appreciate whatever else was being done to serve Islam and take advantage of any opportunity that might be available.

He visited a *d'awah* center which was engaged in an excellent reform work in the community. He highly appreciated its work and effectiveness of its efforts. Thereafter, he drew their attention to something which was extremely important in the Western countries – proper education and upbringing of the new generation. If we did not do enough to instill Islamic values in our children and feel contented with the education that they were getting in government schools, its consequences would be very dangerous. Parents might be very religious, punctual in *tahajjud* (pre-dawn prayer), and particular in *istighfar* (repentance for wrongdoings), but their children might become atheists, devoid of Islamic values, and victim of the environment and education. That is, children might turn out to be totally opposite of their parents, their thinking might be fully Westernized and they might have no interest in Islam.

On another occasion, Sheikh Nadwi said:

> If you cannot make necessary arrangement to protect *iman* (faith) and *'aqidah* (basic tenets of Islam) of your next generation and feel helpless in preventing them from falling victim to godless and atheistic ways, I consider your stay in this country as an act of sin.

Upon seeing some unhealthy trends in California, he said in one of his speeches that Muslims, under the influence of unfavorable environment, should not become so compromising that they drift away from the very basic and fundamental principles of Islam. If such things were allowed to happen, it would create differing versions of Islam such as British Islam, American Islam, Asian Islam, and African Islam. We should always keep our eyes on the true model of Islam – the Islam of the early period – so that we all have one Islam and do not deviate from the original version as has happened in other religions.

He said very explicitly:

> There is only one Islam. You should not become so much influenced by the local conditions that you create American Islam, Asian Islam, Australian Islam, African Islam, etc. The basic values and principles of Islam are fixed and universal, and the ability to accommodate regional and local conditions is already built in it. Thus Islam in its core will

> be the same regardless of place and condition, and its fundamentals cannot be altered by local conditions and circumstances.

Sheikh Nadwi did not make his speeches just a formality and did not limit his talk to any specific aspect of Islam. Wherever he went, he looked at the whole picture. He also tried to look at the shortcomings which were either not readily visible or connived at [for fear of offending people]. Before he travelled to Europe, he thoroughly studied the life and thinking of Europe. When he went there, he witnessed (what he had read) with his owns eyes and presented Islam to the people in an effective manner.

In his address at the University of Engineering in Berlin, Germany, he first acknowledged special traits of Germans and their important contributions in philosophical sciences and then told them that [given their talent and ability] they should have studied Islam and benefitted from its teachings. Islam is still intact in its original form and is full of inspirations for the mankind to advance and prosper by channeling its capabilities in the right direction. Thus Europe could benefit from Islam in making better utilization of its progress and achievement for itself as well as for the rest of the humanity. He delivered the speech in Arabic and its German translation was read immediately.

In his address to Germans, he also told them:

> You have produced many great minds and you are an enlightened nation. You should try to take guidance from Islam. It will enhance your strength and prosperity.

His speeches were published in Arabic and German.

In one of his speeches in USA, Sheikh Nadwi first explained that the teachings of Islam are relevant and beneficial for every place and every time period. He then explained that Islam combines the world and religion together and shows how to fulfill the worldly needs without sacrificing the demands of religion. Thus Islam should have been more acceptable to Europe and America. But it is strange that they have opted for a religion that professes shunning the world. Had Europe (which is racing ahead of everyone in worldly achievements) adopted Islamic principles and teachings, it would have found in them the cure for all of its social and moral ills.

In another speech, he said:

> Christianity is a religion which encourages abstinence and denial of worldly pleasures whereas Islam recognizes the importance of both the worldly and religious needs and allows a person to have both in his life in a balanced way. Thus Europe which has made so much progress in the worldly matters could have found better guidance for itself in Islam than in Christianity.

In his speeches, Sheikh Nadwi gave full consideration to the environment in which he was speaking and to the people he was addressing – their qualities and shortcomings. He used to talk in such a way that the audience got something refreshing and beneficial and felt inspired to improve its condition.

His speeches delivered in Europe and North America have been compiled in the form of two books namely *From the Depth of the Heart* and *Speaking Plainly to the West*. The letters that he wrote from Europe have been compiled as *Makateeb-e-Europe*[5] (Urdu). Upon Sheikh Nadwi's advice, I had written the book *Do Mahine America Men*[6] (Urdu).

---

5 Approximate translation of the title: *Letters of Europe*.

6 Approximate translation of the title: *Two Months in America*.

To Neighboring Countries (Burma, Malaysia, Pakistan, Bangladesh, and Sri Lanka)

First in 1947 and then in 1950, Sheikh Abul Hasan 'Ali Nadwi visited Hejaz and saw the condition of Muslims first-hand in Arab countries. Two or three years later, he got an opportunity to visit Syria (second time) and Turkey. All these visits enabled him to see the Muslim world closely. He was able to see various organizations, movements, and efforts of *d'awah*. He also fulfilled the obligation of giving advice to people of those countries as has been described earlier in this book. But he did not get an opportunity to visit any of India's neighboring countries until 1960 when he visited Burma (now known as Myanmar).

BURMA

Burma, because of its geographical proximity to India and close relationship and communication with the subcontinent during the British rule, was seen as a part of the subcontinent. A sizeable population of Indian origin was also living there doing business. Thus Burma was not a strange country for Indians.

In his trip to Burma, Sheikh Nadwi was accompanied by Qazi Muhammad Moinullah Indori Nadwi, who was an assistant to Sheikh Nadwi in the administration of Nadwatul 'Ulama. Sheikh Nadwi was very warmly welcomed there. He delivered speeches at numerous places and his speeches were heard with great interest and enthusiasm. At that time, Muslim businessmen, mainly immigrants of Indian origin, were very well off there. But they were only casual about Islamic practices – something that Sheikh Nadwi found very alarming. From the holy Quran, he knew very well what became the fate of nations when prophets warned them about good and evil and they did not change themselves; calamities befell them as is mentioned in the holy Quran:

> I see you in prosperity, but I fear for you the penalty of a day that will compass (you) all round. – *Hud,* 11: 84

Referring to the above Quranic verse in his speeches, Sheikh Nadwi said:

> I see abundance of wealth, luxury, and complacency. Contrary to that, I see a very lax attitude in you towards *deen*. I am afraid that the situation may change abruptly and everything may be lost. The history of nations bears testimony to the fact that if people become overly indulged in enjoying bounties of Allah and do not fulfill their obligations towards Him, they are afflicted with adverse conditions. I am afraid that your huge factories and shops may be forced to shut down by a sudden political upheaval.

He drew attention of Muslims [living in Burma] to the need of protecting and propagating Islam in that country. He urged them to introduce Islam to the indigenous population and develop acquaintance with them. Otherwise, they would not be safe. He also stressed that they must become proficient in the Burmese language.

He stayed in Burma for more than a month. He delivered numerous speeches which were heard, but only as a ritual. However, shortly after his return from there, communists came to power and confiscated properties of wealthy people and businessmen in the name of uprooting capitalism. As a result, millionaires became paupers overnight. Many of them took shelter in their old country (India or Pakistan) and many fled to Europe or Africa. Those who had heard his speeches said instantly that his predictions proved right and his warnings of dire consequences were real.

Sheikh Nadwi's visit to Burma was memorable in many respects. The people of Burma used to often remember and recount his advices. They used to listen to his speeches on cassette and get affected saying how accurate were his predictions. The main sponsor of that trip was Sheikh Qari

'Abdur Rahman Qasmi who was acquainted with Sheikh Nadwi from before. The other person who made the trip very beneficial was Sheikh Ibrahim Ahmad Mazahari who was the editor of *Daur-e-Jadid*, an Urdu magazine that was published from Rangoon.

When Sheikh Nadwi undertook the trip to Burma, his elder brother Dr. Syed 'Abdul 'Ali Hasani, who was the rector of Nadwatul 'Ulama, was suffering from heart ailment. While Sheikh Nadwi was away in Burma, Dr. 'Ali's condition became worrisome and he wanted Sheikh Nadwi to return soon. Sheikh Nadwi was informed about it. So he cut short his visit and returned to India. Dr. 'Ali felt consoled by his return.

Apprehending no immediate danger to Dr. 'Ali's health, Sheikh Nadwi resumed his traveling engagements within India. But while he was away to Saharanpur (about 400 miles from Lucknow), Dr. 'Ali suffered a severe heart attack and passed away a day before Sheikh Nadwi could return to Lucknow.

It was the wish of Dr. 'Ali that Sheikh Nadwi should be by his side during his last moments, but it was destined to be otherwise. Upon getting the news of Dr. 'Ali's rapidly deteriorating condition, Sheikh Nadwi tried to return to Lucknow as soon as possible. But when he reached Lucknow next morning, he came to know that his brother had already passed away the previous night and the body had been taken from Lucknow to Rae Bareli for burial. Sheikh Nadwi proceeded to Rae Bareli, but could not reach in time to attend the funeral prayer. For a long time, Sheikh Nadwi felt the grief of not being present by his brother's side in his last moments. However, he continued recompensing his brother for his love and affection using the ways which are permissible in *shari'ah*.

MALAYSIA

Sheikh Nadwi's next trip was to a South-East Asian country,

Malaysia in 1987. Like the Indian subcontinent, Malaysia also was a British colony. Thus when Malaysia gained independence in 1957 and the British left the country, they left behind their cultural imprints all over the country. Ethnic Malay Muslims were in majority by only 2 per cent. But, by being indigenous, they had more rights than the immigrants who had come from China and the Indian subcontinent. Since the entire country was divided among landlords (who were Muslims), each landlord became monarch of his own area after the British left the country.

Malaysia became a federal constitutional elective monarchy in which power is divided between the federal and state legislatures. After independence, Muslims, who were in majority, took responsibility and actively contributed to the progress of the country. As a result, an international university and several Muslim institutions of higher learning have come into existence.

Sheikh Nadwi visited Kuala Lumpur (capital of Malaysia), the northern state of Kedah, and the southern state of Selangor. In Kedah, a *madrasah* was being run under the supervision of people who were associated with Nadwatul 'Ulama. In Selangor, some religious activities had begun under the supervision of a person who was a graduate of the Islamic University of Madinah. Wherever Sheikh Nadwi went, he was warmly welcomed and people listened to him attentively.

Sheikh Nadwi felt that the Muslim intellectuals and leaders of Malaysia were fully aware of their religious and social obligations and he saw a lot of hope and promise in them. They also took good effect from his advices.

A number of Malaysian students, who were studying at Nadwatul 'Ulama, had returned to Malaysia after completing their education due to which Nadwatul 'Ulama enjoyed a position of respect in Malaysia. They started the noble work of *d'awah* and education, and opened *madaris* and schools in their respective places. Sheikh Nadwi was very happy to see their accomplishments.

In Kuala Lumpur, Sheikh Nadwi visited the International Islamic University. He liked the curriculum and overall administration of the university. He gave appropriate advice to the university officials.

The state of Kedah borders with Thailand's southernmost state of Pattani. Both Kedah (Malaysia) and Pattani (Thailand) are heavily populated with Muslims. Since Muslims in Pattani are faced with serious political difficulties, many of them have taken shelter in Kedah. Both of these areas are adjacent to Burma.

Sheikh Nadwi's visit to Kedah was significant because Kedah had a *madrasah* known as Tarbiyah Islamiyah whose management had strong connection with Nadwatul 'Ulama. Two graduates of Nadwatul 'Ulama, Sheikh Ahmad Fahmi Zamzam and Sheikh Muhammad 'Ali Rajab were on the *madrasah*'s management committee and they were very close to the founder Sheikh Yusuf N'emat. Sheikh Yusuf N'emat was a graduate of Al-Azhar University, Cairo and was an *'alim* with a good understanding of *d'awah* and education. Sheikh Yusuf N'emat had made a special request to Sheikh Nadwi to visit his *madrasah*; Sheikh Yusuf N'emat had visited Nadwatul 'Ulama in the past. The visit to Kedah was very friendly.

Several Muslim groups and organizations were working in Malaysia at that time. Leaders of those outfits were right-minded people and had good influence on the government. These were signs of a better future for the country.

While Sheikh Nadwi was in Malaysia, the entire country was embroiled in a hot issue which was triggered by an incident which had recently taken place. Someone had posted on internet a distorted version of the holy Quran and many were taking it as a sign that the day of *Qiyamah* (Doomsday) was about to arrive and the world was going to perish very soon. They were implying that since it was the promise of Allah that He would protect Quran until the day of *Qiyamah* and He had now allowed someone to publish a distorted version of it, it must mean that *Qiyamah* was very imminent. This had made many people very fearful.

Sheikh Nadwi explained that there had always been attempts to distort and adulterate the holy Quran, but mere attempts did not matter until they were allowed to succeed. The danger was only when such attempts were allowed to succeed. Thus it was important to make sure that such attempts did not succeed and Quran remained intact and unimpaired. That is what was meant by the protection of Quran. In this case also, Muslims all over the world vehemently opposed it as a result of which the distorted version was finally removed from the internet.

Due to ill health, Sheikh Nadwi could not stay longer in Malaysia. Nor could he do much work. Yet, the trip was beneficial. It gave encouragement to the alumni of Nadwatul 'Ulama who were working there. He gave them useful advice about how to work there.

During the trip, his health further deteriorated and he became much weaker. After returning to India, the weakness persisted and became so severe (due to bleeding from hemorrhoids) that he could not even go to a nearby place for Eid prayer. He got better after undergoing treatment of Dr. Ishteyaq Hussain Quraishi in Lucknow.

PAKISTAN

Sheikh Nadwi made several trips to Pakistan including a few before 1947 – the year in which India was partitioned and Pakistan was formed. After the formation of Pakistan, his first visit was in 1954. It was solely for his own spiritual enrichment as he wanted to spend the month of Ramadan in the company of his spiritual guide and mentor Sheikh 'Abdul Qadir Raipuri. He had undertaken that journey alone which was unusual to him. During that trip, he also visited his teacher and spiritual mentor Sheikh Ahmad 'Ali Lahori and stayed with him for a few days.

The next trip came within a year in 1955. He was accompanied by his nephew Sheikh Syed Muhammad Thani Hasani at that time. The trip proved beneficial from the perspective of *d'awah* and learning.

Sheikh Nadwi's next visit to Pakistan came in 1978 when he was invited by Rabita al-'Alam al-Islami (Muslim World League) to attend the first Asian conference on *Siratun Nabi* (life of Prophet Muhammad). In that trip, he took with him a few associates which included Sheikh Moinullah Nadwi, his nephew Sheikh Syed Muhammad Al-Hasani (a reputed Arabic and Urdu author), and Sheikh Ishaq Jalees Nadwi. Sheikh Ishaq Jalees Nadwi had reached Pakistan a few days earlier so that he could arrange Sheikh Nadwi's programs in influential circles. Thus Sheikh Nadwi, in addition to participating in the conference, addressed gathering at several institutions and organizations which were involved in *d'awah* and educational efforts. In his speeches, he mainly focused on what should be the role of a Muslim country on the international stage in the present circumstances.

In the *Siratun Nabi* conference, Sheikh Nadwi delivered the final speech in which he drew attention of the audience to the historical statement "Can there be any decline in *deen* while I am still alive?" of Sayyidna Abu Bakr Siddique (a companion of Prophet Muhammad and the first caliph of Islam). Sheikh Nadwi said:

> This is the essence of the entire conference. This is the message that the honorable guests should take with them

> from here. It will continue reminding them about their responsibilities as leaders of their country and heirs of the Prophet. No statement can be better than this. This is what was uttered by the Prophet's successor Sayyidna Abu Bakr Siddique when some tribes attempted to renegade from Islam. It shows Sayyidna Abu Bakr's deep sense of responsibility for being the successor of the Prophet, his level of *iman* (belief), and truthfulness. It was such a resolve that it changed the course of history and the wave of apostasy was changed into a flood of submissions and victories.

Sheikh Nadwi also met leaders who were simultaneously involved in both the religious efforts and politics. He reminded them to work for the welfare of the country and people, and to keep the benefit of *deen* (religion) in the forefront. When he met government authorities, he reminded them to work for improving relationship with India.

The speeches that he had delivered in that trip were published in the form of a book entitled *Hadith-e-Pakistan* (Urdu) from Karachi. That collection was later published as *Dawat Fikr wa Amal* (Urdu) from Lucknow, India.

That was the period when General Ziaul Haq was the president of Pakistan. He had read Sheikh Nadwi's books and articles and was impressed with them. Upon Sheikh Nadwi's arrival, the president expressed happiness and met him. He also sought Sheikh Nadwi's advice. Sheikh Nadwi gave him the same advice that he had given to other political leaders – work on improving the relationship with India – and the president promised to do so.

General Ziaul Haq was a regular reader of Sheikh Nadwi's writings. He had read the foreword that Sheikh Nadwi had written for the seventh volume of *Seera-tun-Nabi* – the 7-volume biography of Prophet Muhammad authored by Sheikh Syed Sulaiman Nadwi in Urdu. General Ziaul Haq was very impressed by the foreword and had announced a monetary award of 100,000 rupees for Sheikh Nadwi. Sheikh Nadwi gifted that award to the widow of Sheikh Syed Sulaiman Nadwi and Darul Musannefin (publisher of *Seera-tun-Nabi*). In Sheikh Nadwi's another trip to Pakistan, General Ziaul Haq came to Karachi from Islamabad to meet him and treated him very courteously.

Due to some misunderstanding between the words *Rabita* (the first word in the name of Rabita al-'Alam al-Islami) and Rabat (capital of Morocco), some members of the Indian parliament had raised objection to Sheikh Nadwi's above-mentioned trip to Pakistan for attending the *Siratun Nabi* conference which was convened by Rabita al-'Alam al-Islami (Muslim World League). In the recent past, a conference of Muslim countries was held in Rabat (Morocco) and India had sent a delegation there. But, the delegates were turned away from the conference saying that the conference was exclusively for Muslim countries and India was not a Muslim country. That incident had created an awkward and insulting situation for India and had prompted some members of the Indian parliament to raise the question: Why did Sheikh Nadwi (being an Indian citizen) go to Rabat which had insulted India? Atal Bihari Vajpayee, who was the foreign minister of India at that time, intervened and clarified that the conference which Sheikh Nadwi had attended had nothing to do with Rabat, Sheikh Nadwi's trip was purely non-political and that there was nothing said or done against India in the conference. Though Vajpayee belonged to a pro-Hindu political party, his action showed his tolerance and broad-mindedness.

Sheikh Nadwi's last visit to Pakistan came in 1997 when he was invited by the Pakistani branch of the World Forum of Islamic Literature to attend its seminar during 24-25 October 1997. He was quite weak at that time and it was very difficult for him to travel. Yet, he went there because he was the president of the World Forum of Islamic Literature and its members were very desirous and insistent upon his coming. Upon hearing that Sheikh Nadwi was coming, the then president of Pakistan, Farooq Ahmed Khan Leghari also decided to participate in the seminar.

Leghari reminded Sheikh Nadwi that before he became the president of Pakistan, he had met him in Geneva, Switzerland, many years ago in a program that was hosted by the Islamic Centre of Geneva. Leghari also said that he had a desire to meet him again. The seminar was presided over by Leghari and Sheikh Nadwi was the keynote speaker. Sheikh Nadwi's speech was heard very attentively and with great effect. The Chief Minister of Punjab, the Governor of Punjab, the Central Minister of Religious Affairs, and the Chief Justice of Pakistan Shari'ah Court were among the attendees.

It was a two-day seminar and the theme was "Journals of Travel to Harmain Sharifain".[7] Scholars, journalists, and learned people, including those who had come from India with Sheikh Nadwi, presented papers and gave lectures shedding light on different aspects of visits to the holy cities of Makkah and Madinah.

That trip was limited to Lahore and Sheikh Nadwi stayed at Jami'ah Ashrafia which is a renowned Islamic institution of higher learning in Lahore. Important and influential persons, learned scholars, heads of religious and educational institutions, and prominent religious and spiritual figures welcomed Sheikh Nadwi and benefitted from him. He visited Raiwind which is the headquarters of Jama'at Tabligh. A detailed account of that trip can be found in the seventh volume (pp 53-57) of Sheikh Nadwi's autobiography *Karwan-e-Zindagi.*

BANGLADESH

Sheikh Nadwi visited Bangladesh twice after it was formed

---

[7] Harmain Sharifain – Holy places of Makkah and Madinah.

in 1971. Both of these visits were purely religious and academic. His speeches were constructive and *d'awah* oriented, and were liked by religious and learned people. He visited religious and educational institutions which warmly welcomed him.

The first visit took place in March 1984. In that trip, he was accompanied by Sheikh Abul 'Irfan Khan Nadwi, Sheikh 'Abdul Karim Parikh, and Sheikh Syed Salman Hussaini Nadwi. In the speeches of that trip, he put greatest emphasis on preserving the Islamic character and identity of the country, and its inseparable bond with Islam. He exhorted *'ulama* and intellectuals to develop proper Islamic literature in Bengali and remain connected with the masses. In one of his speeches, he very clearly told the audience that the well-being, prosperity, and dignity of the country depended on its bond with Islam. If it disconnected itself from Islam, it could never stand firm. He reminded *'ulama* to always remain vigilant so that the country's bond with Islam never became weak.

His speeches of that trip have been published by the Academy of Islamic Research and Publications in the form of a book entitled *Tohfa-e-Mashriq*[8].

Sheikh Nadwi's second visit to Bangladesh came when he was invited by the Bangladeshi branch of the World Forum of Islamic Literature to attend a seminar at Jami'atul Mo'arif Islamiyah in Chittagong. Sheikh Sultan Zauq Nadwi was the main organizer of the seminar and the theme of the seminar was "Islamic Attitude in Literature and Languages of the People of the East".

Since Sheikh Nadwi was the president of the World Forum of Islamic Literature, it was important for him to attend the seminar even though he was very weak. When he arrived in Dhaka, he got very sick and it appeared that he would not be

8 Approximate translation of the title: *Gift of the East*.

able to travel to Chittagong – a distance of about 150 miles. Due to that ailment, he had to excuse himself from a dinner reception that was given by the president of Bangladesh. Though it was very strenuous for him to travel from Dhaka to Chittagong, he undertook that journey and briefly attended and presided over the seminar.

Since the seminar was being conducted on an international level, it was attended by representatives and dignitaries from Bangladesh as well as from other countries. The seminar was successful and beneficial.

That was Sheikh Nadwi's last visit to Bangladesh. In that short trip, he met many people and gave them his advice. People benefitted from his advice in religious and educational matters.

SRI LANKA

On the invitation of Nazemia University of Sri Lanka and recommendation of Sheikh Muhammad 'Ali Al-Harkan, the secretary general of Muslim World League, Sheikh Nadwi traveled to Sri Lanka for a short visit in May 1982. He was accompanied by Sheikh Syed Salman Hussaini Nadwi in that trip. He met prominent Muslims of Sri Lanka and they benefitted from his presence. That was his only trip to Sri Lanka.

When Sheikh Nadwi arrived in Sri Lanka, he came to know that his paper *Raddatun wa la Ababakr laha* (published in English as *The New Menace and Its Answer*) was the real catalyst in the establishment of Nazemia University whose founder Haji Muhammad Nazem was inspired by the paper to launch this undertaking. Haji Nazem is a goodhearted businessman and takes care of all expenses of the institution by himself.

The event organized by Nazemia University was attended by the foreign minister of Sri Lanka, ambassadors of several

Arab and Muslim countries, and local Muslim leaders. Sheikh Nadwi in his speech said:

> It is widely believed that Sri Lanka is the country where our father, your father, and the father of the entire human race, Prophet Adam had descended from the paradise. And Prophet Muhammad has said: "O people! You all have the same Creator (Allah) and you all have the same father (Adam). Thus you are brothers of each other because of two relationships – having the same Creator and having the same father." This declaration of the Prophet is the most fundamental basis of human brotherhood and the most important clause of the international human rights charter. Thus if Muslim countries call for the universal brotherhood once, you (the people of Sri Lanka) by virtue of the claim that you are the inhabitant of the birth place of human race, deserve to do it ten times. You should be its advocate and flag-bearer.

6

Publications

Sheikh Nadwi's Publications

SHEIKH Nadwi wrote extensively in Arabic and Urdu. His published articles, lectures and books number about 200 in Arabic and 300 in Urdu. Many of his publications have been translated into English and several other languages. The following is a brief introduction to some of his writings. Keeping in view the interest of English speaking audience, the order in which books have been listed below is slightly different from that of the original biography. Also, pertinent information such as publisher's name, year of publication, ISBN, etc. have been provided for the books which have been translated into English as it may help readers in obtaining them.

1. *Seerat Syed Ahmad Shaheed*

This book was originally written in Urdu. It has not yet been translated into English.

It is a biography of Sheikh Syed Ahmad Shaheed (d. 1831). Sheikh Nadwi wrote it in 1938 or 1939. The book served as a great booster to Indian Muslims who were experiencing great depression and despair under the British imperial rule at that time. It infused a new vigor and resolve in Indian Muslims to continue fighting for a free and dignified life.

It covered in detail the life and mission of Syed Ahmad

Shaheed who had led the largest reform movement of its type in undivided India. The mission of that movement was to bring social reform among masses and revive *khilafah* (caliphate). The book had two volumes. The first volume had 125 chapters and 588 pages. The second volume had 150 chapters and 588 pages.

2. *Islam and the World: The Rise and Decline of Muslims and Its Effect on Mankind*

It was originally written in Arabic as *Ma Dha Khasar al-'Alamu bi Inhitat-il-Muslimin* and the English translation was rendered by Dr. Mohammad Asif Kidwai. It was first published by the Academy of Islamic Research and Publications, Lucknow (India) in 1982 and reprinted by the UK Islamic Academy of Leicester of UK in 2003 (ISBN: 9781872531328).

This book was very instrumental in re-invigorating self-confidence and pride among young Arab intellectuals who had become shaky and skeptical about Islam and Muslims. It had started as a series of essays that Sheikh Nadwi had written to draw attention of Arabs towards their obligation as Muslims. He wanted to present the history of religious and political accomplishments of early Muslims, why Muslims despite being the best nation fell from the height of success and what made others accomplish great achievements. He wanted Muslims to understand the dynamics of the rise and fall of nations and do what was needed to regain their lost glory.

When Sheikh Nadwi was close to completing this book, he got an opportunity to go for *hajj* and stay in Hejaz for several months. During that stay, he met learned scholars from various countries and exchanged his views with them. That enabled him to further augment and refine the content of the book which was finally published in 1950 by Lajnat al-Ta'aleef wal Nashr of Cairo, Egypt under the supervision of Dr. Ahmad Amin. Its acceptance and popularity far exceeded any expectation. It along with *Seerat Syed Ahmad Shaheed* introduced Sheikh Nadwi to the Muslim world as a distinguished scholar, writer and thinker. It has also been translated into several languages including Bengali, English, French, Malaysian, Persian, Turkish, and Urdu.

3. *Muhammad Rasulullah: The Apostle of Mercy*

It was originally written in Arabic as *As-Siratun-Nabawiyah* and the English translation was rendered by Mohiuddin Ahmad.

It is a biography of Prophet Muhammad. Facts and events are presented in a logical way with due consideration to the taste and mindset of the new generation. The social, economic, and political conditions that existed in the Arab peninsula, especially in Makkah and Madinah, in the pre-Islamic period have been presented in detail without which one may not fully appreciate the beauty and success of Islam.

4. *Muhammad: The Last Prophet*

It was originally written in Urdu as *Seerat Rasool-e-Akram* and the English translation was rendered by Dr. Shah 'Ebadur Rahman. It has been translated into Hindi also.

It is a short biography of Prophet Muhammad. It is in fact a collection of narrations that were prepared by Sheikh Nadwi for gatherings of *tabligh* (propagation) and *islah* (correction). It contains not only an account of the Prophet's virtues, miracles, and historical events relating to his life, but also a focused discussion on the aspects of spiritual discipline and moral reform that the Prophet preached – underscoring the importance of seeking Allah's favor, sympathy for human beings, and serving mankind.

5. *Pathway to Medina*

It was originally written in Arabic as *al-Tareeq ilal Madinah* and the English translation was rendered by Dr. Mohammad Asif Kidwai.

It is a collection of several articles and speeches on the life, mission, teachings, and accomplishments of the Prophet. Its Urdu translation was published as *Karwan-e-Medinah* which included a number of poems (exalting the Prophet) in Urdu and Persian as well. Its Persian translation was published from Zahedan, Iran.

6. *Muhammad: The Last Prophet, A Model for all Time*

It was originally written in Arabic as *Seerat Khatimun Nabiyun Lil Atfaal* and the English translation was rendered by Iqbal Ahmad Azami. It is a short biography of the Prophet. The English translation was reprinted by the UK Islamic Academy of Leicester (UK) in 2006 (ISBN: 1872531105).

7. *Islamic Concept of Prophethood*

It is a collection of lectures that Sheikh Nadwi delivered at the Islamic University of Madinah in 1963. It was originally published in Arabic as *An Nubawwatu wal Ambia fi Dhauil Quran wal Sunnah*. The English translation was rendered by Mohiuddin Ahmad. The theme of the lectures was the special qualities of prophets, their mission, their services to mankind, and the finality of the prophethood of Prophet Muhammad. It is one of the most famous books of Sheikh Nadwi.

8. *The Life of Caliph Ali*

It was originally written in Arabic as *Al Murtadhaa* and the English translation was rendered by Mohiuddin Ahmad.

It is a biography of the fourth caliph Sayyidna 'Ali bin Abi Talib. It enumerates the unique qualities of Sayyidna 'Ali and his family, his contributions, his role in the regimes of his predecessors, the difficulties of his regime, and the role and contribution of his sons Sayyidna Hasan and Sayyidna Hussain.

It also sheds light on the divine wisdom in the order in which the four caliphs were appointed.

9. *Saviours of Islamic Spirit*

It was originally written in Urdu as *Tarikh Dawat Wa Azeemat* and the English translation was rendered by Mohiuddin Ahmad. Though the Urdu version consists of five volumes, the English version has only four with topics slightly rearranged. It has also been translated into Arabic, Persian, and Turkish.

It covers important revivalist movements that took place in the last 13 centuries of Islamic history and shows that there has been an uninterrupted infusion of new blood which has kept Islam alive and vibrant to this day. It also covers prominent personalities who were at the forefront of those movements.

The first volume covers the first seven centuries of Islamic history and gives a detailed description of the lives and contributions of 'Umar bin 'Abdul 'Aziz, Hasan Basri, Imam Ahmad bin Hanbal, Imam Abul Hasan al-Ash'ari, Imam Ghazali, 'Abdul Qadir Jilani, 'Allaamah Ibn Jauzi, Sultan Nuruddin Zangi, Sultan Salahuddin Ayubi, Shiekhul Islam 'Azzuddin bin 'Abdus Salam, and Jalaluddin Rumi.

The second volume covers the eighth century Hijri and gives a detailed description of the lives and contributions of Sheikhul Islam Hafiz Ibn Taimiyah and his illustrious disciples Hafiz Ibn Qaiyam, 'Allaamah Ibnul Hadi, 'Allaamah Ibn Kathir, and Hafiz Ibn Rajab.

The third volume focuses on the important figures of *tasawwuf* (mysticism) and *ihsan* (spiritual perfection). It shows how they were able to win the hearts of people and develop in them qualities of love, devotion, firm faith, and good morality. It gives a detailed description of the lives and contributions of Khawaja Moinuddin Chishti Ajmeri, Khawaja Nizamuddin Aulia, and Sheikh Sharfuddin Yahya Maneri.

The fourth volume is about Mujaddid Alf Thani who, at the time of Emperor Akbar, was facing a situation in which Akbar was openly sponsoring and promoting un-Islamic practices in India. It describes how his steady and non-confrontational approach transformed Akbar's successors and changed the course of history for centuries to come.

The fifth volume is about Shah Waliyullah Dehlavi and his successors. It enumerates their struggle in preserving Islam in the Indian subcontinent.

The English version *Saviours of Islamic Spirit* was published by the Academy of Islamic Research and Publications, Lucknow (India) in 1994 and by Darul Ishaat, Karachi (Pakistan) in 2009 (ISBN: 9789694281933). The White Thread Press of California (USA) has recently produced a set of 10 audio CDs with narratives based upon this book.

The UK Islamic Academy of Leicester (UK) has published a book entitled *Sheikhul-ul-Islam Ibn Taimiyah: Life and Achievements* (ISBN: 1872531725) in 2005. It consists of a portion (about Ibn Taimiyah) of the original book's second volume.

The Islamic Book Trust of Kuala Lumpur (Malaysia) has published a book entitled *Lessons of the Crusades and the Mongol Hordes: Salahuddin al-Ayyubi and his Successors* (ISBN: 9839154664) in 2006. It consists of two chapters (on Nuruddin Zangi, Salahuddin Ayubi, and Tatars) from the original book's first volume.

10. *The Four Pillars of Islam*

It was originally written in Arabic as *Al Arkan Arba'a fil Islam* and its English translation was rendered by Dr. Mohammad Asif Kidwai.

It delves into significance, objective, and virtues of the four fundamental pillars of Islam – *salat* (worship), *saum* (fasting), *zakah* (poor-due), and *hajj* (pilgrimage to Makkah) and how they affect human life. It also compares them to devotional practices of Buddhism, Christianity, Hinduism, and Judaism.

The Islamic Book Trust of Kuala Lumpur (Malaysia) has recently published a new edition of *The Four Pillars of Islam in* 2011 (ISBN: 9789675062780).

11. *Faith Versus Materialism: The Message of Surat al-Kahf*

It was originally written in Arabic as *As Sarai Bainal Iman wal Maddiyah* and the English translation was rendered by Mohiuddin Ahmad. It explains the Quranic verse *al-Kahf* (Chapter no. 18) in the light of *hadith*, ancient history, and modern knowledge and draws lessons that are pertinent to today's life. A recent edition of the English translation was published in 2007 by the Islamic Book Trust of Malaysia (ISBN: 9839154788).

12. *Glory of Iqbal*

It was originally written in Arabic as *Rawa'i Iqbal* and the English translation was rendered by Dr. Mohammad Asif Kidwai. It is an introduction to the poetic marvel and revolutionary ideals of the Poet of the East Dr. Muhammad Iqbal and how he (Iqbal) had warned mankind of the perils of the Western values and culture.

13. *Religion and Civilization*

It is a collection of lectures that Sheikh Nadwi had delivered at Jamia Millia Islamia, Delhi, in 1942. It was originally published as *Madhab wa Tamaddun* (Urdu) and the English translation was rendered by Mohiuddin Ahmad.

It argues that a proper understanding of the universe, its

creator, and the real purpose of human life are essential for building a just, robust, and prosperous society. It enumerates beliefs and concepts of the earlier civilizations and shows how Islam envisions the formation of a just and righteous society.

14. *Islam: An Introduction*

It was originally written in Urdu as *Islam kaa T'aaruf* and the English translation was rendered by Dr. Shah 'Ebadur Rahman.

It is based upon various writing of Sheikh Nadwi and was compiled by Syed 'Abdullah Hasani Nadwi (teacher at Nadwatul 'Ulama) under Sheikh Nadwi's supervision. It explains fundamental beliefs, religious obligations, and social etiquette in simple terms for common people who don't have time to study voluminous books. Its Hindi translation *Islam: Ek Parichay* was rendered by Muhammad Hasan Ansari. It has been translated into other languages also.

15. *A Guidebook for Muslims*

It was originally written in Arabic as *Al 'Aqeedah wal 'Ibadah Wal Sulook* and its English translation was rendered by Mohiuddin Ahmad. It is a complete code of conduct for a Muslim in the light of Quran and *sunnah* and covers all aspects of life such as belief, worship, manners, striving for the cause of Allah, and supplications for different occasions.

16. *Western Civilization, Islam, and Muslims*

It was originally written in Arabic as *As Sirau Bainal Fikratil Islamiyyate wal Fikratil Gharabiyya fil Aqtaril Islamiyah* and the English translation was rendered by Dr. Mohammad Asif Kidwai. It analyzes the negative influence of the Western culture and values on Muslim countries and how they have created anti-Islamic attitude among Muslim rulers.

17. *Hadith and the Promotion of Islamic Climate and Attitudes*

It is the translation of the paper *Daurul Hadith fi Takweenil Manakhil Islami wa Siyanah* that Sheikh Nadwi presented in 1981 in Makkah in a gathering that was organized by Muslim World League at the time of *hajj* and attended by distinguished Islamic scholars from all over the world. It explains the importance of *hadith* and *sunnah* and the dangers of becoming neglectful towards them.

The English translation was rendered by Mohiuddin Ahmad and published by the UK Islamic Academy of Leicester (UK) in 2005 as a part of *Hadith: Status and Role. An Introduction to the Prophet's Tradition* (ISBN: 1 872531 75 X).

18. *An Introduction to the Study of Hadith*

It was originally written in Arabic as *Al Mudkhal Ilad Darasatul Hadith Nabwi.* It introduces the discipline of *hadith,* phases of its development, its pioneers, and the six authentic collections of *hadith.* It also describes methods and etiquette of studying *hadith.*

The English translation was rendered by 'Adil Salahi and published by the UK Islamic Academy of Leicester (UK) in 2005 as a part of *Hadith: Status and Role. An Introduction to the Prophet's Tradition* (ISBN: 1 872531 75 X).

19. *Studying the Glorious Quran: Principles and Methodology*

It is a collection of essays that Sheikh Nadwi wrote while teaching at Nadwatul 'Ulama. The intent was to acquaint students with the importance of the holy Quran and methods of studying it.

It was originally published in Arabic as *Al Mudkhal Ilad Darasatul Quran.* The English translation was rendered by Qazi 'Abdul Hameed Indori and published by the UK Islamic Academy of Leicester (UK) in 2003 (ISBN: 1872531229).

20. *Guidance from the Holy Quran*

It is collection of Sheikh Nadwi's articles and speeches which expound on the meaning and message of Quran. It was originally published as *Qurani Ifadat* (Urdu). The English translation *Guidance from the Holy Quran* was rendered by Dr. 'Abdur Raheem Kidwai and published by The Islamic Foundation of UK in 2005 (ISBN: 0860374750). Another translation (rendered by Maulana Mahomed Mohamedy) was published as *Quranic Teachings* by Zam Zam Publishers (Pakistan) in 2004.

21. *Qadianism: A Critical Study*

Sheikh Nadwi wrote the book *al-Qadiyani wal Qadniyat* (Arabic) on the advice of his spiritual mentor Sheikh 'Abdul Qadir Raipuri to refute the perfidy of Qadianism. The English translation was rendered by Dr. Zafar Ishaq Ansari.

22. *Islam and the Earliest Muslims: Two Conflicting Portraits*

It was originally written in Urdu as *Deene Islam aur Awwaleen Musalmanon kee Do Mutazad Tasweeren* and the English translation was rendered by Mohiuddin Ahmad. The Arabic translation *Suratan Motadha Datan* was rendered by Sheikh Sa'yidur Rahman 'Azami Nadwi.

Sheikh Nadwi wrote this book when the Iranian Revolution led by Ayatullah Khomeini was still very popular among Muslim masses. He presented a comparative analysis of the beliefs of *Ahlul Sunah Wal Jama't* (mainstream Muslims) and *Ithna Ashariyah* (a branch of Shi'ism) and demonstrated that Ayatullah Khomeini was promoting ideas of those who had been very contemptuous of Sahaba (companions of the Prophet) and were alleged to have tampered with Quran.

23. *Speaking Plainly to the West*

It is a collection of three speeches that Sheikh Nadwi had delivered in England and Germany in 1963, 1964, and 1969. It portrays an ideal Muslim who can invite the West to Islam without any reservation or apology. It boldly points out the weaknesses of the Western society and condemns its blind following by the East. It presents Islam as the most balanced way of life for mankind.

It was published as *Maghrib se Kuch Saaf Saaf Baten* by the Academy of Islamic Research and Publications, Lucknow in 1973. The English translation was rendered by Mohiuddin Ahmad and published by The Islamic Foundation of UK in 1983 as a part of *Muslims in the West: The Message and Mission* (ISBN: 0860371301).

24. *From the Depth of the Heart in America*

It is a collection of speeches that Sheikh Nadwi had delivered at various places in USA and Canada in 1977. In those speeches, he gave important advice to Muslims living in the Western countries. It was published in Urdu as *Nai Duniya America Men Saaf Saaf Baten* by the Academy of Islamic Research and Publications, Lucknow in 1978.

The English translation was rendered by Dr. Mohammad Asif Kidwai and published by The Islamic Foundation of UK in 1983 as a part of *Muslims in the West: The Message and Mission* (ISBN: 0860371301).

25. *Prophet Muhammad in the Mirror of His Supplications*

It is the English translation (rendered by Dr. Shah 'Ebadur Rahman) of Sheikh Nadwi's book *Seerate Muhammadi D'uaon Ke Aaine Men* (Urdu). It sheds light on the Prophet's supplications showing his character in the context of prophetic wisdom and miraculous excellence.

26. *D'awah in the West: The Quranic Paradigm*

It is the English translation (rendered by Dr. 'Abdur Raheem Kidwai) of the speech that Sheikh Nadwi had delivered at the Islamic Foundation, Leicester, UK, in 1991. It was published by the Islamic Foundation (ISBN: 0860372251).

27. *The Role and Responsibilities of Muslims in the West*

It is the English translation (rendered by Dr. 'Abdur Raheem Kidwai) of the speech that Sheikh Nadwi had delivered at the Islamic Foundation, Leicester, UK, in 1992. It was published by the Islamic Foundation (ISBN: 0860372324).

28. *Stories of the Prophets*

It is the English translation of Sheikh Nadwi's book *Qasas-al-Nabiyyin lil Atfaal* (Arabic) which describes stories of various prophets. It was published by the UK Islamic Academy in 2007 (ISBN: 1872531091).

29. *Life and Mission of Maulana Muhammad Ilyas*

It was originally written in Urdu as *Maulana Ilyas aur Unki Deeni D'awat*. The English translation was rendered by Dr. Mohammad Asif Kidwai. It is a biography of Sheikh Muhammad Ilyas Kandhlawi who was the founder of the movement known as Jama'at Tabligh. This book enables the reader to understand the importance and necessity of the effort of *d'awah* and *islah*. Since Sheikh Nadwi was closely associated with Sheikh Ilyas and his work, it includes author's personal observations and experiences as well.

30. *Muslims: Beliefs, Customs and Traditions*

It was originally written in Urdu as *Hindustanui Musalman Ek Nadhar Men*. The English translation was rendered by Mohiuddin Ahmad. It was first published in 1977 as *The Musalman* by the Academy of Islamic Research and Publications, Lucknow. In 2005, it was published by the UK Islamic

Academy, Leicester (UK) as *Muslims: Beliefs, Customs and Traditions* (ISBN: 1872531741).

It sheds light on religious, social, and cultural lives of Indian Muslims and their customs, traditions, habits, and festivals.

31. *Muslims in India*

It was originally written in Arabic as *Al Muslimun fil Hind* and the English translation was rendered by Dr. Mohammad Asif Kidwai. It is a historical illustration of Indian Muslims and their religious, educational, and cultural struggle. It also sheds light on the impact of their rule on the Indian society and culture.

32. *The New Menace and its Answer*

It is the English translation of Sheikh Nadwi's article *Raddatun wa la Ababakr laha* (Arabic) which was published in 1950s in the Egyptian journal *Al-Muslimun*. It may be downloaded from the website http://www.wokingmuslim.org/work/islamic-review/isrevconts-1963.pdf.

33. *Inviting to the Ways of Allah*

It is a collection of eight lectures that Sheikh Nadwi had delivered at Nadwatul 'Ulama when the Department of D'awah and Islamic Thought was opened in 1980.

34. *A Misunderstood Reformer*

It was originally written in Arabic as *Al Imam Al Ladhi Lum Yuwaffa Haqqihi Menal Insaaf wal 'Iteraaf*. The English translation was rendered by Mohiuddin Ahmad. It gives an overview of the mission and accomplishments of Syed Ahmad Shaheed (d. 1831) and his reform movement. It also sheds light on the forces that betrayed Syed Ahmad Shaheed and sabotaged his movement.

Sheikh Nadwi used Arabic and Urdu for his writings and

speeches though he was familiar with English and Persian as well. His writings have been translated into several languages including Bengali, English, Hindi, Persian, and Turkish. Translations into Turkish have been done by Yusuf Karacha. Translations into Persian have been done by Qasim Qasmi, Ibrahim Daamni, and 'Abdul Qadir. Translations into Bengali have been done by 'Umar 'Ali, Sultan Zauq Nadwi, and Salman Qasmi. In English, Dr. Mohammad Asif Kidwai, Mohiuddin Ahmad, Dr. Shah 'Ebadur Rahman Neshat, and Dr. 'Abdur Raheem Kidwai have led the way. Hindi translations have been done by Muhammad Hasan Ansari.

During Sheikh Nadwi's lifetime as well as after his death, efforts have been underway to compile his articles and papers in the form of books according to subject matter. Some of the compilations which have gained widespread popularity are: (1) *Islam ka T'aaruf* (published in English as *Islam: An Introduction*) which has been translated into several languages; (2) *Qurani Ifadat* (published in English as *Guidance from the Holy Quran*); (3) *Islam Men Aurat Kaa Darjah Aur Is Ke Huqooq wa Faraidh*[1]; (4) *Maaliyat Kaa Islami Nizam*[2]; (5) *Islam Ke Teen Bunyadi 'Aqaaid;*[3] and (6) *Meri 'Ilmi Aur Motali'ati Zindagi.*[4]

Similar efforts are underway to compile his speeches and lectures as well. Some of the compilations which have already been published are: (1) *Takbire Mosalsal* (Urdu) is compiled by Dr. Mas'udul Hasan 'Uthmani who is the general secretary of Deeni T'alimi Council, and (2) *Juhde Mosalsal* (Urdu) is compiled

---

1 Approximate translation of the title: *Position of Women in Islam and Their Rights and Obligations.*

2 Approximate translation of the title: *Islamic System of Economy.*

3 Approximate translation of the title: *Three Fundamental Beliefs of Islam.*

4 Approximate translation of the title: *My Literary and Educational Life.*

by Sheikh Nadhrul Hafeez Nadwi, a teacher at Nadwatul 'Ulama. *Takbire Mosalsal* is about the basic religious education whereas *Juhde Mosalsal* is about the Muslim Personal Law and protection of *shari'ah*.

Sheikh Nadwi maintained a balanced and moderate approach in his writings without compromising the basic principles of *deen* (Islam) and *shari'ah* (Islamic code of conduct). He understood how to apply core principles of Islam to contemporary issues and his style of presentation was well suited to appeal the modern mind. He was able to strike a delicate balance between objective criticism and research – something that is quite difficult to carry together.

His writings include biographies of several prominent personalities, critical analysis of prevailing conditions of the Muslim *ummah*, and topics of *islah* (reform) and *tarbiyah* (character building). Some of his writings are of purely academic nature as well. But the theme that transcends all of his work is *d'awah* and *islah*. He wrote several books, both voluminous and short, on the lives of prophets and highlighted their special status and qualities. He also wrote on the history of the contributions and accomplishments of Muslims in religion, culture, and literature which has continued despite political upheavals and disasters.

He also authored books on important topics related to culture and literature. These books are very effective in nurturing young minds and are well suited for inclusion in curriculum. Some of his famous books in this genre are *Qasasun Nabiyeen*, *Al Qaratur Rashidah*, and *Mokhtaaraat Min Adabul Arab* (mentioned in detail in Chapter 4).

He also wrote a number of travelogues which, in addition to giving historical and geographical facts of the countries which he visited, provide a valuable insight from the point of view of a *da'i* and reformer. His book entitled

Apne Ghar Sey Baitullah Tak[5] (Urdu) is a vivid description of his *hajj* trip. Some of his other travelogues are: (1) *Mudhakkarat al-Saih Fil Sharq al-'Arabi*[6] (Arabic), (2) *Daryae Kabul Sey Dayae Yarmuk Tak*[7] (Urdu), (3) *Do Hafte al-Maghrib al-Aqsa Marakash Men*[8] (Urdu), (4) *Barah Din Reyasate Mysore Men*[9] (Urdu), and (5) *Do Hafte Turki Men*[10] (Urdu). Other trips are covered in his autobiography *Karwan-e-Zindagi* which is in fact a history of the entire twentieth century as seen by a *da'i*, teacher, leader, writer, thinker, historian, and reformer.

There is a series known as *Tuhfah* (Urdu) which is a collection of his speeches. The collections in this genre are named after the region where he delivered those speeches such as *Tuhfae Pakistan* (speeches delivered in Pakistan), *Tuhfae Mashriq* (speeches delivered in Bangladesh), *Tuhfae Deccan* (speeches delivered in Hyderabad and Aurangabad, India), *Tuhfae Insaniyat* (also known as *Tuhfae Malwa* which includes speeches delivered in Malwa, a region in Central India), *Tuhfae Kashmir* (speeches delivered in Kashmir), and *Tuhfae Bhatkal* (speeches delivered in Bhatkal, Karnataka, India).

The lectures that he delivered from the stage of Payam-e-Insaniyat (of which he was the founding president) on different occasions have been compiled and published in Urdu, English, Bengali, and Hindi.

Though many of his writings gained widespread acceptance and popularity, the one that earned him most recognition and respect remains his masterpiece *Ma Dha Khasar*

5 Approximate translation of the title: *From My Home to the House of Allah.*

6 Approximate translation of the title: *Diary of the Middle East.*

7 Approximate translation of the title: *From River Kabul to River Yarmuk.*

8 Approximate translation of the title: *Two Weeks in Morocco.*

9 Approximate translation of the title: *Twelve Days in the State of Mysore.*

10 Approximate translation of the title: *Two Weeks in Turkey.*

al-'Alamu bi Inhitat-il-Muslimin (published in English as *Islam and the World: The Rise and Decline of Muslims and Its Effect on Mankind*). Arabs consider it to be among the best books of the century. It has been translated into many international languages and numerous editions have been printed. Although more than six decades have passed since it was first published in 1950, it is still being printed by several publishers in large numbers and is selling like a bestseller.

The other book that has been immensely popular is *As Sirau Bainal Fikratil Islamiyyate Wal Fikratil Gharabiyya* (published in English as *Western Civilization, Islam and Muslims*). In this book, Sheikh Nadwi has presented an objective analysis of the political and ideological leadership of Muslim countries. Colonization of Muslim countries by the Western powers has, according to him, produced three types of leaders and intellectuals. The first type consists of those leaders who completely succumbed to the Western mode of thinking and imposed the Western way of life on their people. The second type consists of those who fully rejected the Western system and chose to remain entrenched in their depleted condition. The third type consists of those who want to benefit from both the systems (Islamic and Western) by taking what is good in the Western achievements and leaving out what is harmful in them. After explaining these three approaches, Sheikh Nadwi implored Muslim leaders to adopt a middle-of-the-road and well-balanced path as it was the only one that can lead to success.

In addition to the books that he himself authored, there were several which were written by others under his guidance and supervision. These include textbooks, biographies, history books, and travelogues. *Manthoorat* and *Mo'allimul Insha* are examples of textbooks that are part of the curriculum of Nadwatul 'Ulama. *Tarikhe Nadwatul 'Ulama*[11] (Urdu) by Ishaq

11 Approximate translation of the title: *History of Nadwatul 'Ulama.*

Jalees Nadwi and Dr. Shams Tabrez is a book in the area of history. Notables among the biographies are *Seerat Maulana Muhammad Ali Mongeri*[12] (Urdu) by Syed Muhammad Al-Hasani, *Sawaneh Maulana Muhammad Yusuf Kandhlawi*[13] (Urdu) by Sheikh Syed Muhammad Thani Hasani, and *Seerat Sultan Tipu Shaheed*[14] (Urdu) by Muhammad Ilyas Bhatkali Nadwi. *Do Mahine America Men*[15] (Urdu) by this author (Rabey Hasani Nadwi) is a travelogue.

The University of Delhi had convened a seminar on the writings of Sheikh Nadwi. The papers presented at that seminar were compiled and published as *Motali'ah Tasanif Maulana Abul Hasan Ali Nadwi*[16] by Dr. Mohsin 'Uthmani Nadwi. Sa'yeed Murtaza Nadwi and Tariq Zubair Nadwi have prepared a directory of Sheikh Nadwi's books which have been published in Arabic, Urdu, and other languages.

Work is underway to publish letters of Sheikh Nadwi. Two volumes have already been published by Syed Hamzah Hasani Nadwi and subsequent volumes are being prepared. Efforts are also underway to publish his discourses (informal sayings) as well; Sheikh Nadhrul Hafeez Nadwi, who is a teacher at Nadwatul 'Ulama, is working on this project.

---

12 Approximate translation of the title: *Life of Maulana Muhammad Ali Mongeri.*

13 Approximate translation of the title: *Life of Maulana Muhammad Yusuf Kandhlawi.*

14 Approximate translation of the title: *Life of Tipu Sultan.*

15 Approximate translation of the title: *Two Months in America.*

16 Approximate translation of the title: *Study of Writings by Sheikh Abul Hasan 'Ali Nadwi.*

Publications by Others on Sheikh Nadwi

Both during Sheikh Nadwi's lifetime and after his death, a number of papers and books were published by various authors shedding light on different aspects of his life. The book entitled *Al-Sheikh Abul Hasan Al-Nadwi Kama 'Arrafatahu*[17] (Arabic) by the renowned scholar and thinker Dr. Yusuf Al-Qardawi is one of them. Others in this genre are *Maulana Abul Hasan 'Ali Nadwi Akaabir aur Mashahire Ummat Kee Nazar meyn*[18] (Urdu) by Mamshad 'Ali Qasmi, *Meer-e-Karwan*[19] (Urdu) by Dr. 'Abdullah 'Abbas Nadwi, *Al Ustadh Abul Hasan Al-Nadwi Katiban wa Mufakkiran*[20] (Arabic) by Sheikh Nadhrul Hafeez Nadwi, and *Nafahaatal Hind wal Yemen bi-asaneed Ash-Sheikh Abi Al-Hasan*[21] (Arabic) by Sheikh Mohammad Akram Nadwi.

After Shiekh Nadwi's death, several scholars and writers of the Islamic and Arab world recognized his contributions in the fields of *d'awah*, research, and publication, and wrote articles and books for that purpose. For example, 'Abdullah bin Saleh Al-Washmi of Imam Muhammad Bin Saud Islamic University, Riyadh wrote his M.A. thesis in which he analyzed Shiekh Nadwi's contributions in Islamic literature and criticism.

Dr. Mohiuddin Abu Saleh published a book from Riyadh, in which he analyzed Sheikh Nadwi's philosophy of education. Muhammad 'Abdus Salam Al-'Ajmi published a research paper on the same topic.

---

17 Approximate translation of the title: *Sheikh Abul Hasan Nadwi as I Knew Him.*

18 Approximate translation of the title: *Sheikh Abul Hasan 'Ali Nadwi in the Eyes of Elders and Leaders.*

19 Approximate translation of the title: *Chief of Caravan.*

20 Approximate translation of the title: *Sheikh Abul Hasan Al-Nadwi as a Writer and Thinker.*

21 Approximate translation of the title: *Breezes of India and Yemen with the Ascriptions of Abi Al-Hasan.*

'Abdul Majeed Al-Salmani of Turkey published a book in which he discussed and analyzed Sheikh Nadwi's views on current political trends and practices.

Mrs. Raf'at of Barkatullah University, Bhopal, India, wrote her Ph.D. dissertation entitled *Maulana Abul Hasan 'Ali Nadwi: Hayat aur Khidmaat* (Sheikh Abul Hasan 'Ali Nadwi: Life and Services). Lutfur Rahman of Bangladesh wrote his Ph.D. dissertation entitled entitled *Ash-Sheikh Abu Al-Hasan wa juhooduhu fi tajdeed Al-fikr Al-Islami* (Sheikh Abu Al-Hasan and His Efforts in the Revival of Islamic Thought) at Cairo University.

Sheikh Muhammad Qamruz Zaman, a renowned scholar and writer from Allahabad, India, published a book entitled *Nuqoosh wa Aathare Mufakkire Islam* (*Personality and Character of the Islamic Thinker*) in which he presented and analyzed Sheikh Nadwi's views and thinking.

After Sheikh Nadwi's death, seminars were held at various places to commemorate his life and services. The most notable among those were convened by the Oxford Centre for Islamic Studies (United Kingdom) and the Lahore branch of the World Forum of Islamic Literature. Other seminars were convened by The University of Delhi, the Istanbul branch of the World Forum of Islamic Literature, the Departments of Arabic Literature and Religion of Aligarh Muslim University, Jami'ah Syed Ahmad Shaheed, Katoli, Lucknow, and Jami'ah Islamiyah Kashiful 'Uloom, Aurangabad. Proceedings of these seminars have already been published.

The publications in Urdu include *Sarguzasht* (*Memoire*) by Dr. Nafees Hasan of Delhi, *Sawaneh Mufakkire Islam* (*Biography of an Islamic Thinker*) by Sheikh Syed Bilal 'Abdul Hai Hasani Nadwi, *Hayat, Karname aur Malfoozaat* (*Life, Achievements and Sayings*) by Muhammad Hasan Ansari, and *Nuqooshe Hayat* (*Portrait of Life*) by Dr. Shah 'Ebadur Rahman.

The publications in Arabic include *Al-Sheikh Abul Hasan Ali Hasani Nadwi Al-Da'i Al-Hakim wal Morabbi Al-Jaleel* (*Sheikh Abul Hasan 'Ali Nadwi: A Prudent Da'i and Great Teacher*) by Sheikh Muhammad Ijteba Nadwi, *Al-mas'ha Al-adabiyah fi kitabaat Ash-Sheikh Abi Al-hasan Nadwi* (*The Literary Touch in Writings of Sheikh Abu Hasan Al-Nadawi*) by Sheikh Syed Muhammad Wazeh Rasheed Hasani Nadwi (published by the Lucknow branch of the World Forum of Islamic Literature), and *Al-Sheikh Abul Hasan Ali Al Hasani Nadwi: Al Imamul Mofakkir wad Da'iatal Adeeb* (*Sheikh Abul Hasan Ali Nadwi: A Leading Thinker, D'ai and Scholar*) by Sheikh Syed 'Abdul Majid Ghauri (published by Dar ibn Kathir, Damascus).

Sheikh Salman Qasmi of Bangladesh has published a book in Bengali. In Iran, research work is going on in Persian on Sheikh Nadwi's life and work. Dr. Safeer Akhtar of Idarah Tahqiqaate Islami, Islamabad, has published a book entitled *Maulana Abul Hasan Ali Nadwi: Hayat wa Afkaar key Chand Pahlu* (*Sheikh Abul Hasan Ali Nadwi: A Few Aspects of His Life and Thought*). Darul Kitab of Deoband, India, has published a book entitled *Maulana Abul Hasan Ali Nadwi: Hayat aur Karnamey* (*Sheikh Abul Hasan Ali Nadwi: Life and Achievements*) by Sheikh Muhammad Asjad Nadwi.

Majlise Nashriyate Islam of Karachi has published a book entitled *Nazranaye 'Aqidat* (*A Gift of Homage*) by Sheikh Fazle Rabbi. Another work of Sheikh Fazle Rabbi is *Maulana Abul Hasan Ali Nadwi Key Khutoot* (*Letters of Sheikh Abul Hasan Ali Nadwi*). Sheikh 'Abdul Karim Parikh has published *Maulana Ali Mian Key Khutoot* (*Letters of Maulana Ali Mian*).

Some books have been published focusing on a specific aspect of Sheikh Nadwi's personality. The Academy of Islamic Research and Publications has published a book entitled *Maulana 'Ali Mian aur Ilme Hadith* (*Sheikh 'Ali Mian and the Discipline of Hadith*) by Sheikh Abu Sahban Ruhul Quds Nadwi who is a teacher at Nadwatul 'Ulama. A publisher from Mumbai has published a book entitled *Maulana Abul Hasan 'Ali Nadwi aur Tasawwuf* (*Sheikh Abul Hasan 'Ali Nadwi and Tasawwuf*) by Shamim Tariq.

Several Islamic and literary magazines published special issues to commemorate Sheikh Nadwi's life and work. Delhi's widely circulated weekly magazine *Nayee Duniya* took the lead and published a special issue on the fifteenth day after Sheikh Nadwi passed away. Nadwatul 'Ulama published special issues of its magazines: fortnightly *Al-Raid* (Arabic), monthly *Al-Baas Islami* (Arabic), fortnightly *Tameere Hayat* (Urdu), quarterly *Karwane Adab* (Urdu), and quarterly *The Fragrance of East* (English). Special issues were also published by *Al-Da'i* of Darul 'Uloom, Deoband; *Al-Sahwatul Islamiyah* of Darul 'Uloom, Hyderabad; *Sautul Quran* of Ahmedabad, Gujarat; *La Raib* of Kolkata; *Al-Shariq* of Azamgarh; *Fikre Islami* of Darul 'Uloom Al-Islamiyah, Basti; *Al-Furqan* of Lucknow; *Bange Dara* of Lucknow; *Ar Rasheed* of Multan (Pakistan); and *Al Haq* of Khatak (Pakistan). As a special issue, Jami'atul Hidayah, Jaipur, published a collection of Sheikh Nadwi's articles. *The Urdu Book Review* of Delhi published a series of articles covering works and accomplishments of Sheikh Nadwi.

The above publications illustrate how greatly Sheikh Nadwi's services and contributions have been appreciated. His work and accomplishments are still being recognized although six years have passed since his departure from this world. May Allah make these efforts yield good results! May Allah make these efforts beneficial for Islam, Muslims, and the entire mankind! May Allah enable people to turn to Him and become true followers of Islam!

Glossary of Arabic Terms

ah-lul-sunnah	–	followers of the traditions of Prophet Muhammad
'alim	–	Islamic scholar
'aqaaid	–	tenets of Islam
'aqidah	–	singular of *'aqaaid*
as-samad	–	self-sufficing
awraad	–	regimen consisting of recitation of Quran and remembrance of Allah
bay'ah	–	oath of spiritual allegiance
da'i	–	one who calls people towards Allah and His religion
d'awah	–	calling people towards Allah and His religion
deen	–	religion, Islam, way of life
dhikr	–	remembrance of Allah
d'ua	–	supplication, prayer
fitnah	–	perfidy, deception
ghaib	–	unseen
haadi	–	guide
hadith	–	tradition of Prophet Muhammad
haq	–	truth
hijrah	–	emigration
'ibadah	–	worship, prayer
ihsan	–	devotion to Allah
ikhlas	–	sincerity
ilhad	–	godlessness
imam	–	one who leads congregational prayers in mosques
iman	–	belief, faith

islah – reform
islah batin – internal rectification
istighfar – repentance for wrongdoings
istighna – expecting nothing from anyone except Allah
jihad – struggle
khalifah – deputy, one who has earned permission from an elder to render spiritual guidance on his behalf
khilafah – permission to render spiritual guidance on behalf of some elder
khulfah – plural of *khalifah*
kufr – rejection of faith
madaris – plural of *madrasah*
madrasah – school of Islamic learning
mard-e-momin – man of faith, believer
masajid – plural of *masjid*
masjid – mosque
millat – nation, people, Muslims
momin – believer
nifaq – hypocrisy
niyah – intention
qiyamah – Doomsday
salah – prayer
seerah – life
shari'ah – Islamic code of conduct
sheikh – pious elder
shirk – polytheism
sufi – mystic
sufia – plural of *sufi*
sulook – traditions of spiritual training
sunnah – saying and practice of the Prophet
tabligh – propagation
tafseer – exegesis of Quran
tahajjud – pre-dawn prayer
taqwa – piety
tarbiyah – character building, mentoring

tasawwuf – mysticism
tawheed – oneness of Allah
tazkiyah batin – internal purification
tazkiyah nafs – spiritual purification
'ulama – scholars of Islam
ummah – nation
wahi – divine revelation
wazaaif – regimen consisting of recitation of Quran and remembrance of Allah
yaqeen – conviction
zuhd – asceticism from worldly pleasures

Index

'Abdul 'Aziz Rafa'i, 6
'Abdul Ghafoor Jodhpuri, 61
'Abdul Karim Parikh, 23, 56, 145, 163, 215, 239
'Abdul Karim Refi, 189
'Abdul Majeed Al-Salmani, 237
'Abdul Qadir, 232
'Abdul Qadir Jilani, 73, 223
'Abdul Qadir Raipuri, 4, 14, 72, 79, 97, 183-84, 211, 228
'Abdul Quddus Abu Saleh, 135
'Abdul Quddus Ansari, 187
'Abdullah 'Abbas Nadwi, xvi, xix, 56, 175, 183, 237
'Abdullah al-Salim al-Sabah, 100
'Abdullah bin Saleh Al-Washmi, 237
'Abdullah Ibrahim Al-Ansari, 20
'Abdur Raheem Kidwai, 228, 230, 232
'Abdur Rahman Rafat al-Basha, 20, 135
'Abdur Rasheed 'Azmi, 182
'Abdur Rasheed N'umani, 64
'Abdur Razzaq Hamzah, 180
'Abdus Salam Qidwai Nadwi, 167, 175
'Abdus Shakoor Farooqi Lucknowi, 61
Abu Sahban Ruhul Quds Nadwi, 239
Abul Fattah Abu Ghodda, 26
Abul Hasan al-Ash'ari, 223
Abul 'Irfan Khan Nadwi, 176, 215
Abul Khair Barq, 12
Abul Lais Islahi Nadwi, 39, 167
Academy of Arabic Learning, 134
Academy of Islamic Research and Publications, 16, 80, 81, 172, 239
'Adil Salahi, 227
Afghanistan, 90
Ahmad 'Abdul Ghafoor 'Attar, 186-87
Ahmad 'Abdul Hai, 24
Ahmad 'Ali Lahori, 4, 13, 60, 72, 211
Ahmad Amin, 220
Ahmad bin Hanbal, 50, 117, 223
Ahmad Fahmi Zamzam, 209
Ahmad Hassan al-Bakr, 123
Ahmadu Bello, 195
Ahmal Haroon Al-'Asal Al-Hajjar, 63
Akbar, 84, 189, 224
Al-Azhar University, 171, 209
Al-Bashir al-Ibrahimi, 98
Aligarh Muslim University, 43, 48, 238

All India Muslim Majlis-e-Mushawarat, 1, 17, 43, 55, 157
All India Muslim Personal Law Board, xiv, 1, 20, 159
'Alvi Maliki, 180
Amatullah Tasnim, xviii, 53, 69
Ameer 'Abdul Qadir, 189
Ameer Shakeeb Arsalan, 39
Amin Siraj, 190
Ammatul 'Aziz, xviii
Anees Chishti, 56, 145
Ashraf 'Ali Thanwi, 4, 61, 69
'Atiqur Rahman 'Uthmani, 158
Aurangzeb, 27, 84
Ayatullah Khomeini, 228
'Azzuddin bin 'Abdus Salam, 94, 223

Babri Masjid, 23, 162
Bahjatul Bitar, 190
Baitullah, 63, 184
Bangladesh, 125, 214
Barkatullah University, Bhopal, 238
Bharatiya Janata Party, 86
Bukhara, 25-26
Burhanuddin Sanbhli, 56
Burma, 205

Cairo University, 238
Congress Party, 18, 158
Crown Prince Saud bin 'Abdul-'Aziz Al-Saud, 95

Damascus University, 16, 125, 190
Dar ibn Kathir, Damascus, 239
Darul Musannefin, Azamgarh, 20, 213
Darul Qadha, 165
Darul Uloom Al-Islamiyah, Basti, 240
Darul 'Uloom, Deoband, 13, 19, 35, 46, 160, 240
Deene Ilahi, 84
Deeni T'alimi Council, xiii, 1, 16, 80, 150, 232
Deoband, 9, 107
Deve Gowda, 86
Druze, 123
Durga, 154

Farooq Ahmed Khan Leghari, 27, 214
Fazle Rabbi, 239

Gamal Abdel Nasser, 9, 122, 124, 191
Gandhi, Indira, 18, 85, 143
Gandhi, Rajiv, 23, 85, 87
Ghulam Muhammad Deenpuri, 35, 60

Habibur Rahman Khan Sherwani, 106
Haider Hasan Khan Tonki, 13, 40
Haji Muhammad Nazem, 216
Hamid 'Abdul Hai, 24
Hasan al-Banna, 188, 196-97
Hasan Basri, 73, 223
Hasanul Masat, 180

Ibn Jauzi, 40, 73, 94, 117, 223
Ibn Kathir, 223
Ibn Khaldun, 94, 112
Ibn Qaiyam, 40, 73, 223
Ibn Rajab, 223
Ibn Taimiyah, 40, 50, 73, 94, 223
Ibnul Hadi, 223
Ibrahim Ahmad Mazahari, 207
Ibrahim Daamni, 232
Idarah Tahqiqaate Islami, 239

Idarah T'alimate Islam, 113
Ikhwanul Muslimeen, 122, 191, 196-97
Imam Bukhari, 25
Imam Ghazali, 40, 50, 73, 223
Imam Muhammad Bin Saud Islamic University, 134, 237
Imarat Shari'at of Bihar and Orissa, 160
'Imran Khan Nadwi, 167, 169, 175
Inamul Hasan Kandhlawi, 80
Institute of Objective Studies, 28
International Islamic University, 209
Iqbal Ahmad Azami, 222
Iqbal Ahmad Nadwi, xix
Iran, 90
ISESCO Award, 28
Ishaq Jalees Nadwi, 129, 145, 176, 211, 236
Ishteyaq Hussain Quraishi, 56, 129, 150, 158, 176, 197, 210
Islah-e-Mo'asherah, 90
Islamic Centre of Geneva, 91, 197
Islamic Personality of the Year Award, 27
Islamic University of Madinah, 16, 134, 194
Ismet Inonu, 192

Jalaluddin Rumi, 50, 223
Jama'at Tabligh, 14, 80-81, 94, 181, 214, 230
Jama'at-e-Islami, 78, 167
Jamia Millia Islamia, 48, 168, 225
Jami'ah Ashrafia, 214
Jami'ah Islamiyah, 16
Jami'ah Islamiyah Kashiful Uloom, Aurangabad, 238
Jami'ah Salfiyah, Banaras, 46
Jami'ah Syed Ahmad Shaheed, Katoli, 238
Jami'at 'Ulama Hind, 46, 48
Jamiatul Hidayah, Jaipur, 240
Jami'atul Mo'arif Islamiyah, 215
Jawahar Lal Nehru, 94
Jehangir, 84

K'aba, 26
Kedah, 208
Khalil bin Muhammad, 12, 36, 119
Khaliluddin Hanswi, 37
Khawaja Bahauddin Naqshbandi, 26
Khawaja Fariduddin Ganj Shakar, 75
Khawaja Moinuddin Chishti, 50, 75, 117, 224
Khawaja Nizamuddin Aulia, 50, 75, 117, 224
Khawaja Ubaidullah Ahrar, 73
King Faisal, 19
King Faisal Award, 19
Krishan Kant, 23, 163
Kuala Lumpur, 208

Lajnat al-Ta'aleef wal Nashr, 220
Lucknow Medical College, 44
Lutfur Rahman, 238

Madarasatul Islah, Sarai Mir, 46
Madrasah al-Falah, 188
Madrasah Saulatiyyah, 187, 188

Madrasah Uloom Shari'ah, 188
Mahmoodul Hassan 'Uthmani, 150
Mahomed Mohamedy, 228
Majlis-e-Isha'at, 153
Majlise Nashriyate Islam, Karachi, 239
Malaysia, 208
Mamshad 'Ali Qasmi, 237
Manzoor N'umani, 55, 70, 72, 78, 150, 157-58, 175
M'arouf al-Dawalibi, 98, 190
Masjid al-Aqsa, 102
Mas'ud 'Alam Nadwi, 39, 96
Mas'udul Hasan 'Uthmani, 150, 156, 232
Mazahirul 'Uloom, Saharanpur, 46
Michel Aflaq, 123
Mirza Ghalib, 137
Mohammad Akram Nadwi, 237
Mohammad Asif Kidwai, 220, 222, 224-26, 229-32
Mohibullah Laari Nadwi, 175
Mohiuddin Abu Saleh, 237
Mohiuddin Ahmad, 221-23, 225-32
Mohsin 'Uthmani Nadwi, 236
Motamar al-'Alam al-Islami, 99, 195
Mrs. Raf'at, 238
Mufti Aminul Hussaini, 189
Muhammad 'Abdus Salam Al-'Ajmi, 237
Muhammad Ahmad, 61
Muhammad Ahmad Phulpuri, 4
Muhammad al-Mubarak, 190
Muhammad 'Ali Al-Harkan, 95, 216
Muhammad 'Ali Al-Maghrabi, 180
Muhammad 'Ali Kanpuri-Mongheri, 106
Muhammad 'Ali Rajab, 209
Muhammad Asjad Nadwi, 239
Muhammad bin 'Abdullah al-Subayyal, 171
Muhammad Hasan Ansari, 226, 232, 238
Muhammad Ijteba Nadwi, 239
Muhammad Ilyas Bhatkali Nadwi, 236
Muhammad Ilyas Kandhlawi, 4, 14, 35, 72-73, 78, 80, 181, 230
Muhammad Iqbal, 13, 35, 93, 119, 124, 225
Muhammad Ishaq Sandelvi, 153, 175
Muhammad Mohsin Baarom, 187
Muhammad Natsir, 99
Muhammad Nazim Nadwi, 39, 167
Muhammad Owais Nagrami Nadwi, 175
Muhammad Qamruz Zaman, 238
Muhammad Suroor al-Saban, 187
Muhammad 'Uthman, 21
Muhammad Yusuf Kandhlawi, 80, 94, 181
Muhammad Zakariya Kandhlawi, 4, 14, 35, 63, 69, 72, 79, 182
Muhammad Iqbal, 138
Mujaddid Alf Thani, 5, 50, 73, 83-85, 94, 117, 179, 189, 224
Muslim League, 46, 48
Muslim Students Association, 19, 199

Muslim World League, 17, 90, 95, 101, 125, 194, 211, 213, 227
Mustafa al-Sabai, 190
Mustafa Kemal Ata Turk, 121, 122, 192
Mustafa Zarqa, 190

Nadhrul Hafeez Nadwi, 165, 233, 236-37
Nadwatul 'Ulama, xiii, 18, 76, 80, 81, 106-07, 114, 116, 130-31, 167, 208
Nafees Ahmad Siddiqui, 150
Nafees Hasan, 238
Nazemia University, 216
Nuruddin Zangi, 223-24

Oxford Centre for Islamic Studies, 20, 22, 55, 238

Pakistan, 19, 21, 26, 210
Palestine, 125
Pattani, 209
Payam-e-Insaniyat, xiv, 1, 17, 75, 83, 90, 142, 144, 146-47, 234

Qadianism, 228
Qari 'Abdur Rahman Qasmi, 207
Qari Habeeb Ahmad Lucknowi, xx
Qari Muhammad Taiyab Qasmi, xiv, 20, 160
Qasim Qasmi, 232
Qatar, 19
Qazi 'Abdul Hameed Indori, 56, 145, 227
Qazi 'Adeel 'Abbasi, 9, 149, 150
Qazi Muhammad Moinullah Indori Nadwi, 56, 169, 175, 182, 187, 205
Quran Majeed Award, 55
Qutham bin 'Abbas, 25

Rabita al-Adab al-Islami al-'Alami, xv, 135
Rabita al-'Alam al-Islami, 17, 211, 213
Rahmatullah Kairanawi, 188
Raiwind, 214
Rao, Narasimha, 86, 143, 162
Rasheed Ahmad Gangohi, 107
Rasheed Raza, 39
Rashtriya Swayamsevak Sangh, 88
Rehmat Ali, x
Riazuddin Ahmad, 150

Saddam Hussein, 123
Safeer Akhtar, 239
Saharanpur, 9
Sa'id Ramadan, 17, 91, 197
Salahuddin Ayubi, 125, 223-24
Salman Qasmi, 232, 239
Samarqand, 25
Sampurnanand, 153
Sarasvati, 154
Saud ibn Ibrahim al-Shuraim, 171-72
Sa'yeed Ahmad Khan Saharanpuri, 182
Sa'yeed Murtaza Nadwi, 236
Sa'yeedul 'Aamoodi, 187
Sa'yidur Rahman 'Azami Nadwi, 150, 176, 228
Sayyid 'Ali Al-Tantawi, 6
Sayyidna Abu Bakr Siddique, 211
Sayyidna Abu 'Ubaidah, 104
Sayyidna 'Ali bin Abi Talib, 222

Sayyidna Hasan, 222
Sayyidna Hussain, 222
Sayyidna K'ab Bin Maalik, 7
Sayyidna 'Umar, 104
Seeratun Nabi Award, 55
Selangor, 208
Shaad 'Azeemabadi, xv, xvi
Shah 'Abdul-'Aziz bin Saud, 96
Shah 'Abdullah, 5, 88, 98
Shah 'Alamullah, 27, 51
Shah 'Ebadur Rahman, x, 221, 226, 229, 232, 238
Shah Fahad, 88
Shah Faisal, 5, 88, 101, 195
Shah Faisal Award, 55
Shah Fazlur Rahman Ganj Moradabadi, 61, 107
Shah Halim 'Ata Ceyloni, 175
Shah Hasan, 5, 88
Shah Hussein, 88
Shah Khalid, 88
Shah Muhammad Ahmad Partapgarhi, 61
Shah Muhammad Wasiyullah Fatehpuri, 4, 61
Shah Muhammad Yakoob Mujaddidi, 4, 61
Shah Saud, 5, 88
Shah Waliyullah Award, 28
Shah Waliyullah Dehlavi, 3, 50, 73, 117, 178-79, 224
Shahjehan, 84
Shamim Tariq, 240
Shams Tabrez, 236
Shankaracharya, 23, 163
Sharfuddin Yahya Maneri, 50, 117, 224
Sheikh Shaibi, 184
Sheikh Shamil, 189
Sheikh Zayed, 22
Shibli N'umani, 106
Singh, V.P. 143
Spain, 197
Sri Lanka, 216
Sultan Bin Muhammad Al Qasmi, 19
Sultan Hassanal Bolkiah International Award, 27, 55
Sultan Zauq Nadwi, 215, 232
Syed 'Abdul 'Ali Hasani, xi, xvii, 4, 12, 17, 30, 34, 36, 40, 60, 173, 179, 207
Syed 'Abdul 'Aziz Rafai, 20
Syed 'Abdul Hai Hasani, xi, xviii, 1, 11, 106, 141, 173
Syed 'Abdul Majid Ghauri, 239
Syed 'Abdullah Hasani Nadwi, 226
Syed Abul A'ala Maududi, 14, 72, 78
Syed Adam Binnauri, 51
Syed Ahmad Faizabadi, 188
Syed Ahmad Shaheed, ix, xii, 5, 10, 13, 50, 59, 61, 71, 117, 219, 231
Syed 'Ali Hamdani Kashmeri, 117
Syed 'Ali Hasan Fad'aq, 186
Syed 'Azizur Rahman Hasani, 36
Syed Bilal 'Abdul Hai Hasani Nadwi, xix, 1, 238
Syed Fakhruddin Khayali, xi
Syed Hamzah Hasani Nadwi, 236
Syed Hussain Ahmad Madni, 4, 13, 35, 40, 60, 188
Syed Khaliluddin Ahmad Hasani, xvii, 106
Syed Mahmood, 158
Syed Mahmood Hafiz, 185
Syed Mahmood Hasan, 44

Syed Mahmood Hasan Hasani Nadwi, xvi, xix
Syed Mahmood Madni, 188
Syed Minnatullah Rahmani, 21, 85, 160-61
Syed Muhammad Al-Hasani, xix, 1, 8, 114, 176, 211, 236
Syed Muhammad Amin Nasirabadi, 59
Syed Muhammad Ishaq, 51
Syed Muhammad Murtaza Mazahari, 56
Syed Muhammad Rabey Hasani Nadwi, ix, 2, 6
Syed Muhammad Tahir Mansoorpuri Mazahari, 183
Syed Muhammad Thani Hasani, 181, 211, 236
Syed Muhammad Wazeh Rasheed Hasani Nadwi, xx, 176, 239
Syed Nizamuddin, 161
Syed Qutb Shaheed, 6
Syed Rasheed Ahmad Hasani, xvii
Syed Rizwan 'Ali Nadwi, 183
Syed Salman Hussaini Nadwi, 215-16
Syed Shah Ziaun Nabi Hasani, xvii, 29, 59
Syed Sulaiman Nadwi, 39, 41, 113, 133, 167-68, 212
Syed Talha Hasani, 41, 119
Syed 'Ubaidullah, 31
Syed Waliyur Rahmani, 165

Taif, 84
Tajul Masajid, 167-68
Takiya Kalan, 11, 51
Tandon, Purushottam Das, 153
Taqiuddin Hilali, 12, 38, 119, 167
Taqiuddin Nadwi, 22
Tarbiyah Islamiyah, 209
Tariq Zubair Nadwi, 236
Tashkent, 25
Tatars, 224
Timur Lang, 25

'Ubaidullah Balyawi, 181
'Umar Ali, 232
'Umar bin 'Abdul 'Aziz, 96, 117, 223
'Umar bin Hasan Al-Sheikh, 96
United Arab Emirates, 19
University of Delhi, 236, 238
University of Kashmir, 20
Urdu Book Review of Delhi, 240
USA, 18

Vajpayee, Atal Bihari 86, 144, 213

World Forum of Islamic Literature, xv, 1, 20, 26, 135-36, 140, 171, 215
World Muslim Congress, 99, 195

Yadav, Mulayam Singh, 87
Yasser Arafat, 125
Yunus Saleem, 23, 163
Yusuf Al-Qaradawi, 237
Yusuf Karacha, 232
Yusuf N'emat, 209

Zafar Ahmad Siddiqui, 150
Zafar Ishaq Ansari, 228
Zakaria Barri, 20
Ziaul Haq, 5, 21, 102, 212